THE WITCH'S WAY TO WEALTH

The Every Witch's Guide to
Making More Money—Faster
& Easier Than Ever!

JESSIE DaSILVA

Cover design by Sara Pulver
Cover photograph © Heather Drymon
Internal Illustrations © Getty/Ganna Bozhko, Getty/Alina Kotliar, Getty/kotoffei, iStock/Ramziya Abdrakhmanova, iStock/PICTEORICO, iStock/elenabs, iStock/Inna Kharlamova, iStock/Moto-rama
Internal design by Laura Boren/Sourcebooks

The characters and events portrayed in this book are fictitious or are used fictitiously. Apart from well-known historical figures, any similarity to real persons, living or dead, is purely coincidental and not intended by the author.

Published by Sourcebooks
P.O. Box 4410, Naperville, Illinois 60567-4410
(630) 961-3900
sourcebooks.com

Cataloging-in-Publication Data is on file with the Library of Congress.

Printed and bound in the United States of America.
MA 10 9 8 7 6 5 4 3 2 1

To Jill, Joe, & Jack.

My first clients, my best friends, my siblings.

Table of Contents

PART 3: HOW TO KEEP MANIFESTED MONEY

PART 4: HOW TO MANIFEST EVEN MORE MONEY

Preface

What Magic Really Is

Welcome to what is probably the most *unique* personal finance book to ever grace the shelves of your local bookstore.

But before we begin, I want to clarify why a book on magic is also on shelves and tagged online with personal finance, business, personal development, self-help, or, you know, almost every category other than religion and spirituality.

It comes down to what many people don't realize is a central tenet of the witchcraft community: **Magic is science, and science is magic.**

Speak to any witch worth their purification salt and they'll tell you that so much of what science is now proving in quantum physics, neuroscience, psychology, even many medical studies are concepts and practices that have been deeply rooted in witchcraft for thousands of years.

Well, those same scientific principles also specifically apply to money magic.

Yes, this book will include information on spells, herbs, crystals, astrology, and more of what I am sure you associate with typical witchcraft.

However, it will *also* cover budgeting, finding a job that pays you what you're worth (which is of course more money), tried and true business strategies, and *more.*

Money magic is finance, and with the right outlook, *finance is money magic, too*.

Introduction

Yes, I Know This Book Is Weird

I wasn't always the successful, authentic, badass witch living a weird and wonderful life writing books about how to get rich off magic.

Years ago, I was a very respectable lawyer with very respectable jobs. I worked as an assistant state attorney general, I worked for Bloomberg Law, I had *credentials*.

And you know what else I had?

Debt. Stress. Anxiety. Fear. And a habit of living paycheck to paycheck that I couldn't seem to break, no matter how many self-help or personal finance books I read.

Meanwhile, I had always had a penchant for anything a little *woo*. I'm that friend who interprets your weirdest dreams, whips out her tarot deck when you're having relationship problems, and warns you to drive carefully whenever Mercury goes retrograde.

After years of treating those interests as separate from my career and money management, it suddenly dawned on me: Why not look for a magical solution to the problem? At best, I would find a way to make earning and managing money more fun and in line with my interests.

At worst, I would be exactly where I was with a high-paying job that still scarcely covered the bills. Thus, I started researching and using manifestation—a spiritually focused practice of making your dreams and desires reality—and money magic.

What followed was a literal upending of my entire life.

I was fired from my prestigious legal job. I started a business that replaced my income. I've helped clients land jobs that doubled their salaries or start businesses that made them $150,000 in their first year. I've helped companies learn how to explode their profits by tapping into their workers' potential. I landed a feature in *Forbes*, which gave me a brand-new title, "The Millennial Money Witch." And, ultimately, I wrote the book you hold in your hands right now.

Trust me when I say I know this book is weird. I wrote it, so I'm aware. I'm *still* trying to explain it to my parents.

But as someone who's probably read all your self-help and personal finance favorites, let me say one thing before you decide it's too weird for you.

You've *been* reading about magic.

Those gurus you love—Marie Forleo, Jen Sincero, Brené Brown, Tony Robbins, Tim Ferriss, Robert Kiyosaki, and the rest—have been spoon-feeding you a watered-down version of magic and calling it "mindset work."

Those authors are *fantastic* starting places. But this weird little book? It just may be the book that changes your life. Because their work isn't even the tip of the iceberg. Each one of them is a mere snowflake on the tip of the iceberg that manifestation and mindset can unleash in your life.

What I'm teaching you is every aspect of manifesting money with magic—explained with quantum physics, neuroscience, psychology, religion, personal finance, and more. We'll also explore the spiritual practices that will give the *oomph* necessary to make real financial change in your life.

So, to answer the questions you undoubtedly had when you picked up this title.

Does this author actually believe in magic? Yes, though you might be surprised what I include in that category.

Should I be committed? Maybe. But maybe you should read this book before you decide. Because I changed my life by tapping into the power and principles outlined in these pages. And I know they will change yours, too.

PART 1

The Nature of Money

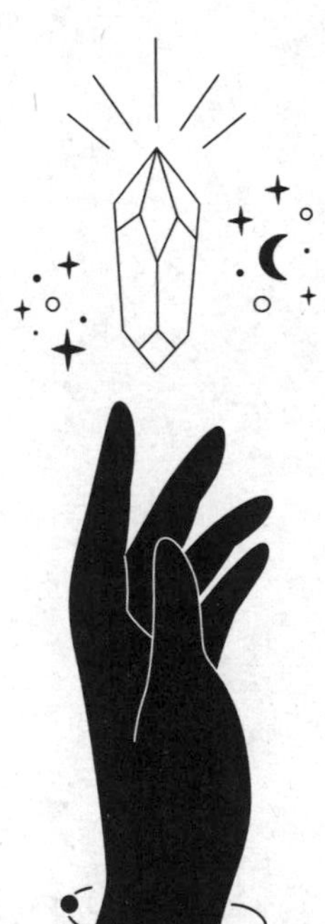

The Energetic Nature of Money

Once upon a time, I thought about money probably the same way everyone else does: as a finite resource. It's something you're either rewarded with for hard work or something you lose when you don't spend it wisely.

I was also riddled with notions about the morality of money.

In my past, money was a necessary evil. I shouldn't think about it or want it or use it except to cover my basic needs.

So exactly how did this relationship with money serve me? Well, it didn't. No matter whether I made $40,000 or $80,000, there never seemed to be enough. Besides rent, there were utilities, the ever-growing price of groceries, vet bills for my cat, and more expenses just to exist. And, of course, as my salary grew, I wanted to live a little, too. Sue me! Going out for dinner here and there, a trip to visit a friend once or twice a year… I lived a really basic but somehow really expensive life.

I found that I was always resentful of living in what felt like an endless cycle of my salary pitted against my wants and needs.

There had to be more to life, more than my forced dynamic with money. Working nine to five seemed like such a long time to do *anything*, even something I thought I loved like lawyering and reporting. And there was a difference between doing something you love because you want to do it versus doing it because someone will take away your only source of income if you don't.

Even when I made plenty of money and lived modestly, I felt like I was getting ripped off. But to admit I wanted more money? Oh, honey, *never*.

No, no, for past Jessie, playing by the rules and being nobly poor while changing the world was the only proper or right way to live.

God forbid that my desire for money turned me into one of *them*.

You know who I'm talking about. The rich bitches of the world. The Jeffs, the Bills, the Waltons...*them*. The one percent.

I blamed money for why those companies exploited so many. Because if you have too much money, it will ultimately corrupt you.

"*Not I*," said the little hen.

I will stay down here with the other 99 percent and refuse to admit that I had any wants or needs outside these little treats I granted myself now and then.

Of course, it wasn't true at all. We all want money. That's no surprise. But we're all terrified to admit *how much we truly want*—not just enough to survive, but enough to thrive.

What's funny, or perhaps what's predictable, is that so many other aspects of my life followed that same pattern of thinking it was wrong to *want* what I *wanted*.

Not only was my relationship with money lackluster, but my relationships *in general* were.

I carried so much resentment for the friends and family who constantly asked me for support. And not just the emotional support of holding space while someone cries about their breakup on the phone. I'm talking about ranting about the same problems over and over again without ever taking my sage advice. Loaning money to relatives who couldn't seem to get a handle on their finances as much as I repeatedly tried to get a handle on mine. Always coming close to paying off my credit card debt, but never actually becoming debt-free.

I was so angry and so very afraid to let it out. Even in my career, I deeply hated having to play kiss-ass to my bosses, to pretend to be a Pollyanna in professional settings when I curse like a sailor, and to tone down my fashion sense to make it acceptable for office dress codes. And for what? So they could pay me pennies and heap more work and responsibility on me as a reward for being a high performer.

And don't even get me started on my dating life, which was littered with trash men who swore they wanted intimacy and commitment, but constantly let me down and broke my heart.

Looking back now, what I see is the common denominator: me.

I'm not saying everyone deserves a free pass, but the truth is that I didn't *say* anything. I *accepted* the dynamics at hand and even *encouraged* them in some cases!

I carried a definitive split between what I said I wanted (enough money to live comfortably and thrive) and what I subconsciously believed I was allowed to have (just enough to scrape by).

I would eventually learn that at the most basic level of magic and manifestation, that split in desire between the conscious and subconscious was the reason why nothing I tried to better my situation seemed to work for long.

The most fundamental building block of spellwork, money magic, and manifestation is called a thoughtform, which describes the energy generated when your conscious and subconscious beliefs match. It sounds easy, but we can rarely identify our subconscious beliefs based on what we logically know to be true. It's called the *sub*conscious for a reason, and the best way to discover what's down there is to look at your life and see where you aren't getting the results you want.

The truth is that all of us have been conditioned from childhood onward by society, our parents or caretakers, the media, our communities, and so on to accept bullshit when it comes to making money.

A story from childhood really highlights how early I, like many, lived in that dynamic, even though it isn't about money.

All the aunts in my family were renowned for buying me and my three siblings atrocious clothes for Christmas. If they weren't two sizes too big, they were plastered with polyester dragons or flowery grandma curtain prints.

Yet every year, I smiled and thanked them and waited for a few days after Christmas to call and ask for the receipts because the clothes didn't fit (which was true, but not honest). My parents always told us to say something in the moment, but we had already been too conditioned by them to be agreeable to dare mention our needs at that point.

And then when I was ten years old, my great-aunt came down for a visit from Canada and blew every bad Christmas outfit out of the water.

She bought me and my sister matching jewel-tone onesies.

They looked like outfits for four-foot-tall toddlers.

I took one look at that fuchsia monstrosity and practically screamed, "NO THANK YOU. I DON'T WANT THIS!"

My outburst was immediately met with cries from my aunt and grandparents of, "Try it on before you say no!"

Did I say no? Of course not! Because I was a child and the instructions I had about life were compromise, accept the result, and deal with the feelings on your own.

The point is this: I could have stopped there and kept my foot firmly planted at this boundary, but I didn't. I tried on the onesie.

Once I did, the crisis somehow got worse. I could not accept this. If

I did, I knew I would only be gifted *more* onesies in the future. This was my Alamo, and I finally drew my line in the sand.

I begged, pleaded, and insisted: "Kids will make fun of me. I can't wear this. It looks like it's for a baby. I'm almost in middle school!"

Finally, the grown-ups relented. I let out a sigh and was excused from the table to read until it was time to clear the table. Unfortunately, that ingrained behavior didn't stop there. That memory might not seem like it had anything to do with money, but I lived in different versions of that moment for the next eighteen years on every scale imaginable—in my career, my relationships, and more. I learned not to stand up for myself in what I deserved, particularly from money, unless the situation was egregious.

Fast-forward five years later and I don't even recognize that woman anymore.

I had it *all* wrong.

And I learned it by taking the first step of just acknowledging what my conscious will was. I admitted that what I wanted more than anything in the world—more than making a difference, more than having a family, more than being a good person—was money.

Does that sound shallow?

Well, it's true!

But not for the reasons you likely suspect.

I want money because I want **power.**

Not the kind of power that would leave me drunk on running a billion-dollar corporation off the backs of minimum-wage employees, unpaid interns, and cheap suppliers who may or may not rely on literal slaves.

I want the kind of power that gives me some fucking sway in this world. The kind of power that affords me and those for whom I wield it more freedom, opportunity, or, hell, even just some flexibility.

I want to be so rich that when I speak, lawmakers listen.

I want to be so rich that I can pay reparations to people and not worry about my bottom line.

I want to be so rich that when I *do* choose to have a family, I can do it without worrying about how much I need for doctors' visits and new clothes every year and whether I can afford a babysitter so I can continue to run my business.

I want to be so rich that I can afford grand acts of kindness like $1,000 tips to servers on their second or third shift of the day or paying off an artist's student loans so they can create without Sallie Mae breathing down their necks.

Would you believe me if I said you didn't need to be in the top one percent to afford this kind of lifestyle?

It's true. You don't even need to be a millionaire.

If you often find yourself dreaming of this kind of life but feeling stuck in this endless cycle of earn, spend, burnout, then I've got news for you.

All you want in this world is money, too. And the power it affords.

And I'm going to show you how to get it, keep it, and make it work for you.

To get you there, I need you to first accept wealth as your *conscious* will. So, for the rest of this book, I want you to decide that your foremost goal in everything I teach you will be to make money—and lots of it.

Money Is Infinite and Renewable

Before we can tackle the activities that dredge up all the subconscious muck around money we've been carrying around, it's crucial to reframe how you look at money. If you continue to view it as a finite resource, it's far too easy to fall into guilt when we focus on acquiring more of it. We tend to think of making money like this: "If I get more money, then the person giving it to me will have less of it." Even if the person giving it is an employer, it's easy to think getting a raise for yourself takes away from the same budget that could give raises to your coworkers or friends.

Misconstruing money in this way is a picture-perfect example of a roadblock that will naturally undermine any kind of manifestation or money magic you might attempt.

So, first, you need to understand exactly how money is *infinite*.

If you've come even remotely close to anything regarding money mindset, manifestation, and so on in the past few years, you've definitely heard the phrase "Money is energy."

It's a saying that's repeated among all manifestation experts but rarely explained.

Unfortunately, they often say that because they don't know *why* money is energy. They just know it is.

Well, I'm here to explain it to you. And you don't need to live through a ride on a financial roller coaster or take ayahuasca in the desert to understand it either.

When people say, "Money is energy," they're saying two things:

First, money has no *intrinsic* value.

Second, money is a *renewable* resource.

I know those both sound bananas, but just hear me out.

Money only bears value because we as a society have collectively agreed to it.

Without humans, money is just paper, cloth, metal, and so on.

You can see an example of this concept playing out in history. During the American Revolution, then-General George Washington continually wrote to Congress about how his troops were starved, weak, and low on supplies, begging legislators to send more money.

The problem was that Congress kept sending American dollars, but merchants would only accept the British pound.

Those merchants likely didn't believe the Americans would actually win the revolution, so it served them better to accept British pounds as the legitimate currency.

That belief made American dollars worthless.

So, you see, money without societal agreement is only worth as much as the scrap materials it's made from.

Then why use money at all? Well, because it's a standardized method of transaction.

Before that collective agreement to create currency, we lived in a trade society. It might sound ideal to barter your goods or services in exchange for different goods or services from others. Except for the fact that there's no guarantee that your bartering partner values your goods in the same way as they value theirs.

I might believe that a sweater that took me a month to knit should cost the same as a month's worth of eggs for my family. And when that farmer has an abundance of eggs, they might agree. But what happens in the summer when it's warm and there's no need for knitted goods? And what if their chickens aren't producing as many eggs? Will they still feel like a month of eggs is a good trade?

That's where currency comes in and standardizes transactions.

And ultimately, that's what money is: a physical representation of transactions between buyers and sellers.

It's even in the word *currency*. Its Latin root is the word *currens*, which literally translates to "current."

So, just as water moves in currents in rivers and the ocean, so too must money. It only has worth as long as we all believe it does and it serves its purpose of representing the potential flow of goods or services exchanged.

And just as belief can affect the value of goods in a trade society, belief can also affect the value of currency on multiple levels. On a grand scale, belief is what causes the stock market to rise and fall. On a small scale, belief keeps us in low-paying jobs or undervaluing our time when setting business rates.

The second part of "Money is energy" is that it is a renewable resource. That means it's less like fossil fuels and more like sunshine.

Money as anything but finite might sound bonkers to anyone who has ever experienced being broke, losing a job, or borrowing from a friend. If you take money from someone, you have what was theirs, right? They now have less and you have more. It makes sense!

Except that money doesn't come from a well with a concrete bottom. Not only is its printing controlled by the government, but it's also increasingly digital.

It's easier to wrap your head around money being like sunshine when you receive payments via online banking, PayPal, or Venmo. At the end of the day, your money is just a sequence of numbers on a screen passing over the airwaves of the Wi-Fi in your home.

If that still feels a little esoteric, imagine walking through your neighborhood. All of your neighbors have some amount of money coming into their hands and leaving them. At the very least, everyone is paying rent or their mortgage either online or in their mailboxes. If they have cars, they're sending money to pay for them or paying for the insurance every month. And they're receiving payment from a job, Social Security, or even a trust fund. As you walk through your neighborhood, it's not hard to imagine that money is exchanging hands at different moments of the day. Maybe someone got a refund in their bank account. Maybe someone else got birthday money in a card from the mail. Either way, money is flowing through the air everywhere you go.

If that still feels tricky, imagine visiting a café or a fast-food restaurant. Everyone in line is transferring digital numbers from their accounts to the corporation's. The corporation is sending electronic paychecks to the employees. Anytime you walk into a store—even if you don't buy anything—money is still flowing through the air between all sorts of parties involved in the business of running that store.

Once you realize it, you can start seeing the air as if it were pregnant with money, and if you can shift your mindset, you feel as if you could almost reach out and grab it.

Maybe it's easy to understand the concept, but you still don't believe it's true for you. I get it. It's hard to feel like you're entitled to the money being paid and received inside a McDonald's, especially if you're there because it's one of the cheapest meals available to you.

Well, there's more than one way to tap into the feeling of money being all around you.

For instance, there's a meditation practice that seeks to create an effect of inner peace and abundance by taking walks and noticing what *is* abundant, even if it's not money.

Want to try it? Let's go back to your neighborhood for a moment. If you live on a tree-lined street, it would be easy for you to walk around in the middle of autumn and say, "My goodness! Just look at *all these leaves*. I can't even *count* how many leaves there are! There are easily thousands of leaves on this street!" If you live in an urban area like New York City, you can remark on how many bricks are in every building, how many people are on the street, how many car horns you hear. It doesn't matter what's in abundance. All that matters is that you notice it.

If you can have fun and get playful with this exercise, it will be even more effective.

Money Is Just a Tool

Now that you can see how exactly money is just energy, you can dispel the myth that it's also the root of all evil and, by extension, that you are evil for wanting ridiculous amounts of it. So many of the judgments we received growing up created this idea that money turns people evil. It's easy to understand why you run the risk of your magic or manifestation backfiring if you don't reframe this concept as well.

Money is neither inherently bad, nor is it inherently good. At the end of the day, money is just a tool, no different than a hammer.

If someone uses a hammer to build free houses for the homeless, we could collectively agree that the hammer was used for good. But if someone takes a hammer and uses it as a murder weapon, it's just as easy to say the hammer was used for evil.

However, the hammer itself isn't morally good or bad in either scenario. It's the *use* that is good or evil.

You see this within tiers of rich people all the time. If you're someone like me who laments the fact that billionaires could use their money to change the world, chances are you've done some reading about resource hoarding and how the top one percent in the world have exploited their way to the top.

Many billionaires would have us believe they worked their asses off to become the billionaire they are today, but in actuality, many of them are just privileged white, straight, cisgender people who benefited from supportive homes and used employee exploitation to attain success and largesse.

These aren't visionaries. They are strategists and exploiters. What made so many of them richer than the others in their industries is sheer commitment to disregarding employee well-being to raise the bottom line.

Take Amazon for example. Amazon was accused of not allowing warehouse workers to use the bathroom while they were on shift so they could meet the promise of Amazon Prime's two-day shipping. And what were these employees paid to hold their pee and risk a bladder infection?

The minimum wage of $7.25, which had steadily declined from a rate reflective of the average warehouse worker pay of $20 an hour in 2000.[1]

This wasn't the only option for Amazon to meet the self-imposed deadline of two-day shipping. They could hire more employees, open more warehouses, or even—God forbid—extend Prime to three-day shipping.

But that wasn't happening because when people are going through bad times, they'll take the jobs they can and put up with the harsh working conditions to make ends meet. And if Amazon could get away with high turnover and meeting Prime deadlines without paying more than minimum wage or giving bathroom breaks, they would.

This is why so many loathe Amazon CEO Jeff Bezos. Because there are possibilities for reaching the same goals without exploitation, yet he chooses to maintain exploitative practices again and again.

Once you reach billionaire status, it's nearly impossible to spend all the money you have in your possession fast enough to lose it all before you die.

With his money, Jeff could maintain multimillionaire status and still:[2]

- Give clean drinking water back to Flint, Michigan, which costs $50 billion.
- Save 300,000 children worldwide from dying of preventable diseases by paying $23 billion to get all of them vaccines.
- Pay for the education fees, books, and school supplies of 10 million children for just $7.5 billion.
- Pull 850 million people across the world out of extreme poverty and into higher poverty levels for just over $1 billion.

And he would *still* be a multimillionaire!

But don't forget the hammer! Jeff's money isn't at fault here. It's his desire for hoarding resources.

So, is it even possible to become a billionaire without exploitation? Many argue no, but that it's OK to never attain billionaire status because being a millionaire should be good enough. One case proves this: our lord and savior Dolly Parton.

Dolly has donated *so much* to charity over her career that it seems no one can accurately estimate what her total net worth would be without those donations. In 2021, *Forbes* estimated Dolly's net worth at $350 million[3] while other sources place her at $650 million—nearly double.

Just to drive home the point that Dolly is wealthy AF, let's review some of her wildly successful sources of income. Her catalog of music makes up about a third of her income at around $150 million, thanks in part to her decision to keep all of her publishing rights by *starting her own publishing company* at twenty years old. That includes the rights to the hit song Whitney Houston made famous in 1992, "I Will Always Love You." Royalties from *that song alone* have made Dolly $10 million.

In 1986, she started her own theme park, Dollywood, to stimulate the economy of Sevier County, Tennessee, where she grew up, even though her financial advisors were against it. Her 50 percent stake rakes in about $165 million a year. That figure *doesn't* include the extensions since 1986, including a water park that makes her $20 million, a resort and spa earning $15 million, and eight restaurants and dinner theaters in the area.

She also started a production company focusing on independent films and television, such as a little TV show in the '90s called *Buffy the Vampire Slayer*. She financed it even after the original movie tanked at the box office because she believed it was a story worth telling. And let's not forget all her new merchandise like her signature perfume, Scent from Above.

Suffice it to say that Dolly is synonymous with "dollar" at this point.

But remember! She's not a billionaire because of all those donations. Charity work has peppered her career since the beginning, but let's review some of her more noteworthy donations over the decades.[4]

In 1988, she founded The Dollywood Foundation in her hometown to decrease the dropout rate by giving every seventh and eighth grader $500 when they graduated from high school. That would be more than $1,300 today. She opened a 30,000-square-foot eagle sanctuary in Dollywood in 1991. Four years later, she started the Imagination Library, which now sends *one million books per day* to children all over the world. Back in 2007, she performed a concert to raise $500,000 toward building a hospital in Sevier.

More recently, she ran a telethon to benefit the victims of the 2016 Tennessee wildfires that raised $13 million for the hardest-hit residents. Then she started her own fund to give $1,000 a month to six families, which she continues to provide today.

The following year, she gave $1 million to the Monroe Carell Jr. Children's Hospital at Vanderbilt University Medical Center in honor of a niece who had been treated for leukemia there.

And in 2020, she donated $1 million to Vanderbilt's vaccine efforts, which directly contributed to the development of the Moderna vaccine for COVID-19.

This isn't even close to all of her donations. It also doesn't include the time she's donated, such as reading bedtime stories online during the pandemic,[5] or the investments she made to stimulate other struggling communities. For example, the office building she bought with her royalties from Whitney's cover to support a historically black community in Nashville.[6] That investment was part of the reason why the community attracted restaurants and other attractions that turned it into the booming borough it is today.

So, is it possible to become a billionaire without exploitation?

Yes.

Meanwhile, Jeff Bezos spent $5.5 billion to take a penis-shaped rocket ship to space *for four minutes* to get away from a dying planet he can pretty much afford to fix.

Money is just a tool. The way it's used is what determines whether that use is good, evil, or something in between.

And here's the catch:

If you wish you had Jeff's money so you could change the world in the ways you know in your heart it could and should be improved... If you would pay off school lunches for the children in your community, send someone to college, buy houses and give them away to the homeless...then I've got news for you:

The world needs you to be rich.

You—yes, you—need to be the change you wish to see in the world. However, I believe the data backs me up in saying that you could make a much bigger impact if you committed to making money and giving as much away as your goals demanded than you could by staying noble and poor but working yourself to death in the name of change. If you can accept that it's your *duty* to become wealthy so you can change the world for the better, this will amplify and expand all your growth opportunities and then your spellwork and manifestation strategies.

So, let's get rich! The world needs you.

Show Me the Money (Magic)

- **Money is energy** means that money moves freely like a current (hence the word *currency*) and it's a renewable resource like solar power. Whatever flows away from you will return *because that's what money does*. If you think about how many digital transfers are happening at any moment over Wi-Fi, it's easy to think that money is flowing all around you!
- **Money is a tool.** A tool alone is neither good nor evil; it's *how* one *uses* the tool that makes a difference. People can use it for corporate greed or to better the lives of others. Money itself is *not* the root of all evil.

ACTIVITIES

- What's abundant around you right now? No matter if it's bricks or leaves, make a list of the abundance surrounding you. Imagine the kind of people who would *love* that form of abundance. Sit with the feeling of being rich in something others would love to have.
- Money is neither good nor evil. The only morality that can be assigned is to its *use*. What are other resources onto which you tend to place judgment? For example, if you hate spiders, list out the ways they benefit you and the world around you, such as trapping mosquitoes.
- Find your money role models. Who uses money in a way that you would love to use it? Write what you love about them. Place a picture of them somewhere in your home so they can serve as a visual reminder of the good you can do with money. If you don't have one, use this QR to borrow one of mine!

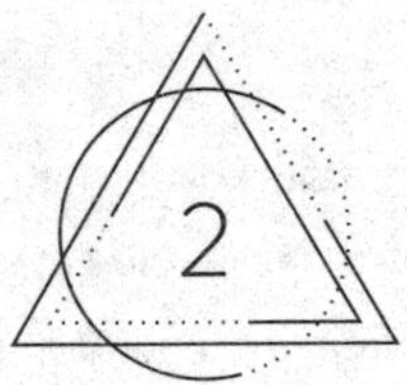

Magic and Manifestation 101

When I say, "I grew up Catholic," what I mean is that from birth until about age twenty-seven, I went to church almost every Sunday. I attended Catholic school from kindergarten through twelfth grade. My favorite show was *Touched by an Angel*, which my mom, my sister, and I watched religiously (pun intended). And I was beaten over the head with the message that all the topics I felt drawn to—like astrology and tarot cards—would send me *straight* to hell.

Because I was afraid of disappointing my parents even more than I was afraid of hell itself, even more than I was afraid of dying, I only ever read my horoscope or picked tarot cards from a digital deck on the AOL spirituality page late at night when no one could see. Then I would feel a wash of guilt that I had somehow betrayed God, go to bed, and pray for forgiveness like I had just watched the kinkiest internet porn available in the early 2000s.

So, how did I go from *that* to writing a book and building an entire business around magic?

Well, aside from the fact that Catholicism—with all its chanting, rituals, incense, saints, and more—*easily* lends itself to witchcraft, there's one source to thank more than others.

My mother.

While she would vehemently deny any identification as a witch, I would disagree.

First of all, this woman has more altars in her house than any church I've ever been to. They center around statues of holy *women* like the Virgin Mary or Saint Thérèse of Lisieux, bedecked with flower offerings, mementos, and other religious paraphernalia.

Now, Christian/Catholic statues don't really differ much from statues of other deities. They're not holier or fancier. If you've ever been dragged through a religious store, you would understand what I'm saying. I mean, my mom's main Mary statue *glows in the dark*. That same Mary's hands also broke off at some point in the '80s. My mom accidentally taped them back on backwards and *hasn't corrected that since*.

Second, my mom loves anything to do with manifestation—as long as it has the right branding.

Her first obsession was the 2000 book *The Prayer of Jabez*, which encouraged Christians to use a brief prayer said by a man in the Old Testament, for whom God lifted a curse and blessed.[1] The prayer goes like this:

"'Oh, that you would bless me and enlarge my territory! Let your hand be with me, and keep me from harm so that I will be free from pain.' And God granted his request." (1 Chronicles 4:10 NIV)

The book basically encourages people to use this prayer because in keeping the request for blessings open-ended and completely surrendering to God, Jabez received more blessings than he ever believed possible. And while some have criticized it as a form of prosperity gospel, that prayer brought my mother a lot of comfort, as it gave me years later when she gifted me her copy of the book before I returned for college.

Then in 2006, my mom got swept up in the documentary craze that taught the world that your thoughts could create your reality. *The Secret*. (We couldn't *not* talk about *The Secret*!)

She practically ran into the house, brandishing the DVD borrowed from a coworker after they watched it during their lunch break. She immediately made me and my sister sit down to rewatch it with her.

I was hooked and moved on to the book, which I read in one sitting. And while I didn't do much other than take in the information and test my visualization powers on traffic lights, focusing all my might on the color green, I realize now that my mom had planted seeds in me that would take another decade to sprout.

The exposure I had to the law of attraction as presented by *The Prayer of Jabez* and *The Secret* gave me the inspiration to search for modern methods for manifestation at the start of my spiritual journey—though I didn't know that would eventually lead to witchcraft.

Psychic or Psycho?

I first discovered manifestation in the midst of a quarter-life crisis. I was thirty-one years old and living in my dream city of Washington, DC. I made good money working for a pretty notable nonprofit with the kind of job title and work that others found fascinating. And yet…I couldn't seem to get excited about my career anymore.

I'd left what had previously been my dream job at Bloomberg Law, reporting on criminal justice issues for a legal audience, because I thought I had gotten sick of sitting on the sidelines and wanted to be part of the change. But at this point, it had been a year and a half and I still felt restless, bored, and confused. And let me tell you, for someone known among their friends and family for being the ultimate hype woman who took any excuse to celebrate, I felt like Casanova with erectile dysfunction—except the Viagra prescription I got hadn't worked.

I knew how to get the kind of jobs other people pined for at salaries they assumed were out of reach, but that didn't feel like the issue anymore. I wasn't sure what I wanted—or, more likely, I didn't think I *could* have it.

Meanwhile, I was experiencing some coincidences that were becoming too weird to ignore.

I've joked my entire life about being psychic, taken multiple friends to visit Cassadaga (a Florida town where most of the residents are psychics or mediums, or both), and I've always, *always* had an affinity for anything to do with witches and magic. There's a reason Halloween is my favorite holiday, after all. But just because I felt naturally drawn to anything occultish didn't mean I put stock in it. It felt a bit like my love of murder mysteries and true crime—pure entertainment.

But everything had gotten so weird I couldn't ignore it anymore. Everywhere I went, every interaction I had, every thought I had seemed connected. I would have mundane dreams about my life only to find myself in the exact scenario days later. People would call me or text me within seconds of me thinking about them. I would have a conversation with one person and say a uniquely specific sentence, only to chat a few days later with a completely unconnected person and hear my words repeated back to me. I would think about something, and someone around me would say something nearly identical within moments.

It had been about a couple months of this, and I had become *thoroughly* freaked out. I didn't know what was happening, so I asked one of my best friends from elementary school, who had been a practicing witch for nearly fifteen years at that point. She said it sounded like I was experiencing some sort of awakening of psychic gifts. I'm pretty sure I laughed, but I still heard her out. After all, *I* had reached out to *her*.

That led me down a Google search spiral, reading anything that could pass as reputable and not scammy. When it comes to what's reputable among psychics, I've since learned that an ethical psychic will generally freely give as many resources as they can to guide others and will never tell you that the only way to resolve a problem is to pay them gobs of money. I'll get into this more in a later chapter.

So, I combed the first page of Google to read whatever I could find on spiritual awakenings, psychic gifts, and whether these were skills that could be channeled, honed, and trained. That's when I found a podcast called *So You Think You Are Intuitive* by a psychic medium named Natalie Miles and thought to myself, "Fuck it. What harm could more information do?"

Natalie's stand-alone episodes are designed to act as a course on tapping into your psychic gifts, and the more I listened to them, the more I realized I could turn those coincidences between my brain and surroundings *off and on*. And when I turned them on, I could laser focus into what people felt and thought in a way that was eerie. It wasn't like how it seems on TV. I couldn't hear anyone's inner dialogue. Rather, I would feel their emotions like they were mine with the same intensity, and I just knew information without knowing why or how. When I started trusting that I would have these random thoughts for a reason and say what was on my mind, people were astonished at what I knew about them.

I probably should have been more freaked out than I was, but considering I had spent twenty years convinced that my letter to Hogwarts had somehow gotten lost in the mail, I instead felt excited and motivated for the first time in years. I practiced using my newfound gifts with the tarot cards that previously sat under a thin layer of dust, automatic writing in response to questions from friends, and read everything I could about spiritual gifts and psychic powers. I started a tarot journal, wrote manifestation letters based on May McCarthy's *The Path to Wealth*, and incorporated little rituals to feel powerful from Laurie Cabot's *The Witch in Every Woman*.

And, of course, I devoured the early episodes of Natalie's podcast, including the guest conversations. One would change my life forever.

Natalie sat in conversation with a young woman named Lacy Phillips, who was apparently a well-known manifestation expert. She had cracked the code on the basic formula and principles behind manifestation, building a fortune on a membership website called To Be Magnetic that taught the formula in its basic form and as applied to popular topics like love and money.

As I listened, I realized this was *not* the think-good-thoughts-and-get-what-you-want practice described in my mother's tomes *The Secret* and *The Prayer of Jabez*.

Instead, it felt like **common sense**, as if Lacy were reminding me of a lesson from elementary school I already learned but had forgotten.

To summarize this life-changing practice, Lacy's method works as follows:

Everything you experience is a direct result of what you believe you deserve on a subconscious level. When you decide you want something *new* or *better* than what you've always had, you need to increase your self-worth so you feel completely deserving of it.

You can achieve this in two ways. First, you use meditations designed to help you dig into your subconscious to find what experiences led you to believe you can't have what you want and then create new, artificial memories to overpower the original ones to reinforce a new set of beliefs and higher degree of self-worth. Second, you find examples of people who prove that you, uniquely, can have exactly everything you want.

The moment you claim what you want in writing, the universe will begin to rearrange to deliver your desires to you. Along the way, you'll receive little bursts of inspiration and ideas that might seem connected or might not. When you act on those ideas, they'll often lead to ideas or opportunities that get you closer to what you're manifesting.

However, because you're simultaneously pushing back against years of belief leading you to accept less than what you deserve, the universe will send you tests to see if you'll settle for less than what you want or act in accordance with a higher level of self-worth. These tests are not about passing or failing, but instead about taking your temperature to see how much progress you've made toward the level of belief and self-worth needed to get your results. If you settle or don't act in a way that shows you have belief, your manifestation will merely take a little longer to arrive.

For example, when I was in the early days of my business, I was so desperate for money that I would ignore my intuition when I had doubts about potential clients. I needed money and they were willing to pay me, so why wouldn't I agree to take them on?

Inevitably, they would wind up becoming problem clients. Often they would not apply any of the advice given to them, which meant they never made more money, and then they would stop paying me altogether. Even though I had contracts in place and could send them to collections, I was still powerless to recover what I was owed without a lawsuit that would probably eat up the amount due anyway.

When I started listening to that voice and either telling those potential clients I wasn't the ideal coach for them or not inviting them onto a sales call altogether, I began attracting better clients. Nothing had changed with my business strategy or the content I wrote and, in fact, my prices were *three times* higher than they had been. My money manifestations still showed up, but it took longer when I acted from a place of low self-worth.

That's why the bigger the manifestation or the lower your belief in your ability to achieve it, the longer the manifestation will take to arrive.

The last test is often a form of silence—no tests, but also no progress—for days or weeks before your manifestation appears.

As I heard Lacy's explanation in the podcast and, later, inside her membership, it clicked for me. When I completed one of her foundational courses, I wound up having an emotional breakdown (or was it a break*through*?), having realized that I had built my life choices around a deep-seated belief that "dreams are for other people, not for me."

I spent an evening sobbing that the reason I could be everyone's else's hype man but couldn't get my dick up for my own career was because I filtered all of my career decisions through a requirement that told me to play it safe and reliable, that I couldn't reach for more because I would likely fail. The realization spread like ink in water as I looked back on my entire career's trajectory.

That belief was why I picked journalism as my major while being a talented young writer who feared not getting enough job prospects with an English degree. Journalism was a *profession*, and I had heard too many adults make jokes about English majors not getting jobs over the years to even consider that major, despite my love of literature and writing. It was why I took a public relations job when I couldn't find a journalism job during the recession. It was why I went to law school when I realized I hated public relations. And it was why I jumped from private practice to government work to legal journalism to nonprofits in six years and was already restless and listless again. I was desperately searching for a career path that I could tolerate that wouldn't put me at risk in terms of both earned income *and* the approval of my family and society—because *dreams were for other people, not for me.*

It broke my heart to learn this about myself. I thought about myself as a preteen obsessed with theater who memorized dialogue from her favorite plays, belted out show tunes every free moment of the day, watched the Academy Awards every year, and daydreamed about the acceptance speeches I would give on my way to an EGOT. How did I go from being so thoroughly convinced about such big dreams to *this*?

I swore to myself the next career move I made wouldn't be something tolerable or logical. Instead, I would figure out exactly what my dreams were as this adult I had become—no matter what anyone thought of them—and I would do anything necessary to see them materialize.

Why Manifesting Money Is Different

It's probably no surprise I fell in love with To Be Magnetic and became a slut for discovering and healing all of my limiting beliefs. I found so much success with Lacy's membership, including the clarity that I wanted to start and run my own business, a love for money mindset that became an integral part of my coaching, a deeper connection in my relationship that saw us move past our fears of commitment to get engaged, and more self-worth than I had ever experienced.

For those reasons alone, I *still* consider myself a massive fan of her and the platform and actively recommend it to everyone, especially those who can't afford life coaching. Honestly, if I had a referral link from them, I probably would have landed a free lifetime membership by now.

Yet as I advanced as an entrepreneur, business consultant, and life coach, I started noticing some holes in the method that kept it from *always* working for me on a very specific and crucial topic—money.

When it came to manifesting money, To Be Magnetic functioned like the cologne Sex Panther from *The Anchorman*: "Sixty percent of the time, it works *every* time."

It worked perfectly up until a point when, like most methods, experts can't always explain *how* to keep making a method work except to say, "Try doing it again, but harder, stronger, and for longer this time."

And while everyone is encouraged to put their own spin on the manifestation process, no one likes the feeling of endless experimentation without the assurance that what they're doing will work. I would eventually turn to magic to fill in the gaps in my knowledge, but before jumping into the meat of it, let's talk about why manifesting money is different than manifesting, well, just about everything else.

People usually turn to manifestation for love, money, goods, or opportunities. Most of those topics are sufficiently specific that the formula popularized by Lacy works for everything. You ask for what you want and confront your limiting beliefs, which often reveal new layers to what we authentically want.

For example, so many people manifesting love will initially focus on physical attributes like the standard "tall, dark, and handsome" order plenty of people have for male-identifying partners. They might have plenty of other character traits alongside that list, but often, it's difficult for them to let go of certain physical requirements in the beginning. Then when they confront their subconscious, they might learn that the reason they wanted someone tall, dark, and handsome is because that's what they associate with heteronormative masculinity. And the reason they want someone heteronormatively masculine is *actually* about someone who makes them feel safe and cared for that they're *also* attracted to.

Well, anyone who's ever been on a dating app can tell you that plenty of people who identify as men can be tall, dark, and handsome—and make you feel definitively *unsafe*. So, they can edit their list and call in someone with a specific profile of characteristics that allow that person to feel a certain way when they're together.

The same thing goes for *goods* and *opportunities*, which could include anything from a deal on a pair of limited-edition shoes to one on an entire house. You list out qualities, do some subconscious digging, and rewrite your list to something more authentic to you.

Take the deal I got for this book, for example. I had a book deal on my manifestation list for *years* before it ever became a real possibility. When I was finally scouted by an editor and signed with an agent to guide me in the process, my manifestation list sounded like this:

- Six-figure book deal,
- Top-five publisher,
- Editor with good taste who doesn't try to edit out my voice, who understands my mission and personality, and
- Publisher willing to invest in promotion for me and my book.

When I got in touch with what I authentically wanted, I realized I didn't actually care how much I made from the advance because I was using it as a substitute for true *belief* in my brand and the mission of my manuscript. The same went for the publisher's ranking. Saying I wanted a top-five publisher was also a substitute, but for my belief in *myself*. I thought if I could land that, it would mean my book had potential, that the idea was legitimate, and that it *could* be a bestseller. So, I rewrote my list:

- I don't care about the advance, but I *do* want a publisher that will put money into marketing my book and making it a bestseller;
- Editor with good taste who doesn't try to edit out my voice, who understands my mission and personality; and
- Editor and publisher are both vision holders for my potential as an author and see me as having great potential for future works.

I wound up getting a decent advance for a first-time author, my editor is my biggest fan, the publisher's marketing department loved my vision for promoting the book, and the publisher's entire mission is to publish new, female-identifying voices. In our negotiations, they told me they like to work with *authors*, not singular manuscripts.

Even though I heard other pitches, I knew I had found the one once I dropped the ego trappings.

However, manifesting money is a totally different ball game.

There's no way to distinguish the *kind* of money you want. Money doesn't come with characteristics. While you can manifest a job, a business idea, or opportunity to make money, that's not the same as manifesting money itself.

Because there's no way to more specifically manifest money, any qualification you attempt to place on it naturally becomes a cap.

Let's say a small-time fashion designer wants to call in $10,000 in one month from their brand. Does that mean they don't want opportunities to do well-paid, full-time costume design for a movie? Does it mean they would turn down a well-paying potential fashion job at a big designer or even a fashion college? Does it mean they don't want birthday money? What about finding $20 in their jacket pocket?

Asking for money to come from a specific source in your life naturally caps you because that excludes all other potential sources for funds. And who's to say this designer couldn't make *more* than $10,000 in a single month? Often, the amount is also related to our own internal limitations.

The other way money differs from manifesting love, opportunities, and goods is how it often affects us during the process of becoming manifested.

Generally, the moment we ask for something on a manifestation list, we'll start getting little signs that it's on its way. In her book, *The Path to Wealth: Seven Spiritual Steps to Financial Abundance*, May McCarthy calls this "seeing the birds."

She compares manifesting to seafaring. In the olden days, traveling by sea meant you could be surrounded by nothing except miles of blue water for weeks if not months at a time. Yet before the person manning that little basket atop the mainmast even had a glimpse of land, they would get an important clue that the ship was approaching land: birds.

Miles before seeing the shore, sailors would begin seeing more and more birds. It reassured them that they were getting closer to land. Similarly, seeing signs that your manifestation is close can be seen as reassurance that it's on its way.

Let's say you're manifesting a trip to Hawaii. You might start seeing ads for Hawaii on the subway or a billboard on your way to work. People you pass on a walk might be talking about taking a trip to Hawaii. You go shopping and find a sale on Hawaii-scented candles. Maybe you get an invitation to someone's birthday, and it happens to be at a tiki bar or have a luau theme. No matter what, you can see all those signs as a heads-up that your opportunity to take a trip to Hawaii is fast approaching.

Now, the same can be said with money, of course, but it tends to present with some trickiness.

Let's revisit that fashion designer with the $10,000 goal for the month, and let's assume this time they're asking for a general $10,000 *minimum* with no preference as to where it originates. As they sell items of clothing or otherwise receive money—maybe someone pays them back for dinner from a few months ago, or they get a surprise check in the mail from overpayment on a bill—a common tendency is to keep count of how much they made so far in the month. They hit the snag when they turn around and count down to see how much they still need to make to hit that $10,000. That internal dialogue usually goes something like this:

"OK, so far, I've sold five jackets for $300 apiece, ten shirts at $50 each, and a custom suit for $800. Plus, Jen paid me back for dinner a couple months ago, which was an unexpected $100. And it's only a week into the month! I'm killing it! How much is that?"

They pause to do the math and then...

"That's $2,900! Which means I need to make $7,100 to hit $10,000 in the next three weeks. Woof. That's a lot. Let me divide that by three. OK, that's only like $2,366.67 a week to get there! Not bad! I got this!"

The next week, they sell a total of $500 and, like most of us, they start to spiral.

"Wow, now I need to make $6,600 in two weeks to make that $10,000 minimum! That's $3,300 this week alone. If I don't make that, there's no way I can make the full goal in my last week. Maybe I should run a sale. Maybe I should lower my prices. Maybe I need to..."

The trickiness is that when manifesting a big chunk of money, people tend to focus on the money they don't have yet. And if there's a moment when the flow seems to cut back, it becomes much harder to celebrate your progress and focus on how far you've come. If you don't hit the goal at all, how possible will it feel to set money goals moving forward? Probably not very. And, as you'll learn later, feeling like something is attainable for you is *everything* in manifestation work.

It's not the same with that trip to Hawaii. If all of a sudden you have a week where you don't hear or see anything that reminds you of your trip to Hawaii, you generally won't spiral. You go about living your life, hopeful that all the signs you've seen to this point are just like the birds sailors see before reaching land, and excited to know you might be taking a trip sometime soon.

The reason it's difficult to manifest money the same way we manifest love, opportunities, and goods is because it's more similar to manifesting a *feeling* than it is to manifesting a *thing*. Remember how money is energy? Emotions are types of energy, too.

As Neale Donald Walsch wrote in his book *Conversations with God, An Uncommon Dialogue, Book 2: Living in the World with Honesty, Courage, and Love*, "Emotion is energy in motion. When you move energy, you create effect. If you move enough energy, you create matter.

Matter is energy conglomerated. Moved around. Shoved together. If you manipulate energy long enough in a certain way, you get matter."

We'll get into the science of how that works in the next chapter, but for now, it should be enough to understand that emotions are merely a channel to the results you crave. What good is having the dream job or dream partner if you're unhappy, right? The same goes for money. If money automatically meant happiness, then celebrities and billionaires wouldn't go through painful public divorces or die by suicide.

Now, I know most people reading this book would refer to the alleged quote from French playwright Françoise Sagan in response to that—"Money may not buy happiness, but I'd rather cry in a Jaguar than on a bus"—and they would be *absolutely* right. A certain amount of money can and does buy happiness. That's the entire reason why I wrote this book!

What I mean by sharing this perspective is to understand that just as money is energy and a tool, so is it a *pathway*. When it comes to manifestation and magic, we can't treat money the same way as we would for calling in homes, jobs, cars, and more. Instead, we need to treat it like something more ethereal, more personal, and more like a state of being. Abundance, wealth, and financial freedom are *feelings*, not things.

Alright, Alright, Let's Talk About Magic Already!

Whenever my brain seizes on a new interest, my solution is to *learn everything I can* about the topic, practice everything myself until I understand how the method works, tweak it based on any gaps I see, then teach the improved method to others to observe how it plays out for them. I guess you can take the gal away from the scientific method, but you can't take the scientific method outta the gal, right?

Anyhoo, that's exactly what happened when I began looking toward magic to fill in the gaps of what I found missing in my manifestation practice.

I began with the communities I was already in, asking how they filled in the gaps of their money manifestation work, but found a troubling pattern instead of answers. No matter how long people had been working on their self-worth, practicing manifestation, using psychic gifts, many of them seemed to think that if manifestation practices weren't working, it was because they needed more healing or unblocking. No one seemed to believe that they could manifest money while they were in the process of healing. So, they would just keep at it or, worse, pay for energy-healing sessions or get readings from intuitives who promised to help them heal enough to receive their money manifestations—*yikes*.

That's when I turned to experts and resources based in magic. I refused to believe that getting desired manifestation results required me to reach a place of being perfectly healed and whole. If that was the case, then celebrities wouldn't struggle with substance abuse, mental illness, or eating disorders. And having been diagnosed with an anxiety disorder at twenty-nine and ADHD at thirty-four, I knew that I would likely face symptoms of excessive worry and negative self-talk for the rest of my life. I couldn't and *wouldn't* hold myself to a healed-and-whole standard.

And thus began my journey to find modalities that would work without the need to seek perfection and instead allow me to channel the hot-mess energy of my life into results.

The first inkling I had that magic held the answer came from none other than a meme. Specifically, one that was just plain text on a white background that read:

"Other witches: !!ALWAYS! CLEANSE BEFORE!!!! RITUALS!!!!!!! OR IT WILL NOT WORK!!! AND YOU! WILL DIE!!!!!

"Me *wiping Cheetos dust off my hands*: Alright, sluts, here we go."

As someone who considers the Cheetos-dust coating on her fingers a *delicacy*, I knew that any modality that allowed for that wide a difference in practice was fine by me.

Of course, I had no idea what practicing magic really entailed. I started with talking to my best witch friend and podcast cohost, Kayleigh, who had been practicing since she was about eleven years old. The main lesson I learned from her is that just about anything can count as magic, which is why you can see so many brands of witchcraft and witch culture.

People identify as traditional or folk witches (those who practice in line with their family heritage or geographic location), kitchen witches (those who predominantly practice magic in—surprise!—the kitchen), hedge or green witches (those involved in plant- and garden-based practices and sometimes herbalism), hearth witches (those who practice a combination of kitchen and hedge witchcraft), cosmic witches (those who use astrology), augury witches (those who use divination), eclectic witches (those who practice a hodgepodge of magic from various places), and more.

This doesn't even cover belief systems, though I won't get into those. This isn't a book designed to tell you *what* you believe, but to help you figure out how to practice in a way that works for you and your bank account *in conjunction* with whatever your beliefs are.

Witching 101

Kayleigh also taught me some basics, such as the importance of the moon in performing spiritual rituals or casting spells. Each phase of the moon comes with its own special juicy energy that can lend some power to your rituals. Although I'll list those phases specifically, all you *really* need to remember are the full moon and the new moon.

The full moon is when it's big and bright, while the new moon is when it's completely dark. What ritual or spell will be best for those phases? Well, just think about what the moon will do in the next few days. The full moon will begin to shrink, so you'll get the best results from rituals and spells focused on anything to do with release, shrinking, or removal. The new moon will begin to grow, which means it's perfect for spells of increase, amplification, or manifestation. See? Easy!

Here is the breakdown for each moon phase:

- **New Moon:** This is the best energy for planting the seeds of your desires, so rituals or spells for new manifestations are ideal.
- **Waxing Crescent:** This phase when the moon looks like a silver sliver is ideal for nurturing anything inside you that will attract your desires. If we stick with the plant theme, this would be that initial sprouting phase where you let your seed germinate on its own.
- **First Quarter:** When the moon looks like half a wheel of cheese, it's a perfect opportunity to call in, well, opportunities. Rituals and spells can focus on the external. Think of this as watering your seeds or adding a little fertilizer to help them grow.
- **Waxing Gibbous:** Right before the moon reaches its full phase, it emits an energy of support for any desires that feel stagnant. Focus rituals and spells on stick-to-itiveness and stamina to reignite motivation. For those of us with black thumbs, this is the part of cultivating a houseplant when you remember you put it outside and forgot to water it for several days, panic, check on it, realize it's doing fine, and add a little water before putting a reminder in your phone to water it again in the future.
- **Full Moon:** The full moon is basically a blank slate. It has the most powerful energy of all the phases, so it's best to channel that energy into any *big* issues or manifestations in your life. Think of it like your plant is *thriving* and now you can take it in any direction you want.

Do you want to repot it or plant it in the yard so it can grow bigger? Do it. Want to cultivate some clippings for your friends? Well, snip, snip, bitch!

- **Waning Gibbous:** Now that the moon is *juuuust* starting to shrink, it's the time to focus on reducing the small obstacles. Think of this as pruning your plant where you cut back on small stuff that isn't getting you closer to your goals.
- **Third Quarter:** Once we're halfway to the new moon, it's time to address any bumps in the road we might have encountered on the way to our manifestations. This is ideal for troubleshooting rituals and spells to deal with unexpected obstacles that have arisen. Using the plant metaphor again, this is when you spot a random problem with your plant like a black spot or sudden drooping.
- **Waning Crescent:** When the moon has returned to that toenail sliver, it's time to go balls to the wall on banishing anything that's acting as an impediment to your life or the result of your manifestations. Think of this like a bug infestation on your entire plant or a mystery disease; you need to be ruthless with cutting back and treating whatever is harming that plant.
- **Dark Moon:** The few days before the official start of the lunar cycle with the new moon, the sky will look dark and the moon will look absent. This is a time to turn inward and face the radical truths about how you get in your own way, how you allow the outside obstacles to block you, or to consult your gifts for guidance on how to proceed in alignment with your goals. Imagine you've gotten rid of the disease that took hold of your plant. This is the time to rebalance the pH of the soil, figure out what started the infection in the first place, and take measures to prevent future infections.
- **Eclipses:** While they're not exactly a specific moon phase, we experience multiple lunar eclipses throughout the year. Eclipses can bring

chaos into our lives that ultimately leads us to better futures. Catholic astrologer Susan Miller describes the effect of eclipses as the movie trope of crossing a treacherous valley over a rope bridge, only to have it fall apart behind you. You cannot return the way you came. Some witches say to never work magic during eclipses because of this powerful energy, but I find that if you channel it into something that desperately needs a change of course or some kind of shake-up, you'll see incredible results. Finally, even though the plant metaphor is probably getting old, I would compare this to my seventh-grade science fair project where I tested the effects of growing seeds by exclusively watering them with a variety of liquids—namely, water, Coca-Cola, orange juice, and Budweiser beer. Surprisingly, the plant watered with Bud grew the tallest and strongest, albeit super crooked, which leads me to believe that eclipse spells are a bit like cracking open a cold one with your plant boys: a nice treat that might be surprisingly beneficial for them.

The other part of working with the moon cycles is understanding the astrological signs the moon is in. It's easy enough to figure out the timing. The new moon is always whatever the sign of the season is, meaning you can look up the dates for each zodiac sign. All new moons match the season. Full moons, however, are the sign on the opposite side of the zodiac wheel. So, let's say it's March 1 and we're solidly in Pisces season. If it were a March 1 new moon, it would be a new moon in Pisces. If it were a full moon, though, it would be a full moon in Virgo.

The signs are important because they're related to various energies and characteristics that make your spells work better. Learning what they represent can take time. As they say, astrology is a *language*. So, for the sake of convenience, I'll do a quick rundown of the qualities and energies that are typically associated with each sign:

Aries (March 21–April 19): Action, impulse, leadership, initiative, control, power, strength, lust, sex, anger

Taurus (April 20–May 20): Comfort, luxury, groundedness, relationships, money, beauty (people and things)

Gemini (May 21–June 20): Creativity, changes in direction, inspiration, fresh perspectives, communication

Cancer (June 21–July 22): Family life, nurturing, emotions, healing, reflection, fertility (for all types of growth)

Leo (July 23–August 22): Courage, social life, breaking out of your shell, makeovers, abundance, positivity, self-image, radiance

Virgo (August 23–September 22): Healing, everyday habits, organization, detailed planning, health

Libra (September 23–October 22): Relationships and partnerships, romance, balance, charm, flirtation, and playing devil's advocate

Scorpio (October 23–November 21): Transformation, death and rebirth, deep emotional exploration, shadow work, psychic powers, divination, sexual energy, fertility

Sagittarius (November 22–December 21): Travel or newness, scholarship, learning, truth seeking, legal issues, protection

Capricorn (December 22–January 20): Discipline, ambition, career goals, money stability, financial planning, business

Aquarius (January 21–February 18): Community, reputation, social network, friendship, overcoming addiction, technology, humanity, big ideas

Pisces (February 19–March 20): Dreams, mediumship, psychic abilities, artist pursuits, philosophy

Having a framework of topics for when to perform rituals or magic of any sort already got my wheels turning. Money is one of those topics that exists in us like a web with tendrils touching every facet of our lives. It infiltrates our families, our love lives, our self-esteem, our time management, and everything else. Even if I used the zodiac to guide the topics I worked on, it already felt like a huge step forward. I felt ready to move on to spellwork.

I started Googling spells on a variety of money-based topics and felt a little disappointed at what I found. Everything seemed to be merely a mash-up of rhyming verse, lighting candles, and other seemingly inane activities like burning spices or melting ice on top of written lists. All of them referenced extra tasks like "cast your protections," "cleanse your space," "stand in front of your altar," or "close your circle when finished." It felt as if I came into Hogwarts as a transfer student and missed a prerequisite. The concepts were easy enough to research, but they didn't answer the most burning question I had: What made the motions and words of ritual a spell versus a weird Tuesday night?

What Makes a Spell a Spell?

I bought a fuck-ton of books on magic and began to read. What I learned is that the reason you can be a Cheetos-dust witch is the same reason we don't walk around in complete magical disarray from words and actions we take on the daily.

There's a group of people who are so twitchy about language and magic. They believe that everything you say aloud is a spell. Whenever you say something remotely negative—even just venting—they will shush you with the ferocity of a parent on their last nerve.

"Careful what you say!" they exclaim. "We cast spells all the time!"

I usually try not to tell anyone that they're dead wrong, but...these people are dead wrong.

If everything we say is a spell, then I have years of complaints to file with the universe because I've shouted, "*Fuck me!*" in frustration too many times to have been so chronically underfucked when I truly needed to be.

What I learned is that what makes a ritual a spell is a polyamorous marriage among a slew of different elements: channeling emotions, mental focus, meditation, subconscious beliefs, the ritual itself, living in tune with your desires, and the actions you take after your ritual. And, honestly, that's skimming the surface because a spell *also* incorporates all the other elements we discussed above like the moon phases, the energy of the zodiac season, the chakra system, and other topics we'll get into later.

So much goes into magic and spells that getting started can feel overwhelming. But when I examined all of these facets and really looked at them, I saw a much simpler pattern emerge—and it's much easier to remember.

The truth is that you can turn anything into a spell as long as you follow three general steps:

1. Align your intentions,
2. Embody them deeply, and
3. Take inspired action daily.

Honestly, if you stopped the book right here (please don't) and only used those three steps to approach all your goals in life, you would be golden. But as I'm sure you've guessed, there are activities and methods that expand on these principles so you can have a more targeted effect when you set out with specific money goals.

And *speaking of* those money goals, that brings me to one final point before we carry on with our journey: the phases of manifesting money.

Where You Are Matters

As I deepened my practice in money magic and manifestation and taught others how to do the same as an integral part of their career or business strategies, I realized that manifesting money comes in three overarching categories. Each one encapsulates a spectrum of goals and circumstances with different processes and activities for each.

First, there's manifesting money for the first time. No, I'm not necessarily talking about the first time you ever received money. It's more so about your first foray into money magic and manifestation work. It doesn't necessarily mean that the person in question is broke, though that's a pretty common situation. After all, why would you be turning to magic if you hadn't tried everything else? Rather, people in this phase probably don't have the relationship with money that they want. They likely feel anxiety or fear around making it or losing it. They want to make more of it and stop stressing about the process. They might even be making a good amount of it, but they don't feel fulfilled by *how* they make it. Think about me at the start of this journey working in the legal field. I had enough to support me and my partner, but I was miserable and I couldn't seem to save or get ahead without seeking new jobs to increase my income. That's the first bucket.

Second, there's *keeping* manifested money. So many people start their money manifestation journeys, learn how to increase their income, but wind up in the same place they started over and over again. No matter how much they make, it seems spoken for the second they make it. They're not even necessarily overspenders. Oftentimes, people make a ton of money but wind up with massive bills that eat up everything they manifested, keeping them from ever getting ahead. Sometimes, overspending comes from a seemingly good place, too. These are often the people who attempt to catch up on debt when they have more money, only to make it harder to pay the minimums in lower-income months.

Finally, there's manifesting *more* money after you've hit your glass ceiling. This isn't just about first-world problems for Richie Riches. This can look like landing your first *thriveable* wage when it seems like every company exec thinks it's brag-worthy to pay $15 an hour, which isn't livable in most major metropolitan cities. It can look like an attorney with a budding law firm who can't seem to crack a seven- or eight-figure year, which would allow them to hire the staff they need to expand and offer more pro bono work. Sometimes, this isn't even money. It can look like the super-successful entrepreneur having five- or six-figure months, but who can't seem to book paid speaking gigs or get media attention no matter what they do. Even if it's a juicy plateau, it's *still* a plateau.

All of these buckets come with their own challenges and themes. While the same three steps still apply, you'll see how they take on different flavors through each evolution of your money manifestation journey. Along with those steps will come activities and methods tailored to fit the approach needed to break out of your cycle and connect with your money goals that much faster.

Show Me the Money (Magic)

- **Manifestation is more than positive thinking.** The baseline formula to manifest, founded and popularized by expert Lacy Phillips, is (1) reprogram your subconscious limiting beliefs to increase your self-worth, (2) find people who show you that what you want is possible, (3) pass tests, and (4) follow your intuitive nudges.
- **Manifesting money is about emotions.** Most people crave money for intangible results like security and freedom, making its manifestation closer to manifesting love than to manifesting goods or opportunities. That means a big part of manifesting money is to dive into *why* you crave it and what emotions you want to feel.
- **Magic does not require perfection.** Intention is the name of the game, so as long as you focus your energy on changing your beliefs, any type of magic you pursue will work.
- **The foundation of spellwork is above you.** Understanding the energy and meanings of the moon phases along with learning the language of astrology will help you identify what spells to cast and when.
- **Words alone do not make a spell.** The three steps of any spell are: (1) align your intentions, (2) embody them deeply, and (3) take inspired action daily. If the words aren't said with intention and embodiment, you have no reason to worry.
- **There are three distinct phases of manifesting money:** Manifesting it for the first time, keeping the money you've already manifested, and manifesting *more* money after you've plateaued.

ACTIVITIES

- Think about everything you've been wanting or manifesting recently. Ask yourself why you want each of them. Do you actually want everything, or are some of the items on your list acting as substitutes for emotions and feelings? Reflect on your desire for money, too: What does it mean to you? Why do you want it? Is money the only avenue to receive what you want? If not, make a list of other ways you could get the results that money would provide.
- What birds have you been seeing that could indicate your manifestations are on their way? Make a list of everything so far and add to it as you see more proof.
- Look up the moon phase and zodiac sign for today. Based on the meanings of the moon phase and sign, what would be some good money-based activities you can do today that will benefit from this energy?
- Do you know which phase (or phases) of manifesting money you're in right now? Write that down, along with a description of your circumstances that support your guess.

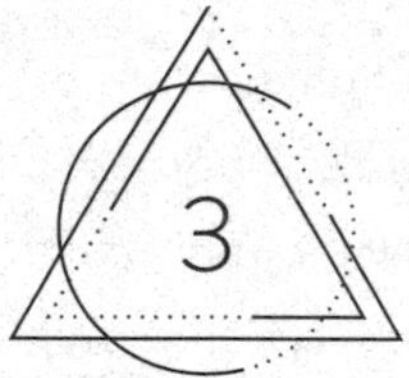

The Science of Magic

I wasn't huge on science growing up. But just as I'm not good at math until there's a dollar sign in front of a number, I can get behind science when it promises to make me money.

Why does the science behind magic even matter? Well, first, it will probably make for great evidence in court in case someone tries to commit me. Second, these are literally the reasons, the *how* and *why* magic works.

Effective magic begins with something called a thoughtform, a.k.a. energy generated when your conscious and subconscious desires are on the same page. Knowing that magic and manifestation are based in science makes it more believable that these practices are *legitimate* and will actually *work*. It helps you align your subconscious and conscious beliefs!

When it comes to our conscious beliefs, it's all too easy for doubt or that friend who considers themselves a Very Practical Person to throw off our game with scientific arguments that make a whole lotta sense. Remember, I was a lawyer before I became the Millennial Money Witch. I needed to know that the spiritual practices I used were backed up by science to *believe* they would work.

Quantum Physics

So, what the hell is quantum physics? It's the field where scientists guess how we know some stuff in the world exists based on how the stuff we *can* see exists. It reviews how our universe works and explores the unexplained. While other sciences seek to learn just about the physical things we can see, quantum physics requires scientists to think and theorize about what we can't.

Let's start with the basics and work our way up. You probably remember the lesson on matter from grade school: "Matter is the stuff that makes up everything in the universe." Everything that contains matter is made up of atoms, which contain protons and electrons, a nucleus, and even smaller parts called quarks and leptons.[1]

What makes up the difference in how matter is arranged is how many atoms are packed together and how close they are to each other. So, the fundamental difference between solids, liquids, and gasses is the density of those atoms. Think of it like a party. Solids are packed clubs with sweaty people grinding up on each other with a line out the door where the bouncer can only let people in as others leave. Liquids are more like a fundraising gala where there's a great turnout and people mingle from an appropriate distance while sipping on wine. Gasses are like when introverts hang out by independently scrolling social media and texting each other memes from across the room.

All that to say that everything we see and everything we are is made of the same universal material, just in different forms. That means your body and mind are composed of the same material as stars, dirt, elephants, and even this book or device you're holding right now.

Wild, right?

What allows us to see or experience the different forms of matter are not just those little building blocks, but the rate at which they vibrate and how we experience those vibrations. Remember the parties; there's a big difference between bumping and grinding at the club and an introvert's night in.

You've heard the old riddle, "If a tree falls in the woods, but no one is around to hear it, does it make a noise?" Well, we know that sound is created through waves, but if no creatures, people with ears, or recording devices are around to experience those waves, can you really say that sound has occurred?

It's the same thing with our eyes. Matter can only exist when we are able to perceive its light waves with our senses. Without a person or creature with the sensory ability to process matter, you could make an argument that the matter doesn't exist. That means *subjective* experience is what creates reality, rather than objective. In other words, the world begins in our minds.

Let me borrow a lesson from law school to explain what I mean by subjective versus objective.

In the first year, they teach you that not all of the law is written. Most of it is interpreted by the courts through cases, which results in rulings that govern how lower-level courts are required to apply the law moving forward. Those rulings are called precedents. Judges base their decisions that explain precedent on the understanding of "a reasonable person of sound mind." That means a judge isn't ruling from their personal opinion, but attempting to decide how an average reasonable person would understand a law and behave based on that understanding. Makes sense, so far, right?

My point is that objectivity is still based on a collection of individual and *subjective* beliefs. True objectivity doesn't exist! If it did, it wouldn't change. It would be a universal, unchanging truth like gravity.

Let's bring this back to science. If objectivity doesn't exist, then we can agree that an individual's subjective experience is the true origin of matter's existence in the material plane. Scientists from the University of

Aberdeen and the University of California even explained in a January 2022 paper for *Science Advances* that due to how our brains experience reality, everything we see is 15 seconds behind reality.[2] Basically, nothing exists without our ability to experience it through our senses. If we can agree on that, it means we can take it a step further and say that reality exists because our brains create it—a concept quantum physicists and neuroscientists alike are actively proving with research.[3,4]

This is, quite literally, exactly how magic works. In Mya Om's *The Un-Spell Book: Energy Essentials for Mastering Magick*, she breaks down the most basic concepts for new practitioners. The first and most foundational topic she covers is visualization, the practice of seeing inside your head instead of with your eyes. This is what generates the power behind the spells. Even *The Secret* uses this method in its most simplistic method of manifestation. Quantum physics taught us that reality is created by our brains, which means that all we need to do to create our desired reality is to see it as vividly as possible in our minds as if it were happening right in front of us—visualization.

What's different about Om's approach, though, is the understanding that not everyone comes with the same ability to visualize. You might have seen the following picture on social media, which asks you to rate how capable you are of seeing an apple in thought alone (pretend that the first image is in full color).

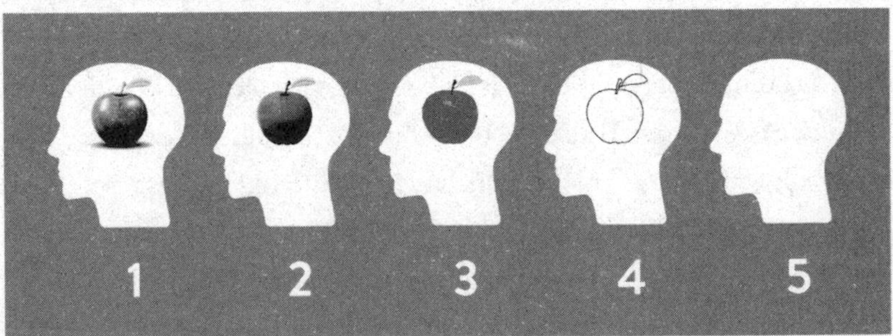

Om understands that plenty of people naturally fall on the other end. So, she provides lots of activities on how you can develop your visualization skills using a physical apple and relying on your memory. She does this because seeing the end result of your spell is what creates the energy to make it happen.

Do you see now why conscious belief is so important as the basis of magic and manifestation? The more we engage our senses in the process of visualizing our desired lives, the more likely it is for our minds to then create that reality around us. Spells just take it a step further by focusing on one specific result.

Creating reality through subjective experience isn't the only thing our brains use to influence reality. They also use the vibrations produced from the electricity generated in our bodies.[5]

Biology and Regular Ol' Physics

Remember the states of matter and the vibrating molecules I told you about earlier? Well, the vibration is made up of different waves of electricity. Everything in the universe emits a unique combination of vibrations. Living beings, specifically, emit more gamma, theta, and beta waves. The more conscious a living being is, the more gamma waves they produce. Scientists theorize that the vibrational frequency of gamma waves could explain why humans are able to feel and think as we do.

So, why do these vibrations matter? First, it means that our bodies emit an energetic frequency. That's the reason why we can feel someone staring at us from across a room or why we can feel the presence of another person even if we can't see them. Our bodies are detecting the electric frequency of our surroundings all the time. We are emitting and receiving vibrations at all times. This is how living beings connect, regardless of distance. For example, people's heart rates and breathing have been found to synchronize in intimate settings, such as when sharing a bed, or in public like a crowd intently focusing on a performance.[6] However, this phenomenon has also been found to occur on a large scale. A study found that five participants living in different countries across the world synchronized heartbeats when they listened to the same meditation at the same time.[7]

That's because the vibrations of the earth were tapped into the participants and the electromagnetic field allowed them to connect to each other. That's why spells get a boost from being performed in a group. When everyone focuses on similar end results, their energies sync together, powering up the manifesting energies of everyone involved in the group. It's one of the reasons why spell circles are so popular; they offer the opportunity for practitioners to get extra juju behind their spells.

That power-up isn't just limited to people. Everything that carries vibration impacts us.

Consider those YouTube or TikTok videos showing someone playing a violin bow against a metal plate holding grains of sand. As the plate vibrates from the sound of the bow, the sand forms patterns all around the plate. When the bow plays another note, the sand creates a different design.

A similar experiment was conducted using sound vibrations in water. As scientists used sound waves to shake up water, the water rippled in unique, intricate, geometric patterns.[8] Considering that the human body is made up of 80 percent water, it's understandable how sound could affect us.

If you've attended a concert by your favorite musician and enjoyed the reverberating tones vibrating through your chest that left you feeling lighter, you've experienced a form of sound healing. Simply put, the sound's vibrations cause the water in your body to change ever so slightly and leave you feeling better.

It's why rhythmic sounds from chimes, gongs, the ocean, organs, sound bowls, and more are frequently found in spiritual practices. Not only do meditation and prayer heal one's mind and body, but the cryomatics of those instruments boost the healing effects.

Being able to sense this frequency in other people strengthens based on the time your bodies spend connecting. Parents are a great example of this. They can usually tell when their teenagers are getting into trouble, even if they're across town and haven't spoken to them.

Neuroscience

Our brains are *so* powerful. It's incredible what scientists are learning about how our brain's circuitry can affect our lives.

Let's go back to the example of being able to accurately read someone's character or emotional state. It's not just about the electric frequency that their bodies and brains are emitting—otherwise everyone's emotions would be completely transparent. Rather, the brain is performing a thorough and lightning-fast process.

It goes by many names: intuition, gut feeling, instinct, sixth sense, and more. It's also one of the most powerful tools you can use in magic. Intuition is how we receive guidance and messages on how we can better achieve our magical goals.

No matter the name, it happens instantaneously. Many people can't explain how or why it occurs. "I don't know how I know, I just *know*" is the oft-repeated mantra of those who claim they can size someone up in the first few minutes of meeting them.

Well, the science of what's happening when we use our intuition is this: The brain scans through millions of data points through all its stored memories in the hippocampus, neocortex, and amygdala and looks for patterns from its past experiences to make a decision about the safest way to proceed in the current moment.

Your brain bases its data off of your subjective opinion of your lived experiences. And because your brain's entire function is to keep you safe and balanced, it probably ascribed good or bad judgments to those experiences. That means you'll likely act in a way that you *subconsciously* believe will keep you safe. Casting money spells works in the exact same way. The magic that powers a spell is simply your mindset. And if part of you subconsciously doubts that the spell will work, it will fall flat.

Anyone who's ever sabotaged themselves by spending money can understand this concept.

A popular coaching metaphor that compares your brain to an air conditioner goes like this: Imagine that your sense of familiarity in life is the setting for room temperature. When you start to perceive yourself as failing, you'll kick into overdrive and hustle until you make the money you need to stop feeling like a failure. But if you continue on that hot streak, your brain will cool you down so you don't get *too* hot. That's when you stop checking your bank account or budget or decide you've earned a treat and wind up overdrafting when an unexpected bill hits your account. At the end of the day, a consistently successful financial life comes with unknown problems and challenges for those of us who didn't always have it. Your brain will always pick the devil it knows over the devil it doesn't.

Can you guess how this might affect your brain when it comes to creating the life you want or making more money as an adult? If you grew up poor, with abuse or neglect, or even just lived with judgmental parents, the data you collected is skewed toward the problems you know—like poverty, pain, or disappointing your parents or yourself. Your brain attuned itself to those problems as its default setting because it knows how to live under those conditions. Being rich, happy, and feeling proud of yourself are too different, and who *knows* what kind of problems they come with. Like Biggie said, "Mo' money, mo' problems," right?

The good news is that you can change your brain, and that includes its circuitry!

By becoming more aware of the references you had around money and showing yourself those beliefs are not true or not *always* true, you can start to show your brain that it's *safe* to have whatever you want.

You can do this through meditation, journaling, and taking different actions. Meditation allows for increased emotional regulation and even develops new gray matter in the prefrontal cortex, the problem-solving part of the brain that lives right behind your forehead.[9] And not only does journaling feel reeeeeaaaaal good, but it also makes it easier for you to process any trauma you experienced and free up brain power to focus better during the day and sleep better at night.[10]

In Byron Katie's absolutely inspired book *Loving What Is*, she talks about using self-reflective questions as pattern interrupters to shift brain function from the amygdala and brain stem—the survival parts of the brain—into the prefrontal cortex. In other words, you can switch off your fight-or-flight tendencies and get into problem-solving mode.

Katie's formula, known as "The Work," is to notice the trigger, journal about it, then ask yourself four questions: (1) Is it true? (2) Can you absolutely know it's true? (3) How do you react/what happens when you believe that thought? and (4) Who would you be without that thought?

These questions require you to examine what feels like default programming and give you the ability to find proof showing you that the data your brain is using isn't actually needed or useful.

You can not only journal on what happened that set you off, but also take the beliefs you have and find out where they came from, who shaped them, and whether you want to believe them anymore. At the end of Part 1, you will find journal prompts that can help you dig up some of these beliefs and follow a formula that will help you start the process of breaking them.

So, what do you do when the data you're working off is off? Well, you gotta replace it with *new* data so your brain can update its analysis. This is the other half of neural reprogramming in which you can literally change the associations you have in your mind around the limiting beliefs that hold you back from reaching your full potential.

The way your brain does this is by understanding that it's possible for *you*, uniquely, to achieve exactly what you desire. One way to rewire your neural pathways is through the use of "disconfirming experiences."[11]

A disconfirming experience is one that directly contradicts the past experience of trauma. Doing so shows your subconscious that it's safe to take scary actions that can lead to success. Even if this doesn't work out as you hoped, the fact that you lived through it is enough to show your brain that making bold moves toward your goals is safe to do.

Our brains' entire job is to keep us alive and well. Remember the air-conditioning example? Our brain wants to keep us in a safe space that is predictable because that offers the most likely outcome for survival. The way we permanently raise the setting closer to what we want to achieve is to take some small risks and survive.

When I initially started my business, I was a job hunt coach. In my legal career, I had developed my own way of growing my professional network from nothing and using email as a way to meet new people (#introvertproblems) to tap into the hidden job market. I developed a system that worked so well for me that I found my last legal job entirely through networking and never sent in a single cold job application.

So, naturally, when I started a business, I relied on this formula and the mindset adjustments I had to make for that system to work. But I had never run a business before and I didn't even know any entrepreneurs. My entire friend and family network consisted of people who worked nine-to-five jobs. While my dad had started plenty of side businesses over the years, none of them ever really picked up and he would drop them after a few weeks. I had no examples of successful business owners, and almost everyone thought I was crazy for leaving behind my legal career, even if they didn't say it.

Those first eight to nine months were some of the rockiest I had experienced. I gave away too much information to people I wanted to help. I had poor boundaries. I undercharged my worth. I procrastinated. But worst of all, I was inconsistent. I started, stopped, and got overwhelmed and discouraged far too easily. And this was even with a coach! Most of the time, I was depending on her pep talks and belief in me to get me started again, rather than going within myself.

Until I had a realization. In the depths of my self-pity after another spurt of self-promotion that didn't seem to do any good, I had a moment of clarity and asked myself, "Why do you keep doing this? What are you so afraid of?" I sat down and started writing in my journal, just word vomiting up whatever came to mind. At the end I read it and got the message quite clearly. I was afraid that if I worked consistently at promoting myself every day and it didn't work, I would feel like a failure and everyone would judge me for being a failure.

"That's it?" I thought to myself. "I'm afraid of a *feeling*?"

In that moment, I found it so silly to fear a feeling. After all, I was already experiencing fear and I was alive and well. So, I asked myself, "Well, what happens if you work hard every day for a straight month and nothing happens? What will you do?"

I took a moment and thought to myself, "I will just try a new approach. If it really doesn't work, I'll just...try something else."

That didn't seem like that bad of an outcome, so I decided right then and there that I would truly give it my all for thirty days. That was it—thirty days of effort, and after that if it wasn't working, I would pivot. At this point, I had already cashed out my savings and a 401(k), so I figured, what the hell did I have to lose?

So, I did it. Every day I posted something to social media that taught a small lesson around job hunting or mindset shifts to make for your career. I talked about my own experiences and what I had learned about them. And every time I also talked about what I taught and the program I'd created to help people. By the end of the month, I made just over $3,000. It was the first time I made enough money to pay my bills and didn't wind up fighting with my partner over paying rent.

That was a fundamental lesson that showed my brain that I can work hard and get a payoff. That I *could* build a business. I lived through an experience I feared, and because I showed myself it was possible to take a risk and achieve, I knew I could do it again.

The cool thing about your brain is that even when you fail, your brain will still build a new, better neural pathway based on that experience.

Let's fast-forward about six months. COVID-19 hit the United States and the economy came to a screeching halt. I knew no one would be hiring new employees for a while, so I needed to pivot. I realized a *ton* of people would need support on how to start an online business. After all, I had made some seriously great money from one-on-one coaching and a six-week workshop. So, I hired my first online business manager plus a copywriter and launch strategist to sell a six-month program for increasing your business income. Both of them were working hard and I felt so free. I was flying high! This was it. The moment everything would turn around, when I would start making money in my sleep and become an internet-famous business coach with a six-month waiting list. And I was *so* ready.

Unfortunately...not a single person enrolled.

To say my launch flopped is an understatement. It bombed. And not only that, but I completely ran out of the money I *had* made because I hired two independent contractors. It was so bad that my rent check bounced. So, not only did I not make any money, but I lost the money I *had* made.

The experience sent me into a tailspin where I wound up losing all my leads and clients a few months later.

You would think that experience would make me afraid to launch anything again or to market myself. And at times I still feel a twinge of nervousness. But a lot of power comes from facing one of your greatest fears and living through it. The experience showed my brain that I could fail and *survive*. I lost my money and made it all back a few months later. Now, I knew that no matter what I was afraid of happening, I could live through it. And that lesson truly unleashed a commitment and bravery that I never had before. Because I knew that no matter what happened, I would be fine in the end.

Of course, I recognize how privileged I am to have a strong network of friends and family who would never let me wind up without housing. I know not everyone has that luxury. But to your brain, it's all the same: facing failure in whatever way *and surviving* is what creates the new neural pathways that allow you to continue making progress and believing that it's safe to do so.

But where does all this panic come from in the first place? Some of it is from our lived experiences or mental illnesses, of course, but a lot of it can feel like a general sense of panic and dread that we can't quite place. You can thank your brain for that, too. And your grandparents.

Epigenetics

Epigenetics is the study of genes inherited between generations. But this isn't just your average genetics topic. This is looking at the genetic contribution of several generations. Some basic ancestor math shows the significance of this topic.

Just knowing that every person is born of one egg cell and one sperm cell means that everyone has had four genetic grandparents, eight great-grandparents, sixteen great-great-grandparents, thirty-two great-great-great grandparents, and so on. If you trace any person's ancestral lines, you will see they're descended from twelve ancestral lines and 4,094 ancestors over the course of 400 years.

Now, here's some wild information that drives home the impact. At only four months old, when a fetus develops ovaries, it also produces all of its future eggs.[12] That means a pregnant person carries not only one unborn child, but all that child's offspring. That means all of us lived inside one of our grandparents!

Because pregnant people carry not only their unborn offspring, but a second generation as well, the conditions they experience can leave an imprint on two generations at once.[13] The phenomenon is referred to as the "three-generational footprint." This doesn't just include health and diet, but mental state as well.[14]

Studies have shown that children born during or after times of war or famine, or who suffered other traumatic experiences, had an increased risk of anxiety, depression, and a host of other mental and physical illnesses.[15] People feel anxiety because their brains release adrenaline hormones that put them into survival mode, keeping them prepared to fight or flee at any moment. The flood of hormones in the body becomes part of the fetus's development, making it more likely that the person will naturally have increased responses to stress, including a predisposition to heart disease.[16] That's why parents who use surrogates are often so concerned about the carrier's mental and emotional health throughout the pregnancy. Genes might predispose someone to certain disorders, but fetal stress can also determine whether those genes present after birth—sometimes as far ahead as adulthood.

So, if your brain's job is to keep you alive, but you've come from a family line experiencing ongoing trauma like domestic violence, famine, or war, your brain is more likely to naturally overproduce adrenaline because that's what was programmed into your egg when you lived inside the fetus that was your parent.

This is why it's important that when evaluating the influences on what you believe is possible for your life, you unpack not only your experiences, but those of your parents and grandparents as well. Their experiences, particularly around pregnancy, are extremely important to evaluate as they impact your natural tendencies toward anxiety and stress.

Because these disorders can manifest differently in family members, conversations with others are important, too. Anxiety, depression, and ADHD all run in my family—a fact I only learned when I got diagnosed with generalized anxiety disorder at age thirty and put on antidepressants. Shortly after, my brother was diagnosed and placed on the same medication. Then my sister got diagnosed. And then my youngest brother.

As I learned more about the chemistry in my head and how it presented in me, I couldn't help but think of my mother. She and I are so similar, not just in personality but the ways we worried about ourselves and our loved ones and the codependent behaviors that appeared alongside that worry. We both struggled to stand up for ourselves out of fear of rocking the boat, preferring to suffer in silence and act like martyrs later. We get accused of being nags because we repeat concerns so often, when half the time, we forgot we said anything and we're reminding ourselves. We get told we're buzzkills because we want everyone to be safe and hearing party stories stresses us out. We've both struggled with an obsessive fear of death, which I now know to be existential obsessive-compulsive disorder.

Because we were diagnosed pretty closely to each other, my brother and I were learning a lot about anxiety around the same time. I remember talking to him and saying I suspected GAD ran in our family.

"I know," he said.

"Yeah, it's so obvious that Mom has anxiety," I replied.

"Mom?" he asked in disbelief. "I was talking about Dad. What makes you think Mom has anxiety?"

I was just as shocked to hear my brother thought our dad had anxiety as my brother was when I mentioned what I had seen in our mom. We compared notes and realized how differently anxiety manifested in each of us and thus how it manifested differently in each parent.

But it makes sense, considering that all four of my grandparents emigrated from different countries. When my grandmothers were pregnant, they were experiencing culture shock, loneliness, missing their siblings and parents back home, still learning English, and raising toddlers at the same time. My maternal grandmother lived in poverty in the South Bronx while my grandfather drank away much of his paycheck. She was also a victim of domestic violence. I can only imagine how that experience affected my mother growing in her womb and my siblings and me growing in my mother's.

The Witchy Form of Epigenetics

Since focusing a lot of my business around magic and manifestation, I've found a version of this in nearly all of the witchy and spiritual clients I've met over the years: the witch wound. The term "witch wound" refers to the pain that everyone who identifies as a woman or a spiritual person carries from the witch trials. It's based on the theory that the souls of those who lived during that time reincarnated into developed nations in a modern age when practicing witchcraft and exploring spirituality outside of Christianity no longer comes with a high risk of death.

At their core, the witch trials were a mass femicide in Europe and the Americas that peaked during the 1600s but spanned four hundred years in total. While anyone was technically at risk, women were overwhelmingly targeted. The most popular reasons, however, were based in *otherness*.

Otherness came in many forms back then: bright-red hair, practicing a different religion, having a pet that seemed a little *too* bonded to you, spurning the advances of a man in power, making money from midwifery or herbalism, saying crazy shit while drunk, being related to people who fit those descriptions, and plenty more.

We often think about the witch trials in terms of pop culture like *The Crucible* or *Hocus Pocus*, watching with curiosity that makes us wonder, "Maybe they *were* witches, though." That thought process, though titillating and tempting, does a disservice to what a cruel and torturous time it was to be a woman or someone living on the fringes of society. It's estimated that almost as many people died in the European and American witch hunts[17] as U.S. military were killed in the Vietnam War.[18] About 75 to 80 percent of those killed in the witch trials were women. In many countries today, people can still be executed for suspected witchcraft.

Poor women at the time lived in absolute fear of false accusations that could arise from the most innocuous missteps. Best-selling author (and a friend of mine) Stacey Halls conveyed this so well in her book *The Familiars*, which tells the tale of a young midwife accused of witchcraft and the young, pregnant noblewoman trying to save her.

What I've found is that the fear of that time in history runs deep in our souls, even now, and usually shows up in four ways.

- **A life lived in fear and hiding:** At the very least, those who lived with the fear of being falsely accused during the witch trials dealt with a constant need to shrink themselves to avoid the detection of anyone's eye or ire. Now, they often engage in people pleasing, struggle to set boundaries, or feel frozen by perfectionism. Essentially, they dim their shine to stay safe because being noticed had grave consequences.

- **Killed for individuality:** If you were actually killed for being a witch—because you lived as a natural healer, unabashedly used your voice, lived on the fringes, or more—this wound can show up in your life now as self-sabotage. Essentially, success proves risky to your subconscious. On some level, you're afraid that you'll be harmed if you stand out, so you make sure that you never get past a certain comfort level around success.
- **Economic oppression:** The witch trials of the 1600s were not only a mass femicide that left the vast majority of women in outright fear, but also a war against the poor. Two of the only ways poor women could earn a living was through medicinal herbalism and midwifery—two practices commonly condemned as proof of witchcraft. Now, this usually looks like a fixation with money and security. It's often accompanied by a need to sacrifice either money or happiness, an inability to imagine having enough money to feel safe, and a tendency to push financial success away by spending money as soon as it hits one's bank account.

Thankfully, all the activities and work available in this book and the resources I recommend will naturally help you heal whatever witch wound you have. Being aware that it's there can only help.

What does it all mean?

While I could easily write an entire book dedicated to the science behind magic, this ain't that book. Instead, I hope you're starting to see what I've believed all along: science and magic are *exactly the same thing*.

Think about it! People relied on herbalism for healing over the course of millennia before the scientific revolution in the seventeenth century.

As scientists and doctors began studying the body, they came up with cockamamie theories on how the body worked and even stranger ways to treat people. You know the saying, "blow smoke up your ass"? That literally came from the popular practice of smoke enemas in the 1700s, which are exactly what they sound like.[19]

People swore by this practice as a form of resuscitation, with one account describing a man who allegedly brought his dead wife back to life with some good ol' tobacco smoke up her bum. Although I'm fairly certain her revival had more to do with falling unconscious and being woken up by some surprise back-door action.

Meanwhile, herbalists, wisewomen, and midwives were executed for witchcraft because their remedies were so effective that it *must* have been the devil's work.

So, thousands-of-years-old practices were seen as unreliable, but a brand-new treatment of reverse-smoking cigs through your friends' bungholes was totally fine.

Anyway, I say all of this to explain that we are living in a miraculous time. We have the advances in technology to measure, observe, and document previously hidden phenomena—whether that's inside the body or the molecules that make up the world around us. And what they're finding is that some of the most ancient concepts *were right all along*.

Show Me the Money (Magic)

- **Matter matters.** Everything in the physical world is made up of matter. However, the matter only matters based on our experience of it. That means the world around us starts *inside our minds*. If that's the case, then it's not a stretch to believe that you can shape reality through your beliefs.
- **It's all about the vibes, man.** The vibrations from matter's molecules cause everything, including our bodies, to emit electric fields that can influence the world around us. It's why we seem to develop ESP with our close friends and family members and serves as more evidence in favor of manifesting reality from inside our minds.
- **The subconscious calls the shots.** As you grow up and live through a variety of experiences, your brain makes connections to keep you safe from uncertain outcomes. That means if you want to believe you can take new actions and get new results, you need to access those subconscious beliefs so you can confront them and prove them wrong to your brain so it can start creating *new* connections that wire you for success and happiness.
- **Blame your parents.** We can inherit trauma from our parents and grandparents, often through the maternal line. When a person becomes pregnant with a fetus developing a uterus, that fetus will develop its lifetime supply of eggs. If that pregnant grandparent experienced trauma during pregnancy, it would have affected the development of not only the fetus, but its egg

supply as well—predisposing us to mental health conditions, diseases, and stress responses. This makes it more important for us to intentionally access and reprogram our subconscious limiting beliefs.

- **Healing the witch wound.** Because the witch trials spanned such a long time and largely targeted oppressed populations like women and the poor, many people drawn to spiritual practices carry the imprints of that trauma.

ACTIVITIES

- Which scientific explanation behind magic and manifestation was the most compelling to you? Take a moment to summarize it in your own words so it sticks in your brain.
- How vividly can you picture an apple? If vision isn't your strong suit, are there other senses that you can access more easily? What about emotions? Sounds? Tastes? Other internal senses can work as forms of visualization as well.
- Take a recent thought that made you panic about money and journal through Byron Katie's questions: (1) Is it true? (2) Can you absolutely know it's true? (3) How do you react/what happens when you believe that thought? and (4) Who would you be without that thought?
- Do any of the witch wounds sound relevant to you? Does it show up in more areas of life than others?

Write a short, fictional story about the past life you lived during the witch trials that created this wound in you.

PART 2

How to Manifest Money

Magic and Mindset Walk into a Bar

By now you know that all an effective spell boils down to is intention, embodiment, and inspired action. That includes spells that seem really advanced. And while all those steps are equally important, you can't succeed at two and three if you don't first align your intentions.

What does that mean exactly? Aligning your intentions refers to a *union of wills*. That means your conscious desires must match your subconscious beliefs.

In other words, it doesn't matter if you really, really, *really* want more money. If you don't believe you deserve it, if you judge how others spend it, if you're afraid to lose it, if you believe that it's the root of all evil—even if it's only a teeny, tiny, itty, bitty part of you—you will struggle to make money.

This is why you can have a fancy spell with loads of steps and expensive ingredients fall totally flat, even if you took all the actions in total perfection. If you don't *subconsciously believe* that the spell will work *for you*...it won't.

Yet this is also why such simple actions like a dedicated journaling or meditation practice, prayer, breathwork—hell, even a walk in nature—can result in such radical change. All of those practices involve quieting inner doubts so you can *believe* that you are whole, worthy, and deserving of what you want for your life.

If you're thinking to yourself, "Hey, this sounds a lot like some of those mindset books I love to read," then you would be absolutely correct.

Aligning your intentions is mindset work done with the intention of receiving a specific result.

Unfortunately, just because we want things and we *consciously* know that our doubts, fears, and anxieties aren't true doesn't mean we can snap our fingers and suddenly believe what we logically know to be true.

Your brain contains entire legions of obstacles that keep you from believing you're capable of having what you want in a misguided attempt to make you feel safe.

As you'll learn in this chapter, *it's totally normal* for your brain to create these obstacles. Diving into an understanding of how it's benefited you so far in life is the perfect way to sort through all those self-conscious beliefs without shaming yourself for having them. You're human. Your brain is *doing its job* when it's working against you. Understanding why will help you make it work *for you*.

How and Why Your Brain Holds You Back

Remember how we talked about those neural pathways the brain creates based on your experiences? Well, think of trauma as a short-circuiting of those neural pathways. Your brain's job is to keep you alive. Living through trauma, especially in your formative childhood years, communicates to the brain that you are living in a dangerous environment. So, your brain creates a secret, subconscious operations manual to help you survive danger for the rest of your life.

The social services and psychology fields refer to these experiences as "adverse childhood experiences" or "ACEs." Living through these traumas puts people at risk of experiencing further victimization or perpetration as adults. Put simply, this is the reason children of alcoholics marry alcoholics or become addicts as adults, whether it's alcoholism or workaholism.

Essentially, your brain goes into survival overdrive and chooses its proven response: fight, flight, fawn, or freeze. Whichever it lands on becomes its default setting to get you through life.

This is why, once you're years removed from the traumatic experience or environment, you can still slip into coping mechanisms you don't like.

Many people understand fight and flight, right? Those settings create adults who either use anger or run away to deal with their problems. So, let's take a less widely known coping mechanism. Fawning is what I've noticed tends to be common around adult children of explosive parents. What I mean by that group is those with anger control issues, alcoholics, and/or abusers, including those enacting physical, emotional, and verbal abuse.

To survive an explosive environment, your brain realizes it needs to try to guess what your caregiver is thinking or feeling *at all times* so it can, hopefully, guess when the next blowup is coming. On the extreme end, this could look like parenting younger siblings in the evening and keeping them quiet until an alcoholic parent or caregiver drank themselves to sleep. On the mild(er) end, this was knowing you needed two weeks' notice on any sleepover invitations so you had enough time to catch your strict parent or caregiver in just the right mood to ask if you could go.

In the meantime? You fawned over them and their needs. You agreed with anything they said, did whatever they asked without saying anything, and tried to strike the balance between keeping to yourself and engaging with them—all so you wouldn't set them off. Your brain worked overtime trying to navigate the environment, picking up on any and all cues to guide you to safety. It looked for barely detectable signs like facial expressions, shifts in emotion or mood, or environmental signs on what your caregiver was experiencing.

As an adult, you develop razor-sharp intuition. You become a human lie detector, a psychic, or both. And I mean that literally! We all have extrasensory gifts, but adults who used fawning as a coping strategy in childhood quite literally have psychic gifts that other people must work to develop. You thought Sherlock Holmes was impressive? *Pfft.* Spend five minutes at a party with an adult who grew up with an abusive parent, and they'll be able to tell you not only how you feel about the hosts, but your motivations for coming, how you treat your romantic partners, if you like your job, and all your deepest insecurities to boot.

Fawners are also likely to fall into people pleasing in adult relationships. Because they can sense when anything is off, they'll go above and beyond at work to make sure their boss can't find any fault with them. They'll go into overdrive to make their romantic partners feel better, especially if they were the cause of negative emotions. Finally, they're also most likely to deny their own feelings to keep everyone happy, sometimes becoming martyrs who resent their loved ones for not appreciating what they willingly and voluntarily sacrificed for them. If this sounds like codependency to you, then *ding, ding, ding*! You win!

Like those of codependents, fawners' brains have deduced that the best way to survive this life is to bypass all thought processes and go straight to pleasing other people.

Freeze is a bit self-explanatory. Think of a deer in headlights, so afraid of the car pummeling toward it but unable to cross the road to safety. If you're the kind of person who constantly thinks of great comebacks hours after a confrontation, you're probably all too familiar with the feeling of being shocked into silence.

This way of thinking about how your brain operates is the best way to explain exactly how and why you can consciously want something, work really hard to get it, and still never reach that goal. Your brain's secret, subconscious operations program needs an update so you can start believing you're capable of having the thing you truly want.

Many who work in psychology, coaching, or manifestation paraphrase Carl Jung to explain this one: Until you make the unconscious conscious, it will direct your life and you will call it fate.

People might be surprised to know that Jung was the OG when it comes to manifestation work. His research formed the entire basis for everything that's found its way into popular culture and neuroscience today, including all of the spiritual aspects that go along with them.

And before anyone screams, "What about Freud?" at me, you should know that Jung saw him as the father of their field, laying the foundation for his later research before they fell out as bros. The main difference between the two is that Freud saw everything as subconsciously about sex, going so far to say that infants displayed sexual desire toward their parents (wtf). He also believed in a distinct separation between the external world and our minds, while Jung believed in a collective consciousness in which all humans' minds are connected. Jung even believed it was possible for people to direct the energy in their minds and bodies outward to affect the physical world around them.

Basically, Freud started to see Jung as that stoner friend whose theories couldn't possibly be based in science because they were too weird.

But the language and concepts Jung coined literally formed the basis of modern manifestation work. Although Freud might have set the stage by explaining the mind as having conscious and subconscious workings, Jung's explanation for how to view different aspects of the subconscious formed the modern rhetoric around that work.

For example, Jung refers to a part of the mind he calls "the shadow," which comprises all the qualities we have that we try to push away. It's our ugly. The stuff we try so hard to *never* be. In doing so, we stay stuck where we are. The only way to find peace and progress is to accept those ugly parts of ourselves. I'm not talking about cute flaws like having skin rolls when you sit down. I'm talking about the *really* ugly parts of ourselves that we never want to admit that we have. On the extreme end, that's acknowledging we are all racist, homophobic, ableist, privileged, and so on. On the other end, it's lighter terms that feel deeply shameful to many people, like "lazy," "boring," "fat," "spoiled," "stupid," "failure," and many more.

When we feel ashamed around a certain quality or term, we hide it in our shadow like an Easter egg full of dog shit as an attempt to convince our conscious mind that it doesn't belong to us.

This spawned an entire field of manifestation magic known as shadow work. No one source boasts the same approach to shadow work, which really means you're spoiled for choice on how to approach it. However, the goal is always the same: to increase your self-worth and self-love by embracing those shameful qualities, rather than striving to push them away.

Shining Light on the Shadow

But if these qualities are not conscious, how can we identify them in our shadow or subconscious? It might surprise you how easy it is to identify them. It also might make you gag.

Anything that makes you feel defensive or judgmental is likely a quality you placed in your shadow. Basically, if it gets a reaction or rise out of you, it's likely not only something that's *true* about you, but also something you need to embrace.

When I began my own shadow-work journey, the first word I knew I needed to work on embracing was *fat*. It sounds so silly and basic to me now, but at the time, if someone had dared to call me fat, I would have been horrified, hurt, and embarrassed. I battled this word my entire life, no matter what size I was. I never wanted to be seen as or labeled "fat." Part of the reason for that was the standard dose of bullying that came with being a plush child and curvy adolescent trying to squeeze a decadent peach into low-rise jeans during the early 2000s. Part of it came from my mother's own body-image issues that resulted in attempts at bonding with me and my sister by going on diets together, starting when I was around twelve years old. Another part came from overhearing my dad use "fat" as a derogatory term when he was angry. And, of course, there's the constant barrage of media messaging around thinness and a singularly homogenous beauty standard.

All of those experiences and memories piled on top of each other to convey to my subconscious that to be fat meant rejection and shame.

As an adult, I did every diet and workout program under the sun. Atkins? Check. South Beach Diet? Check. Clean eating? Check. Some weird-ass program where all I ate was meat and grapefruit at every meal? Check.

That need to push away the label of "fat" eventually led to an obsession with clean eating and working out as a Beachbody coach who sent those obnoxious "Hey, girl!" messages to all my friends on Instagram and Facebook. Because, surely, the need to form friendships based on the shared desire to be anything but fat was universal, right?

Until I began shadow work.

I realized that no matter how much I weighed or how I looked, I was always afraid of someone calling me fat. It was one of the few words that could immediately rob me of any semblance of confidence. Even after I had done so many so-called body positivity posts about embracing my curves, I couldn't handle negative feedback. People telling me I was brave and beautiful for deciding to love myself as I am? Fabulous! I felt like a queen. And then some random teenaged boy on the internet decided to tell me that it was fine if I liked myself even though I was fat, but my weight was unhealthy and I should still seek to lose weight.

I lost my shit.

How *dare* this *child* tell a strange, adult woman he found on the internet that her body was unhealthy?

I decided to teach him a lesson about the internet and privacy.

From the small amount of information he had on his Instagram profile, I was able to track down his name, his parents' emails, the school he went to, and much more. I wrote a kind but firm email to both his father and school principal detailing his comments and how easy it was to find his information. I asked that they have a conversation with him about internet privacy and thinking about his words before he commented on strangers' bodies. I also stated concern that if he was so willing to comment on a stranger's body, what was he potentially saying to teenage girls he encountered on a daily basis? God forbid he was bullying young women like I had been back in middle and high school.

The emails I sent were respectful and expressed concern, rather than insulting. At the time, I sent them proudly and stood by my actions. I even bragged about sending them on social media as a way of standing up for myself. I never heard back from his parents or the principal. The vast majority of my audience applauded my response, saying they would want to know if that's how their sons were acting on social media. An old law-school classmate, though, took huge issue with it, not only saying she would be livid if someone told her child's principal, but also defending the idea that the child was concerned with my health.

Of course, as any fat person can tell you, trolls are never concerned about a stranger's health. They never seem to make those comments on the pages of thin people, which is what I explained to this classmate, catapulting us into a days-long social media argument that did nothing but sour any true potential for friendship.

When I look back on those actions now, I cringe. What I see is shadow. I could say I loved and accepted my body all I wanted, but my reaction to that one comment shows that my supposed body acceptance was empty. I believed I had found body acceptance after a lifetime of struggling with my weight. Instead, it was more of the same. I was still afraid to be called fat. I was still reacting to that word as an insult, even though, realistically speaking, it's a totally neutral quality in the same vein as "tall" or "short."

When I really, truly decided to work on body acceptance and consciously chose to give up dieting and allow my body to only move the way it wanted—even if that meant not moving at all—a funny thing happened.

If you're expecting me to say the weight finally started to come off, well, I'm sorry to disappoint you, but it was the exact opposite. I gained 60-plus pounds.

The funny thing that happened is that I stopped judging myself. I found more peace in my skin. Rather than deciding my body was wrong at a size 16, I chose to find inspiration that could let me love myself exactly how I was.

That meant I started following a lot of fat people on social media—not just perfectly curated plus-size models like Tess Holiday and Brooke Barrows—but regular ol' fat people just living their best lives. It meant lovingly and silently unfollowing all the weight loss-oriented coaches I already considered friends. It meant speaking up when others wanted to talk about diets, healthy eating, or exercise by letting them know I could no longer discuss those topics and love myself as I was at the same time.

It also meant I told my parents before visiting that I had gained a lot of weight, that I wasn't looking to change anything about myself, and that I would leave if anyone made any comments about how I looked—positive or negative. I told my partner I didn't want him to mock his own dad bod in front of me because I was trying really hard to love my own. I watched more media with fat main characters living their lives that didn't turn on their fatness, like *Sweet Magnolias* and *GameFace*. I stopped using workout videos that mentioned weight loss or even yoga videos that used non-inclusive language like "If you can't do the full pose, you can modify it like this." (Turns out, there's no such thing as modifications in traditional yoga.) I bought bigger, fashionable clothing from Torrid, Eloquii, and Universal Standard.

And, finally, I started to refer to myself as fat in a positive way.

Not "fat, but" but "fat, and."

I'm fat *and* I'm beautiful.

I'm fat *and* I'm smart.

I'm fat *and* I'm healthy.

I'm fat *and* I'm deserving and worthy of anything and everything I want.

Somehow I was surprised that I literally stopped thinking about my body in any kind of negative way, but I shouldn't have been. It took this conscious undoing of exposure to so much of the media and conversations that had naturally filled my eyeballs and brain with the message that my body was wrong and I needed to shrink it. When I began taking these steps, everything around me began to change. The weight-loss ads and before and after photos on my Instagram discover page were replaced with fat activists and anti-diet rhetoric, which, of course, made it easier for me to stay in a loving mindset toward my body. I started seeing recommendations for TV shows with more than just thin, pretty, blond women. I more easily found workout videos that didn't make me judge how well I could move or bend.

Is it any surprise that I began eating with total freedom? My diet was more balanced and enjoyable than it had been in years. I could keep a pint of Ben & Jerry's in my fridge for a month without eating it in one sitting.

I no longer felt the pressure of needing to enjoy it all at once because I knew it was never going anywhere. I could eat it whenever I wanted.

When I decided to start moving my body again after nine months of resting it, it came from the simplest inspiration.

While on a visit to my old stomping grounds in Washington, DC, I ran to catch a bus. *And it felt so good.*

I had tried multiple couch-to-5k programs in the past and even gotten to the point of being able to (slowly) jog a full 5k. Even though I loved it, I gave it up *because I hadn't lost weight from running.* When I finally laced up my Brooks for another go at a couch-to-5k program, I was astounded at what a different experience it was—not because I was faster or less winded than I had been. I was astounded because all of the judgmental thoughts I normally battled when I started a running program *were totally and completely gone.*

Previously, I felt overwhelmed by judgments like:

"Wow, I'm so slow, it's pathetic. People walking their dogs are whizzing by me."

"Everyone driving by is probably laughing at my fat jiggling."

"I'm so out of shape, it's sad."

Instead, I couldn't stop smiling! I kept thinking to myself, "Oh man, does it feel good to jog again!" If I thought about my body, it's because I was focusing on my form and breathing. That first walk-jog session was easily the most fun I'd ever had working out.

It wasn't until much later when I was coaching another client and sharing my lifetime struggle with body image that I realized what the lesson had been in manifesting my future.

You see, I had always been manifesting a future as a thought leader with several books, coaching programs, conferences, TED Talks, and all the rest. Even as young as five years old, before I fully understood what it meant, I talked about being famous.

But the reality of that kind of notoriety with thousands, if not millions, of people knowing your name is that the internet trolls will find you. And if you happen to identify as a woman and wear anything above a size 2, the first insult those trolls will lob at you is "fat."

For me to become that thought leader, I needed to become fat in my own eyes. Only then could I identify with that word and reclaim all of the power from a label that others considered an insult. Before then, I carried an energy that blocked what I wanted. Although I freely shared my opinions and photos, I feared that someone out there would find my account and call me fat. No matter what I consciously wanted, as long as I subconsciously feared being seen for the mere fact that someone would inevitably call me fat, I would never get the influence or notoriety I craved.

Now that the word has no power over me because *I know I am fat and I still feel worthy and deserving of everything I want*, I see anonymous hater comments around my weight as a milestone. Are you really a famous woman in this world if a stranger *hasn't* commented on your body or appearance?

Let me tell you, friends: Nothing takes the wind out of a troll's sails like responding to an anonymous comment of "You're fat" with "I know. And?"

Plenty of people need to take their own journey around whatever words feel heavy with judgment and carry a lifetime of pain behind them. But the surest way to ensure that these shadow words stop dictating your future is to embrace them.

Maybe your words aren't as obvious as *fat* or *lazy*. The best way to identify the shadow words you *do* have is to measure your reaction to them.

Let's say, for example, someone tries to insult you on a feature you absolutely don't have, like purple eyes, which are genetically impossible for humans to have.

"Ew! Are your eyes *purple*? Ugh! Disgusting! That's unnatural. Have you seen a doctor? That's really not OK, dude. It's not normal. It's unhealthy. You should really get those fixed or wear contacts at least."

But you don't have purple eyes. You have brown, blue, green, or hazel. How would you react? Maybe at first you would try to insist you *didn't* have purple eyes, but if they're refusing to accept it, you would probably just give up and brush it off. You would think to yourself, "That person was weird. How could they think I have purple eyes? There's probably something wrong with their vision. I hope they're OK and get the help they need." And from there, you would probably go about your business as usual. You didn't have a reaction because you knew without a shadow of a doubt that you do not have purple eyes.

When we're settled on the fact that we absolutely do not have the quality that someone is judging us for having, we don't have a reaction. That means it's not a part of our shadow.

Yet if someone decided to insult you for a quality that you consider bad or that you worry you have, your reaction will be different.

"Ew, your hair is so *frizzy*."

"Ew, you are so *lazy*."

"Ew, you are such a *failure*."

If you're worried that those words are true, could be true, or you hope to God that no one ever thinks those things about you, your reaction will be a lot different. You'll either come out swinging like "How *dare* you say that?" or you'll shrink, thinking something like "Oh my god, what if they're right?" That's how you determine if a quality or label is in your shadow.

We try so hard not to be those qualities or labels that we subconsciously act in a way that keeps us from being in a position for anyone to ever think that about us. When it comes to money, the shadow can keep us from the bold type of actions we need to take to make the money we want, such as going after the jobs we want, promoting our businesses the way we know we need to succeed, or even from managing our money, period. If you're always broke, why would you want to budget or check your bank account just to remind yourself how broke you are, right?

Popular financial shadow themes I've either needed to learn how to integrate or helped clients integrate include "irresponsible," "cheap," "lazy," "disorganized," "a mess," "failure," and plenty more.

Now, there are so many ways to work on one's shadow. And the goal is to ultimately get to a place where that word doesn't carry any charge for you anymore, like my journey with the word *fat*. However, that doesn't mean you need to be fully healed and whole to move forward with the self-worth you need to start manifesting exactly what you desire in your life, especially with money.

Instead, I like to teach people how to work with their shadow by understanding *why* we have this shadow. If these qualities hold us back from attaining what we consciously desire in life, how is that useful to us?

Well, you need to remember that the brain has one goal at all times: to keep you alive. While our external surroundings have evolved to a relatively safe environment, our brains haven't gotten the memo. Our brains have only evolved to the hunter-gatherer phase of humanity. Back when the majority of humans lived in tribes on savannahs or in jungles, on tundras, and so on, our best chance at survival was keeping life as predictable as possible. Living around the same people, in the same environment, doing the same activities… You get the picture. That means to our brains, danger lies in change, period.

Fear of change makes the most sense within the context of negative change—a job or relationship turning toxic, for example. However, our brains register positive change as a threat, too. This is why if you start to perceive yourself as failing below a certain comfort level, you'll start doing a lot of work to get back to where you are. It's also why when you start to succeed too much, you'll self-sabotage. It's all in an effort to stay within a range of comfort—not too hot and not too cold.

Of course, solutions to reaching your greatest potential are a dime a dozen. But rather than launch into a whole new method, I'll give you a very simple solution:

Thank your brain for doing its job.

You're alive, aren't you? Well, then snuffing out those baseless threats has served you your entire life. Give your brain a cookie for doing a good job and then reassure it that it's safe to move forward.

Literally, take a moment to put your hand on your heart and talk aloud to yourself.

"Brain, thank you *so much* for seeing the threat behind applying to my dream job. I'm safe and alive because you're always looking out for me. That being said, it's still safe for me to send in a résumé, even if we're afraid. No matter what happens, we both live in a safe home, we have food to eat, we have a support system of people who love us, and we are not in danger. So, I'm going to apply anyway, OK? OK."

It might sound silly, but you need to think of your brain like a natural guard dog. It's going to bark at the UPS guy just as much as it would bark at an actual intruder. You didn't get a guard dog so it could tell the difference between threats. You got the guard dog to bark so *you* could identify the threats. Give your brain a cookie for sounding the alarm and maybe take it outside to meet the mail delivery driver.

Other Parts of Your Psyche

The next part of your brain that will hold you back in an attempt to help you is what I like to think of as the ego. Now, Freud came up with this idea of the ego with a specific understanding in mind. Essentially, it's the part of our minds that reads our internal urges, reads what's acceptable in society, and then goes about trying to figure out how to get what we want in a socially acceptable way.

I like to think about the ego as the part of us that worries about what other people will think about us—plain and simple. Now, almost everyone I've ever coached has had a moment where they confess to me that they worry about what other people think and then say, "I know I shouldn't care and I don't know why I do, but I do!" They're embarrassed because as adults, they know that: (1) No one is paying as much attention to them as they think. We're self-involved creatures, so people are rarely thinking about you as much as you believe they are. (2) This isn't high school! As adults, we know that if we spend all our time thinking about what other people think about us, we'll live life in a small box, never attempting to accomplish the dreams we carry in our hearts.

But here's the thing about worrying about what other people think: It's another tried-and-true evolutionary technique that keeps us alive.

Remember when I talked about how our brains still think we're living in hunter-gatherer times, even though it's the Information Age out there?

When we lived in a tribal society, expulsion from your tribe meant certain death. If you were alone in the world, your chances of dying from starvation, eating the wrong berry, stepping on a scorpion, getting eaten by a cheetah, or not being treated for a cold were pretty high. Your survival was literally dependent on acceptance by other people. Letting your freak flag fly and living an authentic existence took a back seat to, you know, being alive in the first place.

So, if you can accept that this fear about what other people will think of you is just another way your brain is trying to protect you, maybe you can cut yourself some slack. Then we can start working with your psyche instead of against it.

Your ego just wants to make sure you don't die from the very avoidable death that it believes will inevitably come from your great-aunt Jean judging your life choices at Christmas.

The first method for acting through this fear of what other people think is to just speak to this very real fear in your brain. Try putting your hand on your heart and saying something like:

"Thank you, brain, for keeping me safely centered in my tribe. I'm alive because you're always looking out for me. But I actually have a great support system that loves me and wants me to be my authentic self, and that includes changing jobs/starting a business/making money moves that matter to me. And if they don't support me, I know I can have open conversations with them about communication and my needs. If they can't respect my boundaries and love me through this change, I can find a new or supplemental support system that will."

Sometimes that's enough to help you move ahead. Other days, it feels like that little doubt devil just will not accept that you live in a relatively safe world, and you can't seem to stop worrying. On those days, all you can do is indulge it.

Think of your ego as like a screaming toddler in your back seat just trying to get its needs met. Sometimes you can speak gently and explain you're almost home and power through on the way to your goals. Then some days you're driving with a headache, navigating rush-hour traffic, and trying to beat an ominous-looking set of rain clouds in the distance. The only solution is to hand that baby a lollipop, their lovey, a teddy, and maybe even a screen playing Cocomelon—anything to soothe them until you get home.

That's when you need to look at what the true underlying fear is behind worrying about what other people think. Is it solely about rejection? And if so, who specifically are you afraid is going to reject you? Is it your parents, your friends, potential employers, your former boss, that really cool cheerleader in high school you realized ten years later you had a baby-gay crush on? All of those people likely attach to another survival-based fear. Think of Abraham Maslow's hierarchy of needs when you consider who you're afraid is going to reject you. Is it more akin to the bottom of the pyramid, which is all about food, shelter, water? Or is it something higher up like creative self-expression or self-actualization? Knowing which fear your brain is protecting will allow you to appease this part of your psyche in a really effective way.

This can happen to any of us, no matter how successful we get. When I was featured in *Forbes* for my business coaching based in magic, I immediately self-sabotaged the success in my business. I mean, I was in a major business publication talking about *money magic spells*. They called me *the Millennial Money Witch*. Before starting my business, I had worked in journalism and law—two of the most skeptical professions out there. Having that article out there meant there was no going back. If everything went south and I needed to find a job, the first thing people would find out about me on Google is that I taught people how to do magic to make more money. Of course, that's not *exactly* what I teach, as you can tell from this book. But that's what they would think. I would look delusional. Who would hire me?

So, I subconsciously tanked my business. I launched a boring-ass program with no magic that flopped. All my leads and clients seemed to dry up at once. On some level, I let my ego call the shots and say, "*Magic?* Oh, no, no, no, no. If we succeed from this media placement, everyone from law school, journalism school, all our former coworkers, and anyone who might ever want to hire us for a 'real job' is going to laugh at us! We'll never get a steady paycheck again!"

As a result, I lost almost all my money and felt like I had to restart from scratch.

How could that have gone differently? Well, I definitely could have made more time to talk myself through the safety of being seen as magical. I could have taken a beat to rest before resharing the link to that *Forbes* article across my social media platforms to remind myself that I was safe to be this fully magical *and* strategic, logical person. Plenty of multimillionaires and billionaires hire spiritual coaches and use magic, too. As you now know, they just call it mindset work.

And if that hadn't appeased this fearful side of me that truly feared I could never get another "real job" or sign another client again, I could have indulged that scared, shaking ego inside me and explored a backup plan.

A couple years after that *Forbes* feature, I was facing another rough patch in my business. I had finally embraced the idea that I needed to implement practical strategies alongside my magical manifestation methods. I was two months into a budgeting system when I realized, "Shit. I don't have enough income to support my business subscriptions and the support I need." So, I started a job hunt *in the legal field*.

Rather than look for attorney jobs, I sought something that would allow me to coach and discovered the field of attorney development that existed at larger law firms. Basically, I could counsel attorneys on finding happiness at a firm by helping them figure out what truly lit them up and offer training sessions on different aspects of the firm and individual coaching sessions geared around mindset and adjustment. And if they couldn't find happiness at the firm, I would help them figure out what else they could do, such as change jobs or careers.

Rather than attempt to distance myself from that *Forbes* article, I mentioned it in my cover letters and résumés. I talked openly about how I saw the intersection of practical strategies and magic with the people I networked with. I explained that magic was literally just mindset work with some flair for the dramatic. I knew that if I was going to find the right position and workplace, it would need to be a place that accepted all of me and would take pride in that *Forbes* article.

While at this point I was still afraid of rejection, it wasn't because I was afraid of not finding a job that could give me a stable paycheck. My fear around rejection was about self-expression. I was afraid of getting hired either under false pretenses or *in spite of* that *Forbes* article, rather than *because* of it.

The funniest part, of course, is that shortly after I let go and allowed myself to job hunt as my full, unfiltered self, I went viral on TikTok to the tune of more than 1 million views. That single video led to a booming business and a slew of opportunities I had only dreamed of before then, including this book, which had been riding the top slot on my manifestation list for years. I started making money again and didn't need a legal job anymore.

So, if you're wondering how to deal with your ego that's working overtime stressing about how other people will respond to your decisions, ask yourself *why* you are afraid of being rejected by them. Once you know the reason behind that, you can zero in on exactly what kind of backup plan will help appease the screaming toddler in your brain. And if your first backup plan doesn't totally stop the screaming, go for the next one. I don't care if you need to come up with Plan B, Plan C, Plan D, E, F, G, or all the way to Z. The goal is to get your ego to give a sigh of relief that lets you feel it's finally safe to continue that drive toward your goals anyway.

Your Highest Self Ain't All It's Cracked Up to Be

The final part of your psyche that can sabotage the path to your goals is a surprising one: your highest self.

If you're new to the woo, you might not have heard this term before. Essentially, it's the part of your brain that's super chill about life. It knows that time is relative, money isn't real, and all of life is just a hologram.

If you're a person of faith, this is the part of you that says, "I don't need to worry because my God has my back and he/she/they will never lead me astray." If you're a nihilist, this is the part of you that says, "Life has no inherent meaning, so why waste any time worrying about this when we're all going to die one day anyway?" No matter what your perspective is, this is the part of you that's able to rise above the everyday challenges and stop sweating it.

Many people mistakenly believe this is the place we should strive to live in all the time. And it makes sense. Who wouldn't want to live stress-free and know that everything will happen the way it's supposed to, right?

Well, if your highest self knows that everything is going to happen the way it's meant to, what incentive does it have to change anything? Instead, it looks around and says, "I don't get it. You have a roof over your head and food in the fridge. Why do we need to change anything? Isn't this enough?"

And the funny part is that your highest self will think this no matter what your circumstances. Your roof could be leaking and the only food in your fridge could be half a Big Mac and some ketchup packets and your highest self will *still* say, "This is enough. It could always be worse. The universe/God supports me. I don't need to worry or change."

The way you get this part of your psyche to get off its ass and start pulling some weight is to give it a mission. But not just any mission! It needs a soul-aligned mission that lights your heart on fire and makes your highest self say, "Wait a second, *that's* what we can do with more money/clients/a new job? We can do *that*? Well, what the fuck are we waiting for? Let's get it!"

In entrepreneurship, coaches refer to this as your "why"—essentially the reason you do what you do. The mistake they make is not clarifying that your why needs to feel really fucking important. It needs to feel like such a crucial life mission that if you don't accomplish it before you die, you will feel like you wasted your time on earth. That's why basing your goals on something like "So my kids can have a better life than I did" or "So I never need to tell myself no when spending money or investing in myself" doesn't motivate you in any real way. Yeah, it might get you started, but it's not enough to sustain you over the long term. It's not enough to outweigh taking big risks or putting yourself out there in a shamelessly bold way.

For me, my why is about changing work culture in America for the better. I want every single worker in the country to know that they can always find a better job that they love doing, that respects them, pays them their ideal wage, and returns the loyalty they *want* to give an employer. And if they can't find that or don't want to, to know that they can build it for themselves. I truly believe everyone has a marketable skill that they can sell without going back to school to capitalize on it. Finally, I want to change companies through my consulting work to create more workplace havens that view their staff as whole people and support them not just through compensation and time off, but with their individual hopes and dreams as well.

When I think of myself coaching people in their businesses and dream job hunts and consulting with companies to show them that supporting their employees naturally increases profits, *I get fucking hyped*. My highest self thinks, "HOLY SHIT, YES. I WANT TO DO THAT."

I also like to take it a step further, thinking about how if I can get rich while doing this, I can then use my money to further create this reality. I imagine myself calling up a local school and paying for kids' school lunches. I imagine pulling a Nicki Minaj and paying off a random fan's student loans. I think about going out for dinner in December and tipping $1,000 to a struggling server. When I visualize baller moves like this, my highest self starts losing her shit like, "WHOA. *That* is what we can do with more clients and money? We can literally start changing the world at a grassroots level? Fuck, yes! Let's goooooooo!"

That's not to say *your* why needs to be as world-changing-focused as mine. It's totally fine if your why is about traveling the world or supporting your kids. But you need to take that shit to the extreme if you want your highest self on board. What's the soul-mission version of that reason? Maybe you want to travel the world because you feel called to experience as many cultures as you can. Maybe by traveling the world you'll realize how small it is and truly feel that interconnectedness of all beings. Maybe it's because your soul craves as many different sensory experiences as it can handle—wind in your hair, beautiful European architecture, the music filling the streets of Mexico City, the flavors of authentic Nigerian food, and so on. Your why needs to feel like something that would kill you to miss out on. And if more money means more travel, what else can that free you to do? Is it to live among different cultures so you don't feel the pressure to return within a certain time frame? How does money become a tool for accomplishing this *soul* purpose of travel?

And if your why *is* your children, why is that? Is it because you've always dreamed of nurturing souls who can change this world or become their safest, unique selves? Maybe it's because you see children as the future and your ability to raise beautiful souls will create a ripple effect changing the lives of anyone they meet along their own journeys. What does the soul mission of parenthood mean to you? And how does money contribute to it? Is it about giving them the opportunity to pursue whatever dreams they hold so you can pay witness to their evolution? Is it that you can show up as a parent to more children like their friends or foster kids if you have more money? When you deepen the connection to this feeling of deep, soulful desire, that's when your highest self gets excited to help you make the changes you crave, including making more money.

Show Me the Money (Magic)

- **Survival of the fearful.** Trauma exists on a spectrum, which is why it's safe to say we've all experienced it. Because of that, you likely have an instinctual response that's actively working against you when you try to make new, positive changes in your life. This response can be fight, flight, fawn, and freeze.
- **The shadow craves safety.** Shaming yourself or even judging others for qualities you view as negative is often indicative of our shadow—the parts of ourselves we push away to feel like we're good people. The answer is to accept that we *are* the qualities we fear, and that it doesn't make us any less deserving of having what we want. It's OK to feel afraid of being seen as something undesirable. That is your brain's attempt to protect you from danger. Thank it and do the damn thing anyway.
- **Take an ego trip.** Your ego fears what people will think of you because it's evolutionarily beneficial to remain in good standing with others. Your chances of survival plummeted if you were exiled from your community in prehistoric times. Once again, your brain wants to protect you, so if you want to feel confident taking action anyway, create a backup plan for what you'll do if your friends or family reject you. Create a backup plan for the backup plan if you need to.
- **Tell me why.** Your highest self is so untethered from reality and your desire for success and riches that it's content to stay where you are. Money is just a construct, right? Well, if you want the power of your highest self, dive deep into how your manifestations can support your soul's mission on this earth.

ACTIVITIES

- What's your go-to survival technique—fight, flight, fawn, or freeze? How do you recognize when it's kicking in? What other actions can you take to bring your processing back into your prefrontal cortex? Journal about a time that you experienced survival mode in response to money-based circumstances.
- Are there any shadow words or phrases that immediately come to mind? Are there any specifically relating to money? Keep a list of them for reference in future chapters.
- Take one of your ego's fears and come up with a backup plan on what to do if it happens. Do you feel better? If not, ask yourself why you're afraid of what will happen if you use the backup plan and *that* fails. Then, come up with a backup plan for that. Keep going until you feel prepared to take action.
- What's your core *why* when it comes to money? What are all the reasons you want it? What's the most powerful and compelling soul-mission that you could complete if you had the money you wanted?

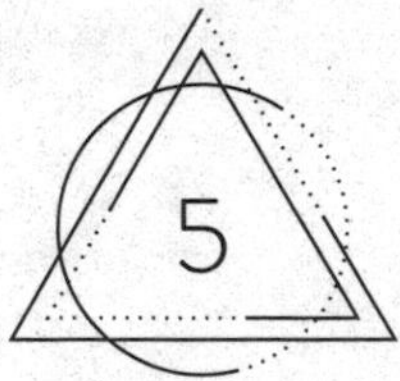

How to Align Your Intentions

As you now well know, the first step in money spells is to align your intentions. Yet in order to do so, you have to first decide what you want when it comes to money. Yes, you want more of it, but I find that writing intentions out helps you better connect with that goal.

When explaining why manifesting money differs from manifesting stuff, opportunities, or experiences, I said naming amounts of money is usually indicative of a self-imposed limitation. Well, this is one of those times where breaking the rule can work in your favor.

The reality is that when you are trying to manifest money for the first time, you need to honor the fact that you're starting from square one. Yes, we want to reach for our potential and call that in, but it first requires us to be honest with ourselves about where we are in the current moment—limitations and all.

In other words, what you write down must feel *believable* to you. So, if you're an entrepreneur and you want to make $10,000 by the end of the month in your business, but you've never made more than $1,000, there's a strong chance it's not going to happen. And if you insist on writing it down and you *don't* make $10,000 by the end of the month, what's that going to do for your confidence on how quickly you can make money? It's going to tank it!

Yet if you decide to manifest $2,000 in the following month and you *actually do it* or, even better, wind up making $3,000, how will you feel then? You'll feel *so* much more powerful than you would have trying to force yourself to go for something that didn't feel believable the first time. And if you can make that first goal of $2,000, you might even feel *more* confident to manifest $4,000 the next month. After all, it only took you one month to double your income, right? Of course you can do it again.

So, when writing your new intentions down, it's always better to *honor where you are* rather than to reach for something that feels unrealistic.

This is especially important because this chapter is all about digging up the subconscious muck and revisiting the trauma that has kept us from actively manifesting money in the past. I'll go ahead and say *I'm sorry* ahead of time because you're probably going to feel pretty low once we're done, but I also promise to give you a way to ensure that revisiting all this trauma doesn't make you quit while you're ahead.

So, before we move on, let's write out at least one money goal, preferably something you could achieve by the end of this book. It can sound like anything, including one of these examples:

- A hot lead on a job making six figures
- A surprise $500
- $5,000 minimum in my business next month
- A new pay-in-full client
- $1 million in profits from my company for the year
- A healthier relationship with money

Other than the goal feeling believable, there are no rules. Make the goal big or small, specific or general, a literal money figure or more tangentially related to money—I don't care.

Once you identify your goal, ask yourself why you want this manifestation. And the more sacred and important that answer feels, the better.

So, rather than writing something like, "So my kids can have a better life," go deep.

"I want a job that makes six figures so I can be a better parent. Six figures will allow me to support the unique individuals my kids are becoming with extracurriculars or private lessons. I can take them on trips to show them the world and all its people so they become compassionate adults. It will give me enough time and breathing room to take care of my own needs so I can fully support them as they make their life transitions into adulthood. By raising robust, compassionate adults, I'm helping to make the world a better place through their influence in addition to my own."

Doesn't that sound *way* more powerful?

The main point is for you to write a list that not only feels like you can achieve it, but also gives you the motivation to push through any difficult assignments as we move through upcoming exercises. Capeesh?

Alright, witches, let's do this.

Digging into the Subconscious

Getting our subconscious beliefs on the same page as our conscious desires is the foundation to everything else! Remember, this is the first step to magic. Aligning our conscious and subconscious beliefs is how we align our intentions.

When it comes to money, a few key influences—like your family, childhood, school, friends, religion, and more—generally shape the beliefs you carry. In this chapter, I'll walk you through an explanation behind the more common obstacles I've seen while doing this work myself and walking hundreds of other clients through them.

This includes explanations, stories, new coping strategies, and journal prompts to help you dig into your subconscious and get it on the same page as your conscious desires.

If you can't access certain memories or you don't know the answers to questions, this is the time to put that natural intuition to work—*play pretend*. Your brain will draw on its subconscious when you treat a journal prompt you don't have an answer to like a creative writing assignment.

As Oscar Wilde wrote, "Life imitates art far more than art imitates life." What he meant is that our subconscious craves the expression of certain emotions and experiences. Art gives our subconscious a set of models and templates on how to express those emotions and experiences. If you've ever said to yourself, "I feel like I'm in a movie!" or been in a place so beautiful it looked like it could be a painting, you've experienced that.

Using journal prompts as a creative writing assignment will force your brain to draw on the subconscious emotions and experiences holding you back.

Now, I made enough recommendations to people who read *You Are a Badass at Making Money* to know how this is going to go down. You're going to try to read all the stories and concepts but breeze through the journal prompts by just *thinking* instead of actually pulling out a pen and paper and doing the damn thing.

Except if you do, you'll literally be skipping over *magic*.

Yep. Journaling is a magical practice. It's easy to dismiss it as solely a resource for therapy and teenagers going through breakups, but remember what I said a few chapters ago? What turns regular ol' words into spells is *intention*, and the same goes for any kind of mundane action. So, if you approach these journal prompts with the intention of discovering your subconscious obstacles and releasing them, you will literally be performing a spell to do just that!

The most basic full-moon spell and ritual you can do is journal. The full moon is all about release and decrease because from that moment until the new moon, it will appear to shrink in the sky. On my laziest full moons, all I do is light a candle before some journaling time and blow it out when I'm done as a signal to my brain that there was a start and end to the ritual.

So, don't cheat yourself here! Whether you decide to turn these journal prompts into a formal ritual, just make sure you're actually doing them. That way, you can identify what lessons you need to unlearn so you can unite your wills and tap into the power you need to make true, lasting magic beyond this chapter.

All in the Family

It's important to understand how you can identify when your mental roadblocks are getting in the way. After all, plenty of people struggle to identify the difference between what feels like an intuitive pull and a nagging fear to take an action that might limit them, such as my decision to start a job hunt when my business was slowing down. For some, that could be an action that gives them financial stability so it doesn't put pressure on their business. For others, that could be an action that makes them feel like a failure who is stepping back from their full genius.

The answer on how your subconscious could be limiting your ability to go after your goals—financial or otherwise—is to look at your childhood.

I talked about how your brain essentially creates a rulebook for survival based on the traumas it lived through, especially in childhood. This is because in your most formative years, you're learning what's going to allow you to thrive and continue receiving love and nurturing. As kids, we think in black-and-white terms and we're whip-smart when it comes to reading body language. A withering look from a caregiver when you or a sibling, parent, or even a TV show character did something wrong can shape a lifetime of decisions built around never, ever receiving that look from them again. Your brain registered that quality or behavior as *not safe,* so in adulthood, you'll do everything you can to avoid it. The wild part is that this can even extend to qualities or behaviors we want to engage in as adults.

For example, I was a li'l ham as a small child. I loved talking to adults. I viewed every new grown-up as a new test audience for my latest reenactment of a favorite movie, an a cappella performance, or dance moves. My mom often jokes that my sister, who is just shy of two years younger than I am, barely spoke for the first three years of her life. Anywhere we went, this is how the dialogue would go down.

Adult: "Hello! Nice to meet you!"

Me: "Nice to meet you! I'm Jessie. I'm five!"

Adult: "Hello, Jessie! And what's your name, sweetie?"

Me: "Her name is Jill."

Adult: "Well, hello, Jill! And how old are you?"

Me: "She's three. Want to see me tap-dance?"

I eventually learned to let my sister speak up for herself, but that only came after repeated reminders from my mother that I needed to include her in conversations and performances. I couldn't hog all the attention for myself.

For a long time throughout our twenties, it seemed my sister and I couldn't thrive at the same time. We went through cycles of one of us succeeding in school or our career only to see the other one struggling. When I was landing cool journalism internships, climbing the ranks of the *Independent Florida Alligator* (billed as the largest independent, student-run newspaper in the United States, no big deal), and catching the eye of some industry bigwigs, my sister was taking and retaking organic chemistry. She had always been the one with high grades in math and science and carried all the pressure from second-generation American parents to become the next doctor in the family.

But when she decided to pivot into law as I had and started seeing massive success as a result—admission into a much-higher-ranked law school than mine, prestigious social justice internships, and slimming down along the way—my life began tanking. I worked at the mall to supplement my first lawyer job, which was so boring I thought I would die at my desk. My car could never seem to work longer than two months at a time. I was then laid off from said lawyer job and unemployed for three months. My relationship, which I had voluntarily made the foundation of my self-worth, was so full of drama that I could never settle into stability with my live-in boyfriend. I accepted a job with such low pay that it wound up making it nearly impossible for me to support myself and enjoy life, even in a small college town. And, eventually, he dumped me, leaving me with this shitty life I'd built around him.

And once I pulled myself out of that and moved to Washington, DC, where I landed my dream job, dream apartment, and dream income? I bet you can guess what happened with my sister.

The reality is that on some level, we were both carrying this subconscious idea that to succeed and shine brightly on our own meant that we were leaving the other one out. We could only succeed for so long because when the other started doing well, we would ever-so-politely sabotage our lives to let our beloved sister have a chance at the spotlight and parental approval.

Thankfully, we both managed to break that cycle and are happily thriving in our careers today. But we lived in that fucked-up cycle for a solid fifteen years before breaking it. It took both of us finding the childhood programming we received from those formative years.

So, how can you start to uncover what self-sabotaging stories might be floating around inside your psyche?

Well, it's called the subconscious for a reason, right? If it were easy to identify, we wouldn't be stuck on these hamster wheels of success, furiously running without making any progress. However, it's always much easier for us to find what's wrong with everyone else in our lives. So, if you want to see what kind of patterns might be running rampant in your psyche, look for matching patterns in your family.

Basically, you need to put your detective hat on and get really curious about your childhood, especially before the age of seven. Many people don't have a freakishly good memory, and even if you do, you can still only view it through your own perspective. Learning more about the circumstances you lived in as a child and thinking of it through the lens of your adult self now can connect some crazy dots between where you are and where you want to go.

Generally, if you can interview your parents or childhood caregivers, that would be ideal. If you can't, go to the people who were adults or, at the very least, older around that time. I was eight years old when my youngest brother was born. I might not have as vivid a memory as my parents, grandparents, or aunts, but I definitely remember more about our home when he was an infant than he ever could.

Also, I know the reality is that sometimes those relationships aren't safe or you might not even have anyone alive to ask about them. In that case, make it up. You heard me! Use the little information you have and think of it like building a character for a novel. So, if you were adopted and you don't know anything about your birth parents, invent those parents in your mind. Make them as real as possible as far as personality, emotions, family, and geography can take you. Once they each feel like a real, solid figure in your mind's eye, answer these birth-related questions for them. The brain is really powerful, so anything you invent is probably going to be closer to the truth of what's holding you back than you would imagine.

If you were adopted at birth, answer these questions for your adopted parents as well. By having double the parents, you can find double the information!

Finally, I know a variety of birth situations exist that I couldn't possibly cover to fit every person out there. My advice to you is the same as above. Do your best to answer with the information you have, interview a caregiver if a safe one is available to you, and if you're missing one or more of your biological or adopted parents, let your brain fill in the blanks, even if the answers are totally fake.

When it comes to your birth, ask these questions to your caregivers, real or imagined:

- What were your caregivers' financial circumstances when they were expecting you? Were they stable? What were their income and expenses like? Did they feel financially prepared to bring you into the world?
- How did your caregivers financially plan for your birth, if at all? How did your birth impact their finances?
- Did your birthing parent experience any physical or mental health-related issues that could have contributed to financial fears before or after your birth?
- Did your caregivers experience any financial traumas before, during, or after you were born? That could be a stock market crash that wiped out their savings, an eviction, a death in the family that required a huge expenditure, or even a large inheritance or winning the lottery.
- What financial preparations, if any, did your parents make when you were born? Did anyone help them or contribute in any way, whether it was money or hand-me-downs?

- Did your parents' careers or financial circumstances prevent them from being fully present in your life as an infant and beyond? If so, why? This could be because one of them needed to work multiple jobs to make ends meet or because they ran a successful business that kept them away for twelve-hour days.
- Were your caregivers on the same page with each other about their finances when you were born and thereafter? How did they communicate about money? Were there any repeat fights, disagreements, or problems during this time? Were they able to come to an understanding or did financial differences lead to separation?
- If your parents separated, what role did money play during their split? Did they say anything about the other's financial situation? How did they feel about any payments or allocations decided on during the process of their breakup?
- Did your caregivers put their financial needs above your needs at birth? That could look like returning to work sooner than expected or leaving their job to stay home with you. Did that prioritization change as you grew? Does your perception of their priorities match what they said? Why or why not?

Some of the answers you get might surprise you. But the most important activity is to look at the answers you received and see how any of that information could relate to you as an adult.

This could be around patterning you see that's holding you back. When I analyzed the circumstances of my birth, I remembered how much my mom really sacrificed when she married my dad. Her parents didn't totally approve of the marriage, and on top of that, she planned to move out of the Bronx for the first time in her life. Not long after the wedding, she had a falling-out with her family. She saved up enough money to buy her parents' home so they wouldn't need to move ever again. In response, her brothers—who lived at home and didn't work—manipulated her parents into bringing a bogus suit against her as a way to get awarded money damages from her savings.

Answering these questions and journaling the answers made me realize how much financial drama had been surrounding my mom close to my birth and in the first few years of my life. It felt like I had been born knowing that story. When I asked about my mom's parents as a little kid, she told me a version of that story explaining that her brothers and parents tried to scare her into giving them the money she worked for years to save.

On some level as a child, I interpreted the moral of my mother's story to mean "If you become *too* wealthy and successful, your mommy, daddy, and siblings will all turn on you and you'll need to cut them off. You can stay poor and have your family, or you can earn more and risk losing them all."

Was it any surprise that I couldn't seem to build any financial momentum in my business? My brain was screaming in terror that if I actually reached the level of financial success that I wanted, I could lose the people I loved. Once I realized this underlying fear, I was better able to soothe myself and start feeling safe and comfortable with earning money.

Understanding Adolescence

Although your brain might have solidified a lot of its money programming in very early childhood, it was still building upon those lessons and refining its rulebook as you grew up. That means the questions can't just stop at seven years old. You need to analyze your own memories of your home and community to get a fuller picture of how exactly you've been keeping yourself safely tucked inside a box of financial smallness.

This means you need to take inventory of your memories around money and analyze your parents' relationships with money and their careers over the years. Consider journaling on these questions:

- What was your first memory of money, meaning the first time you became aware money existed?
- What did your main caregivers do for a living throughout your childhood and adolescence? How did they feel about their jobs/careers?
- How did your main caregivers manage their money? What were their relationships to money like?
- Did one of your caregivers solely rely on the other (or an external source, such as a trust fund or social security disability) to support their needs? How did that affect their relationship with each other? How did it affect their relationships with you and any siblings?
- How did your caregivers speak about money to each other? How did they communicate about money to you?
- What's your perception of what your caregivers used money for? To keep up appearances, to create security, to help others, to manipulate?
- How did your caregivers judge others based on money? Were there any sayings about people that you routinely heard, such as "Rich people are snobs" or "Poor people are lazy"? Were there any specific individuals they either praised or criticized for being rich, poor, hardworking, lazy, and so on?
- Did your caretakers ever encourage you or your siblings to make a living based off of your innate passions and talents?
- Did your caretakers ever receive money through deceptive means?
- If your caretakers were wealthy, did they instill shame in you around flaunting money or needing to hide wealth so others wouldn't take advantage of you?
- Did your caretakers ever experience obstacles to obtaining money

because of their race, gender identity, sexual identity, culture background, accents, appearance, or other factors?

- What were some of your most vivid positive and/or negative experiences with money or work in childhood? List them out by age or school year.
- Do any of your current circumstances reflect anything you uncovered from these prompts?

You might want to revisit these prompts multiple times throughout your life as you begin to uncover different layers of memories and patterns that have been looping through your brain for years. And I know that first one about when you first became aware of money is a doozy, but don't skip it. There's a lot of wisdom from zeroing in on your first real memory of money.

Take mine for example.

I first became aware of money at about seven years old. It was 1994 and my mother finally relented to my begging and said she would buy the VHS tape of *Thumbelina*. I expected to grab shoes and rush off, but instead, she grabbed an old office water-cooler half full of coins and dumped it onto the beige carpet. She told my sister and me how much the coins were worth and how many we needed to make a dollar. Together, the three of us counted coins and rolled them into paper flutes to come up with the $21 we needed.

It took hours—or at least it felt like it did. I was over the activity soon after it started, but still I rolled, focused only on my soon-to-be new princess obsession. When we eventually made our way to Kmart, we took the tape to the register and became that cashier's worst nightmare. One by one, the cashier opened twenty-one coin logs of shame and counted them.

With that being one of two open registers, the line behind us began to grow, each person rushing us with their eyes and probably debating how much they really needed those groceries. Meanwhile, my mother was completely unfazed, smiling and hyping us up about what great counters we were, my toddler brother babbling and drooling on her hip. Not having worked retail in my first seven years of life, I wasn't completely aware of why everyone seemed so mad. All I knew was that it felt like we were in trouble, even though no one was yelling.

I was relieved when we finally made it home and I could fire up the VCR and pop in the sweet, sweet spoils of our suburban adventure. Until I actually watched it, that is. When it finished, I sat there on our gray tweed couch in disbelief. It was terrible! I spent eighty-plus minutes watching animals trying to force a tiny, whiny woman into arranged marriages only for her to marry a tiny, whiny man at the end? Who green-lit this?

I was so angry. I inspected the box, looking for a Disney logo and, not finding it, assumed I had been tricked. And then came a thought that I had no idea would haunt me the rest of my life: "What a waste of money."

When I realized the first true memory I had of money could double as a scrapbooking page for "baby's first buyer's remorse," I was stunned. No wonder that for the majority of my life I was plagued by a feeling of scarcity!

Even when I had money available, I wouldn't buy full-price clothes from Old Navy for myself. For others? Sure. But when it came to my interests or my dreams? I was buying off lists sorted from lowest to highest, even in person. I lived in fear of regretting my purchases. At seven years old, $21 might as well have been $210, $2,100, or $21,000 for all I knew. I moved forward from that memory knowing I didn't want to make any mistakes.

I saw how that was playing out in my life. I was afraid to truly pursue my dreams, always taking safe routes that my parents and society told me would lead to financial stability and abundance. When I graduated during a recession and couldn't get a journalism job, I immediately sold out and accepted a job doing public relations work that I hated.

When I realized in the first week of the job that I couldn't do it longer than necessary, I took the LSAT in January and panic-applied to twenty-seven law schools after most of them had already selected their first-year classes. I went to the school that gave me the most scholarship money, even though I had been accepted by better programs, because it felt safer to follow the money.

(Spoiler alert: About a decade later, my law school would be investigated by the American Bar Association, lose its accreditation, and be shut down on multiple points of fraud that included stacking first-year classes with students who had scholarships so the grade curve would cause them to knock each other out of qualifying for scholarships to save the school from paying on all their scholarship offers for all three years while keeping their best students unable to transfer to better programs.)

After I graduated, it continued. I accepted the first jobs I was offered in my first two job hunts. And when it came to the first three jobs in my legal career, I didn't negotiate my salary at all! In that third gig, I realized a couple years in that I was on the low end of the salary range in my company while my boss refused to engage in conversations about a raise, always moving the goalposts for my performance to delay my requests for another year.

When I decided to leave, it was for another safe job at a well-known nonprofit. I knew in the first month it wasn't a good fit for me (nor was I a good fit for the job), but I stayed because that's what responsible people who don't waste money and good opportunities do. A year and a half later, I got fired—for being bad at the job.

In the end, one early experience of disappointment in buying a VHS tape created a behavioral loop around financial safety that I couldn't break until I became aware of it. Once I did, it became a lot easier to take risks in my life.

As you go through these prompts and explore the caverns of your mind and memories, remember that sometimes these prompts can raise painful memories. Don't hesitate to process them with a therapist, coach, or close friend. Asking for help is never a bad thing!

Once I realized making money through my channels of passion didn't feel safe, I could start taking actions that would let me honor my fear while still taking steps toward building business and wealth. I could act despite the discomfort, which allowed me to make progress toward untangling my financial fate from my seven-year-old self's disappointment with *Thumbelina*.

Seeing Community as Context

While our caregivers and home life arguably have the greatest influences on our relationships with money, we spend enough time away for others to have an influence, too. Reviewing how your friendships, neighbors, culture, community, religion, and other sources of money teaching impacted the way you look at money can reveal more than you realize.

Consider these questions as a jumping-off point to unpack what outside influences might have been impacting your brain's drafting of survival mechanisms:

- What was the socioeconomic state of the community you grew up in? Think about the places where you interacted with more people. This could be extended family, your neighborhood, or your school. The people you were closest to are likely more important.
- How did the people in your community talk about money?
- Did anyone in your community treat you differently—positively or negatively—because of your family's economic status?

- How did the other adults in your life make their living? How did they feel about their careers and money?
- What were the common beliefs or teachings in your culture or religion around money?
- Did your caregivers, family, or friends talk shit about anyone based on money-related issues? This could be gossiping about job loss, breakups/divorce settlements, career aspirations, or other issues.
- Did you know any adults who made money from their passions? How did you perceive their success, happiness, stability, wealth?
- Did you judge anyone—again, positively or negatively—when growing up based on money? Maybe as a kid you thought someone was a show-off because they always brought new toys to school. Maybe as a teen you judged someone as trashy based on how they dressed or where they shopped.
- Do you have any poignant memories related to money involving your extended family, community, or friends?

I mentioned earlier that I attended Catholic school for thirteen years—kindergarten all the way through my senior year of high school. While there were multiple private grade schools in the tricounty area, the high school I attended was one of two Catholic options. Tuition at the other school was way more expensive than ours. As in they had a Zen garden on campus and boat parking for local students. Meanwhile, we had yellowing, laminated signs along the hallways warning us not to mess with the ceiling tiles because they still contained asbestos.

Anyway, going to private school for that long meant I was surrounded by a good number of rich kids. My sophomore and junior years drew a harsh line between the rich kids and everyone else because every time someone got their driver's license, they showed up with a new car. Back in the early 2000s, the hot rides for the girls were cute little Jettas and the guys had either zippy sports cars with spoilers or tricked-out Ford F-150s. (Florida is still part of the South, after all.) Meanwhile, I showed up with a 1990 Lincoln Town Car I dubbed "the Milk-mobile" because my brothers spilled so much milk eating breakfast on the way to school that it always stank.

To be clear, I was grateful to have any car at all. Anything that granted me even an ounce of freedom was a blessing. I also knew that being the first child and younger-sibling chauffeur, my parents wanted me in the auto equivalent of a tank. I drove twenty minutes on I-95 every day to get us all to the school. Had we ever crashed, we all would have survived. Also, cars don't really matter to me! My fiancé drives a dark-gray Toyota Corolla and five years into our relationship, I *still* walk up to the wrong car in a packed parking lot. I know Lincolns are great cars, and my dad definitely thought those wheels were fly as hell. If I were a car enthusiast, maybe I would have appreciated it more.

But our brains don't care about what we logically know to be true. They only care about perception and protection, even if it's fake. All my brain knew is that everyone got a cute, sparkly, silver Jetta when they turned sixteen, and I got the Milk-mobile. What it saw was *otherness*. And anything that can cause potential separation from our communities is a red flag for our brains.

Early Adulthood and Beyond

A lot of manifestation and shadow-work literature stops at adolescence as if your brain is set in stone once you hit eighteen years old. Meanwhile, it's decade-old news that the logical part of your brain—the prefrontal cortex—doesn't stop developing until about age twenty-five.[1]

Maybe it's pessimistic of me, but I tend to think the longer we live, the more ammo we have for either why we *can't* have all the money and happiness we desire or why we *can*.

Think about it! A lot of the people who grow up middle class enjoy a certain degree of financial privilege—myself included—that extends through higher education either because their parents could support them, they received scholarships, or they qualified for student loans. And while people are familiar with the archetype of the broke college student, it's nothing compared to the broke new graduate.

You go from having a fairly stable and straightforward life with minimal money worries to being dumped out into your first job that barely covers rent for the apartment you share with five other new graduates. Most of the time, you're furnishing the place yourself and depending on Craigslist finds or the communal trash in your building.

You can't afford to go out anymore because well-liquor drinks cost $12 a pop and a basket of street tacos is $15. You wait to do any maintenance on your appearance until the holidays when you can go home and let your mom pay for your haircut and a couple work outfits under the guise of bonding. And when anyone asks you how work is or how it feels to be in the "real world," you smile and say everything is great when you want to scream, "I make $35,000 a year and haven't turned the heat on in two years! How do you *think* I'm doing, Aunt Janet?"

And that's the case for the average *privileged* graduate. This doesn't even account for those who didn't go to college, couldn't find jobs in their fields, hail from disadvantaged backgrounds, experience systemic oppression, can't work due to disability, and a plethora of other situations that make it downright shitty to earn money in adulthood.

While, generally speaking, finances tend to improve as we age, that doesn't mean we're free of experiencing financial trauma.

Psychologists use the distinction of capital-T Trauma and lowercase-t trauma to distinguish between two main categories of hurtful experiences that forever change the way you think and behave.[2] Experiences with money are no different.

Capital-T Trauma encompasses the notable, significant experiences that our minds generally go to. When it comes to money, that could include experiences like losing a job, becoming homeless, paying for a divorce, living with an abusive partner out of necessity, declaring bankruptcy, and more. Lowercase-t trauma describes the small, everyday experiences that build up over time. Those money experiences could be working in a career you hate, jealousy over friends who make more money, sending in hundreds of job applications, or even a so-called good experience like spending money on a wedding or house.

The lists for both are endless, which is why it's important to take inventory of the financial experiences you had that left you reeling. Journal on the following questions:

- How did your first job impact your view on making money and working?
- During each job you've held, what did your closest friends do for work? Partners? Roommates?
- Have you ever worked in a toxic job or even just a job you hated? How long did you stay? Why? What made you leave?
- What various methods have you used for managing your money over the years? How did you feel about those methods? What kind of results did you get? Why did you stop using them? Keep in mind that "doing nothing" counts as a method.
- Has money ever impacted your romantic relationships or friendships? How?
- Think about the people you spend the most time around, including social media influencers, reality TV show casts, or podcast hosts. Do they talk about money? If so, what are the majority of their conversations about money like? If not, what do you think their views on money and career are?

- What have been your main motivations for wanting money throughout your adult life?
- Whom have you judged in adulthood based on money or career? They can be real people, reality TV show contestants, or fictional characters.
- Have you ever made a *thriveable* wage from your passions and talents? How about your friends?
- Have you ever made decisions in your career out of fear, rather than authenticity? Why?
- When have you been shady with money? Why?
- Do you avoid talking about money with others? Why or why not? What types of money conversations make you uncomfortable?
- If you're succeeding more than your friends, do you feel guilty? Why?
- Have you ever faced discrimination in your career as an adult? Did it impact how you felt about your job or pay? Did you do anything in response to it? Why or why not?
- What have been your most extreme positive and negative experiences with money as an adult?
- Are you where you thought you would be at the beginning of your career? How does that make you feel?

Remember how I told you I graduated during a recession and immediately sold out to a public relations job I hated? Well, time to spill the weird, lesson-learning tea.

When I graduated in 2009 from journalism school, I left with an award for Most Promising Young Journalist, a prestigious internship offer from the *Las Vegas Sun*, and a job market in which journalists with decades of experience were willing to take entry-level pay to support their families.

Unfortunately, I couldn't afford to accept that internship at the

Sun—the *hottest* spot to work in journalism following a Pulitzer Prize win earlier that year. It wasn't just because of the internship pay, but everything that went along with living in Las Vegas: rent, a cross-country drive from Florida, and the cost of living in a city. So, instead, I accepted a secure job with benefits at a public relations firm in a financially safe town.

And let me say: I was *not* ready for what awaited me there.

Before moving, I found an incredible deal on a fully furnished studio apartment in the rich neighborhood of town over the garage of a larger, adjoining house. It included *everything*, so all I needed to take were my clothes. To top it off, I had access to a washer and dryer, and rent included internet, cable TV, and all my utilities. All for the incredible price of $950. Yes, it was high for the area in 2009, but being an introvert, my home is my sanctuary and I was willing to pay a little more. In fact, I was ecstatic! I could live in peace where I could read, crochet, and watch Netflix DVDs to my heart's content.

Until I got my first paycheck.

I got my job through an alumnus of my independent college newspaper, so I felt the confidence to negotiate my salary, even though I had never done it and *definitely* did it the wrong way. The offer was $24,000, and I was proud that I had gotten it up to $27,000.

Again, *until I got my first paycheck*.

It was for $932. My rent would eat up almost 50 percent of my total income. The figure that personal finance experts recommended was 25 to 30 percent, and now I knew why. I felt instant pressure. I had a monthly bill to repay a small student loan I took out to study for a semester in Washington, DC. My boyfriend, sister, and most of my friends lived two hours away. My PT Cruiser had started violently shivering anytime I woke it up on cold mornings.

Maybe if it had been $932 and work I loved, it would have hit me differently. But also by the time I got that first paycheck, I knew I wanted to leave. I found the work unfulfilling, my coworkers were catty, and the CEO wouldn't allow anyone to eat bananas in the office because he had a freakish talent for smelling them across the building.

A couple months in and I knew I couldn't stay. I tried to take my birthday off only to realize I had three sick/vacation days for the entire year—yes, *slash*, meaning three total paid days off for illness or holidays—because you were expected to work from a company laptop if you were home sick.

Then there was the time my boss screamed at me when I couldn't find the location of an important client meeting because they hadn't updated their Google Maps listing. My phone also died that morning, preventing me from calling while I sobbed and drove around in a blind panic for over an hour. My boss spent the next week working from the empty desk in my office to keep an eye on me, as if my poor sense of direction directly reflected my work ethic. She chewed me out for using the word *Hey* to open an email. When I asked to help on a project under someone else in the office, she told me that "In other firms, some bosses would see that as betrayal."

That experience not only left me desperate—choosing to go to law school so I could delay the job market for three more years—but also scarred. I struggled to show up with any sort of personality in internships and jobs for almost a decade after. I struggled to ask for help or indicate I didn't understand instructions. I couldn't seem to network because I didn't trust anyone who would try to do me any favors. After all, I networked my way to *that* job, and look how it turned out.

For a long time, I saw that season in my life, of giving up a dream opportunity for something safe that turned toxic, as a fundamental turning point. I spent years wondering if that internship could have been the opportunity that led me to the *New York Times* or the *Washington Post*.

I looked at my choices then as a pathetic grasping at some semblance of stability. If only I had the gumption to take a risk, then maybe...

Yet every time I considered revisiting journalism, I told myself I had been out of the game for too long. I told myself that for six years. Until I decided to look at that situation differently.

Six years later, I went through a painful breakup and as I took inventory of my life, I realized that working in journalism was the last time I had been truly happy in my career. When I explored my choice to turn down that internship, I asked myself a question I had always been afraid to voice: Did I actually want that internship, deep, deep, *deep* down? If it had been the *New York Times*, *WaPo*, or *USA Today*, would I have taken the risk?

Abso-fucking-lutely, I would have. I would have given my left tit to work at one of those three! I would have gladly accepted $935 every two weeks to intern there. Christ, I would have paid *them* $925 every two weeks to intern there.

The truth of the matter is that the opportunity wasn't my dream. It was *a* dream opportunity, sure. But it wasn't mine.

I had been a big name in college journalism for my thoughts and approaches on finding new multimedia angles for print stories. I challenged everyone on the newspaper staff to come up with an online exclusive for every story they covered. I led them in groundbreaking, *live* online coverage of the 2008 presidential election. I was famous among my peers for rolling my eyes at classmates who only wanted to write news stories or for making condescending comments like, "Well, you know print media is *dead*, right?"

But when I got real with myself all those years later, I realized I was no different. I didn't want to learn how to code beyond the basics. I got a C in my photojournalism class. I had somehow avoided learning how to record and edit video in my four and a half years of college and I intended to keep it that way.

I just...wanted to write.

And had I accepted that internship, I might have gone on to one of those big papers, but not in the capacity I would have found fulfilling. Meanwhile, I didn't regret going to law school. I'm probably the only person who enjoyed the experience. My legal knowledge felt like a superpower, and the confines of legal writing had improved my skills. Why couldn't I find a legal journalism job? Surely, I was an even better candidate as a journalist with a JD behind my name. I just needed to be in the right place.

That's when I decided I would move back to Washington, DC, and get a legal journalism job no matter what—which is exactly what I did. I went on to write for Bloomberg Law for nearly three years.

Now, when I look back at that first job out of college, I don't feel any regret. Instead, I see a process of becoming. I turned down an internship that wasn't my total dream. I accepted a job that was my first big exposure to a toxic workplace, which would later inform the work I do now. But mainly, I had such a *weird* four months that it makes for a great icebreaker with a lot of my job-hunting clients.

Similarly, I want you to explore your memories of money and career with compassion and empathy for your past self. I want you to find the lessons and blessings that came from them. I want you to get real with yourself so you can start seeing these experiences—whether they're Trauma or trauma—as bread crumbs leading you to the place of empowerment you'll be by the end of this book.

And if this work shakes up feelings that you're struggling to process, don't be afraid to unpack them with a therapist, your therapist friend, or a trusted professional. Confronting our pasts and the ways they've affected us requires a lot of bravery. You're essentially forcing yourself to relive a lot of the trauma you've been through so you can analyze it. It's natural that you might experience anger or grief over situations or beliefs that you didn't have time to process while you were in survival mode. Take all the time you need to feel those emotions.

You can even look at that as an abundance practice. Knowing that you do not *need* to brush off your emotions and live in survival mode anymore, but can take the time and space to *feel* is a form of abundance. Money ain't goin' anywhere, and it will be much easier to call it in once you've given yourself the chance to feel your feelings fully. After all, rich people still suffer, get angry, and cry. They're just doing it in nicer houses and cars. So, you might as well learn to cry now so you'll know how to do it in style later.

What to Do with These Revelations

Chances are, you're probably feeling like a steaming pile of wet garbage on a hot summer day in the middle of Tallahassee, Florida.

I know because that's how I felt when I realized all the shitty influences I had that set me up for obstacles to making and keeping money in my life. It's easy to look at that rundown and feel like a victim or to feel anger for how our caretakers, authority figures, our exes, even our friends fucked us up.

The good news is that *all of it* is fixable.

Yes, no matter how big or small the trauma, it's possible to reduce how much it impacts you. That's why we spent so much time discussing science earlier—so you'll believe me when I explain how you're going to work to change it.

The first step is to take the answers to your journal prompts and look for patterns or themes. What was consistent among the majority of your experiences? Is it "money is the root of all evil"? "Rich people are bad"? "I'll be rejected if I make more money than my caretakers/friends/community"?

Maybe all of those sound relevant. Since this is your first real try at money manifestation, write them all down. Then look for themes among the list of judgments you've made. Your brain is a bit of a caveman, so the goal is to get it to the simplest judgment we can get.

That doesn't mean it needs to sound as literal as "Money evil. Me get money, me evil." Rather, think about how your desire for money can boil down to your brain seeing this as a fundamental personality flaw like "I'm bad," "I'm not important," "I can't have what I want," "I can't trust others," "It's not safe for me to make money," "I'm too much," or something else similarly simple.

Once you have that fundamental judgment identified, go ahead and cry it out. It sucks to realize you think this about yourself on some level, and tears are like farts in that it's always healthier to let 'em out then hold 'em in.

Now, think about which of the memories that came up highlight that theme the most. We want to get the earliest memory we can, so if it's a memory from seven years old or before, you can skip the next paragraph and go straight to the healing practice.

If your memory isn't from before the age of seven, let's see if you can get to an earlier one. Take the memory that *did* come up, and describe all the emotions you felt in that memory. Get as specific as you can. If you're struggling with how to get more specific than "bad," "angry," "sad," then head on over to www.feelingswheel.com to see what you can find that's more specific. Write all your emotions out, then highlight or circle the *most* prominent ones.

Once you have those emotions identified, close your eyes and feel those emotions right now. Experience what it feels like to hurt with that specific cocktail of emotions. When they feel nice and vivid, silently ask yourself, "When was the *first* time I felt this way?" Trust whatever memory comes up.

If the memory is from age seven or younger, feel the pain of that memory and ask again, "Did I feel like this before then?" Give it a few seconds, letting the feelings pulsate for a bit. It's OK if the answer is no, but give your brain a chance to find something older, even if it's fuzzy.

Take the memory in question and either meditate on your own or find some meditation music on YouTube to help you relax into it. My favorites are those designed for somatic healing or with binaural beats. Bring up that memory and imagine it playing out in a way that would have left you feeling confident and reassured that the *opposite* of your wound was true. In other words, if you walked away from that memory thinking "I am insignificant," you need to imagine the memory playing out in a way that would have left you feeling *significant*.

Don't judge what you need. Sometimes we need nice, politically correct responses like an adult figure giving us agency or finally seeing our needs. But if the scenario that makes you feel the best is your current self bursting through the wall like the Kool-Aid man, beheading a high school bully with a katana a la *Kill Bill*, and escaping with your teenage self in a red Corvette while Beyoncé cheers you on—*do it*. It doesn't matter what leads you to the conclusion that you need. It's about creating a memory that can rival (and maybe one day overpower) the one you actually experienced.

After correcting the original memory, repeat to yourself the opposite phrase of your wound, for example, "I am valued," over and over again until the meditation ends.

The more often you do this—whether it's with the same memory or a different one each time—the less of an impact the original memory will carry. Eventually, your subconscious will get the memo that what you initially believed simply *isn't true*. That less-than feeling will begin to fall away, and soon enough, your default setting will switch to the empowering belief.

Show Me the Money (Magic)

- **No cutting!** Journaling is a form of meditation that allows you to access your subconscious more easily. Make sure that as you go through this book, you're engaging in any journal prompts I've set out or journaling on concepts that resonate with you.
- **The apple doesn't fall far from the money tree.** Our baseline beliefs around money often come from what we experienced or witnessed during childhood. Even if you don't remember your lived experiences, your subconscious does. When you explore the circumstances around your parents' or caretakers' lives before your active memory kicked in, you can often find a lot of parallels to your beliefs and behavior around money now.
- **Not a kid anymore.** Adolescence has a way of fucking with our confidence in a truly unique way, thanks to the hellscape that can be middle school and high school. Our beliefs around money are no different. Teens go for low-hanging fruit when it comes to mocking and bullying, so making money is an easy target. The same goes for how they judge each other. Chances are, your experiences during that time began cementing some of those childhood beliefs around money.
- **It's not all good in the neighborhood.** Obviously, we're not around our caretakers twenty-four seven. Another massive influence in our subconscious money beliefs comes from the people in our communities growing up. This could be your friends, their parents, your extended family, your neighbors, and more.
- **Adulting is hard.** It's a rare occurrence that anyone gets a formal,

quality education on money management, which means most of your lessons will come from your earliest days of making and managing money. These experiences likely sealed the deal on whatever beliefs you currently carry around your ability to make money, keep it, and make more of it any time you want.

ACTIVITIES

- What were the most surprising discoveries you made regarding money's role in your life?
- What significance do you see in your first memory of money?
- What negative stories did you create in response to your first adult job? What lessons and blessings came with the experience?
- What patterns or themes did you see in your money influences?
- What is the central belief you had regarding money from your life experiences?
- How did you feel after attempting to heal the main memory that fed into that belief?

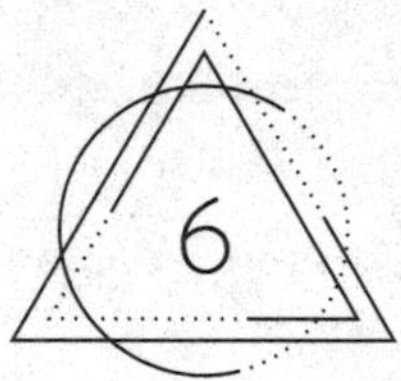

6

Embody Your Intentions Deeply

By now, you probably have a massive understanding of why you think the way you do, why your reality looks the way it does, and the scientific means for changing it. But knowledge on *why* and *how* can only take you so far.

What really makes the difference is *embodiment*, one of the three main concepts I found when I began learning about magic spells.

I already shared the three basic steps of effective spellwork that I've used to change my life and my clients, but in case you don't want to flip back to it, here they are again: (1) align your intentions, (2) *embody them deeply*, and (3) take inspired action daily.

When you read spells, they normally have a sentence that reads along the lines of "Go forward confident in the belief that your heart's desires are on their way." To the untrained eye, that sounds like a throwaway line akin to "And they all lived happily ever after" on the last page of a fairy tale. Except it's not. It's actually an important instruction all on its own.

Spellwork requires a lot of belief, and a big part of true belief is *living as if* the spell already worked. For example, if you cast a spell for more money and spend the entire moon cycle panicking about whether it's going to work and if you'll be able to pay your bills, you would be dedicating your reality-creating energy to the fear around *not making more money*. Instead, you need to spend that time *living as if* you are someone who can easily make more money and pay their bills.

That *doesn't* mean, however, that you come out of casting a money spell and spending money like you're personal shopping for a Kardashian. Instead, you need to think about how someone in the next income bracket above you who doesn't have your same issues with income treats their money. Generally, their focus isn't on buying, but on *balance*.

That means after casting a spell for money, you need to behave in a way where you're not overly worrying about money and you're also not spending from insecurity. That's the difference between "faking it 'til you make it" and "*living as if*." Embodiment is about living your life in a way that makes it easier for you to *believe* your new thoughts.

Embodiment is built through a variety of methods, including routine, environment, boundaries, and more. Yet before you do any of it, you need a model of what to build.

Just as with a money spell after which you want to behave more like a consistently wealthy person who approaches their money with balance, you need to find a model for all the endeavors you pursue in making more money. This touches on both the scientific and spiritual.

Your brain needs to see to believe. When it sees external proof that what you want is achievable, your brain will start to build new neural pathways that make achieving your goals possible. The more people you find who have accomplished similar goals that you relate to, the more your brain is able to make stronger connections that prove you can have that ability, too. Those new connections are created between neurons in your brain. The old neural pathways that connected to the memories that held you back weaken and, therefore, lose their power over you.

The easiest way to start building those pathways is to find role models you can relate to in any way. They can look like you, come from a similar background, have a similar personality, and so on. It doesn't matter *how* you relate to them; all that matters is that you're able to see yourself in them.

Chances are, you're already doing this on some level. When you hard-core relate to a celebrity, a character in a movie or TV show, or a friend, your brain is recognizing them as a mirror showing you exactly what you want or what you're capable of having.

What If I Can't Find Role Models?

Many times when we set about to start making money and the career achievements we need to get there, we can feel alone.

After all, if your family and community were rich and well connected in your industry, they would have helped already, right?

The good news is that there is also a *magical* method for finding role models who can show you that what you want is completely achievable.

In magic, the version of this is called deity work. This is when we pick a god, goddess, or nonbinary deity to sponsor the work we do. Catholicism has a version of this in their pantheon of saints and love for Jesus's mother, Mary. But say that to any Catholic and they will quickly correct you that they do not *worship* the saints or Mary. Instead, they pray to them so the saints can pray *on their behalf* to God. Essentially, saints are the VIP Catholics who can offer you a hookup by putting in a good word for you with the Almighty One.

Similarly, deity work is about invoking the energy of a deity (or saint, even!) by becoming one of their fangirls. And what do fangirls do? They gorge themselves on information about their idols, buy their merch, and spend a lot of time pretending they're friends or lovers.

I'm a Queen and Freddie Mercury fanatic. I saw *Bohemian Rhapsody* in the theater *four* times. I know every word to all their songs. I've watched every interview and documentary I can get my hands on. I saw Queen in concert with Adam Lambert *and* I saw a famous American cover band with a killer Freddie Mercury impersonator. People buy me Queen and Freddie merch for holidays, so I have a framed print of Freddie with one of his cats, three T-shirts, guitar-pick earrings of '70s glam-rock Freddie, and a lapel pin of him in his iconic fist-in-the-air power pose from Live Aid.

Whenever I doubt the belief that I'm meant to be a big-time coach, I think of Freddie persuading the band to sell their van to record their first album, an action that would have prevented them from playing *any* gigs if it didn't work.

Whenever I worry whether I'm being too long-winded or that people will think my book is too weird, I think of Freddie writing a *six-minute rock opera* that broke all the rules of songwriting to become a No. 1 hit.

And whenever I feel insecure, I think to myself, "How would Freddie view this situation? What kind of sassy remark would he make about it?" and then I blare "Don't Stop Me Now" and shake it off.

Fangirling isn't much different than deity work.

I've worked with a variety of deities and saints over the years. My most recent one, who serves as a wonderful example, is Persephone/Kore, the Greek goddess of spring and queen of the underworld.

If you're not familiar with her, let me give you a quick recap of her most famous story that explains the origins of winter. She was the daughter of Demeter, goddess of the harvest and agriculture, and Zeus, king of the gods. Demeter and the goddess then known as Kore worked in concert to ensure the world was a green, beautiful, and fruitful place to live (pun intended). Then one day, Hades, the god of the dead and king of the underworld, popped up from a crack in the earth, kidnapped Kore, and took her to the underworld to rule by his side.

Demeter became so distraught without her daughter that she

couldn't perform her duties and the earth became barren. After enough annoyance from the mortals, Zeus demanded that Hades return Kore to the mortal realm. But she had eaten six pomegranate seeds from a fruit grown in the underworld, which bonded her to the realm. Now, every year, she spends six months with her mother in the mortal realm and six months with her husband in the underworld. And every year, her mother is so distraught at her departure that the earth turns barren and we experience autumn and winter.

Also, after marrying Hades, her name changed from Kore, which means "maiden," to Persephone, which means "she who destroys the light."

At the time, I chose to work with Persephone because I realized that I was so focused on people seeing me as a kind and good coach that I was holding myself back from being effective—and part of me knew I needed to tap more into my darkness to get there.

Back then, I didn't want to be seen as mean if I didn't sugarcoat my advice. I didn't want to get canceled if I said the wrong thing on social media. I didn't want to risk losing out on potential clients by holding my boundaries around how available I was to my followers. Until I realized that all of those concerns were forcing me to shrink myself and *resist* getting discovered in a big way—the exact manifestation I was calling in for myself and my business!

If Persephone could be *both* the goddess of spring and queen of the underworld, then couldn't I be sweet and spicy, too? I mean, that's a barbecue flavor for a *reason*.

So, I started reading everything I could about Persephone. Admittedly, I started with *Lore Olympus, Volume 1*, the webcomic by Rachel Smythe that offered a modern retelling of that myth where the relationship between Persephone and Hades is consensual and romantic and coincides with her learning to love the power that comes from her anger and darkness.

When I first read the story of Persephone as a child, I was horrified at the idea that she could have been tricked into eating food that would keep her locked in the underworld and away from her mother for half the year, *every* year. But reading *Lore Olympus* made me wonder if that was the only way people interpreted the myth.

As it turns out, tons of people read the myth in a completely different light. Instead, they understand it as the story of a young, lonely woman stuck under the thumb of a controlling parent who took the first opportunity at freedom that she got. In the six months she spent in the underworld, she fell in love with Hades and the agency he granted her as his queen. Upon finding out that she would be forced to return to her mother's control, she willingly ate the pomegranate seeds to secure her place. As the adult child of parents whose love manifested as strictness and control for a good portion of my life, that really struck a chord with me. I felt seen and understood.

That story also made a lot more sense in the grander context of other myths. They were, in fact, the only couple that ruled their realm as equals. Not only that, but Hades is the only royal husband in the Greek pantheon who *never* cheated on his wife.

Because of her associations with spring and the underworld, Persephone is viewed as a goddess of life and death. And she follows through with the badassery that conveys. When a nymph had a crush on Hades and tried to make a move, Persephone turned her into a mint plant. She was known for both for encouraging Hades to be more compassionate toward human souls awaiting their judgment *and* for being the harsher and scarier of the two if she believed someone deserved punishment.

In her book on shadow work, *Existential Kink: Unmask Your Shadow and Embrace Your Power*, Carolyn Elliott puts forth an even cooler theory about Hades and Persephone: that they are two halves of a whole person. As a being who contained both darkness and light, Persephone split herself in half and created two deities to house the opposing energies within her. When she decides to accept her fate and ingest the pomegranate seeds, she remembers that Hades was a being of her own creation and now "a lover so selfless, so devoted, and so subservient, that he fully played the role of the malicious villain just because she asked him to."

The first time I read that, I thought to myself, "*Holy shit*. That is the integration I need to access my full power."

Over time, I continued to read about Persephone and created a dedicated space for her on my altar, which is just part of my L-shaped desk. I give offerings I know from my research that she values, such as a flower picked on my walk, a piece of dark chocolate from a bar I'm eating, nice hunks of pomegranate in the fall and winter, a lit floral-scented candle, or even just a small glass of water if I have nothing else. When I place them there, I thank her for being a companion to me and showing me how darkness isn't *bad* or *evil*, but a necessary and *normal* part of humanity. I ask her to continue showing me how I can love my darkness even more.

With time, my resistance to setting boundaries, honest communication, and speaking my mind online began to wear away. About a month after my fangirling, a book editor reached out to say she loved my social media and asked if I had ever considered writing a book. I couldn't respond to that message fast enough!

Although my newfound brazenness can sometimes bite me in the butt, what I've learned is that it's not about making mistakes. It's about how you respond to them. If you have a willingness to listen, admit fault, and learn from the experience, then backlash winds up being a good thing.

Now, I look forward to the day I wind up getting canceled. It will mean I'm finally famous enough to get canceled in the first place.

Rest Is Abundance

I'm adamant about creating my to-do lists around what I *want* to do instead of what I *need* to do.

Of course, some of the things I *need* to do inevitably wind up on the list. That's because I would rather do them than deal with the consequences. I *want* to feed my cat not only because I love her, but also because she will scream at the top of her tiny kitty lungs until she hears me pop that Fancy Feast can.

The other main reason I write lists on want instead of need is because rest is another form of abundance that will help you feel like whatever your money manifestation goal is, it's possible.

If that doesn't make sense, I urge you to recall the incredibly popular phrase, "Time is money."

Generally speaking, that phrase is all about thinking of your time in terms of hourly pay. The capitalist overlords that be have convinced us that rest is a waste of time. An hour spent on your lunch break is a waste of the $36.05 per hour paid for a salary of $75,000.

And, somehow, we've believed it.

We've been brainwashed to think of things like hobbies, socializing, and even *doing nothing* as a waste of time. Plenty of baby boomers out there love to criticize younger folks' commitment to rest as entitlement.

"All these *teenaged millennials* out here want to make $20 an hour *flipping burgers* and get *free college* because they just want everything handed to them! If they spent all that time on their phones *working a second job* or *starting a business*, they could pay for college like I did!"

Aside from the fact that millennials are mostly in their thirties with kids, $20 an hour isn't even a livable wage, and tons of other countries have managed to provide free higher education without going bankrupt, it's easy to hear that kind of gripe and get red-hot with anger.

Those are the kind of statements that start fights over family dinners and comment wars on Facebook while we young folk try to defend ourselves from what we see are factually incorrect judgments. We talk about how much student loan debt we're in, how hard we've worked in our careers, how low our salaries are, how much our rent costs—all in the hope that they can see how wrong they are about us.

In reality, we're worried they might be right.

I know I'm not the only adult who grew up being told they were lazy as a kid because they didn't want to spend all their spare time on chores, would prefer to sleep in than go to church on Sunday, and generally preferred to play over doing their homework on the weekends.

When you crave a deep level of rest or playtime as a kid but your parents work two or three jobs to provide for you and all they ask is for you to help prevent the house from becoming a health code violation every weekend... Well, yeah, wanting to rest or play sounds a lot like being lazy, entitled, and selfish. Who wants to be identified that way?

Meanwhile, baby boomers are *also* acting from a wounded place in these arguments. They desperately crave rest and playtime, and they resent the fact that they didn't get enough when they were kids or young adults. If suddenly all people could relax and rest without worrying about losing money, there's a pretty good chance they'll need to face some uncomfortable questions like "Is it possible I wasted the best years of my life working?" "Why didn't I advocate for my own needs back then?" or, heaven forbid, "Was the sacrifice I made for my family worth it?" Would you want to face the possibility that you had it all wrong?

In reality, the whole argument boils down to another form of scarce thinking.

I don't have enough time.

If time is limited, that means it can be wasted. So, if time can be wasted...and what we want more than anything is money...and time *is* money...then how can we justify rest? We should be plugging away at our jobs or businesses in every spare moment. Rest is only for people who don't need money anymore.

However, time isn't *tied* to money. There's no guarantee that one hour will net you any specific amount of money. Volunteers work plenty of hours and never receive any money. If you stick your hand in an old jacket pocket and find $20, you just made money with nearly no time investment. Yet the belief that time is money runs deep, so we question whether we have enough time for rest or whether we should be focusing on something *more* productive instead.

When I began my business, it was really hard for me to unlearn the "time is money" phrase. After all, I spent more than ten years working for pay based on forty hours a week. It made sense that if I put in the same hours (or more), I would increase my chances of getting paid.

The only problem is that when I overworked myself, I would start getting sick and need to take time off. One time, I rushed down the stairs in a hurry to get to the gym around 9:00 p.m. (when I *finally* called it a day), missed a step, and heard my ankle release a *crack* so loud that the person on the phone with my fiancé said, "That sounded bad. What happened?" Thankfully, I only twisted my ankle, but I found myself stuck from going to my coworking space or the gym for three weeks while it healed.

After a while, I started to realize that working nonstop didn't get me any further along than working at a personalized pace because nonstop work inevitably led to setbacks. In fact, I found the opposite. The more well rested and relaxed I felt, the easier it was to see solutions for increasing my income and follow through on my ideas. When I'm well rested, I'm a better coach, writer, and money manifestor than when I'm tired and burned out. Truth be told, I've made the most money in business either during or right after returning from a vacation.

Rest is abundance because it communicates to you and your subconscious, "I have all the time in the world at my disposal." If time is money, then it seeks to follow that you have all the *money* in the world at your disposal, too.

A Note on Systemic Oppression

In an episode of her TV series and podcast *Master Class*, Oprah Winfrey talks about how her grandmother's wish for Oprah when she grew up was that she would find herself some "good white folks" to employ her as a maid. Oprah knew that would never be her path, but that's beside the point. The point is that because it was all her grandmother knew, it was all she could visualize for Oprah's future.

Modern institutions and systems—such as government programs, higher education, healthcare, or corporate America—have been deliberately built to make it difficult for marginalized groups to find the hope that they could get ahead and threaten the standing of those in positions of power.

One need only look at the United States' housing policies from the 1950s. Research shows that the government intentionally planned to push Black Americans out of good, white neighborhoods and into dilapidated neighborhoods where white people wouldn't need to encounter them.[1]

And for anyone who says that those old policies don't negatively impact class mobility today, you can check out all the research being done on implicit bias when it comes to buying and selling residential property.

A 2022 study from the Federal Home Loan Mortgage Corporation, known as Freddie Mac, revealed that houses with black owners were more likely to be appraised lower than near-identical white homeowners' houses. In 2020, many news articles revealed that homes received higher appraisals and sold faster and for more money when pictures of black homeowners were replaced with pictures of white families instead.[2] There's still a negative bias against black neighborhoods and black homes that impacts Black Americans' ability to build generational wealth at the same rate as their white counterparts.

Unfortunately, this is also a part of manifestation.

You see, the world as a collective consciousness has an ugly side to it. The bias and bigotry that so many harbor influence policies and institutions that then solidify that bigotry into systemic oppression.

So, what does one do when they're living under the rule of system oppression?

Being in that situation makes exposure to people who have accomplished your dreams even more important.

Of course, I'm just a privileged, white-passing woman who grew up in the Florida suburbs. I didn't live through the type of systemic oppression that my black and indigenous friends of color have. Even the bias I experience as a woman will never come close to the experiences of my friends who are women of color, trans women, or trans women of color.

However, my Hispanic mother—who was born and raised in the South Bronx long before it started getting gentrified—raised me with stories about what it was like to live on the wrong side of the racial divide in a major metropolitan area, and those stories are always at the forefront of my mind when I talk about manifestation and magic.

This is a woman who walked past dead bodies on her way to elementary school, experienced multiple evictions throughout her childhood, ate mayonnaise sandwiches when her family ran out of other food, used the oven to heat her family's apartment when the heat was shut off in winter, and more.

Not only did she come from poverty, but she came from dysfunction, with an alcoholic father and brothers who got mixed up in gangs and drugs as early as eleven years old. She experienced a variety of abuse no child should ever even know of. She only learned English once she attended kindergarten, and she's still shy about her slow reading speed today. As a teenager, she once ran away and was homeless for almost a month until the local prostitutes told her she would have better luck with her dysfunctional family than on the streets.

Yet with all of those cards stacked against her, she managed to become a nurse practitioner, save money, move to a country club community in Florida, and have four children who all attended and graduated from college. She managed to get her bachelor's and master's degrees while we were growing up, and when I went to law school, she got her doctorate.

My mother got to where she is by exposing herself to more than just the people she identified around her.

TV shows were a big inspiration to her. She loved *Leave It to Beaver* and *The Munsters*, especially. In *Beaver*, she saw what a family could look like. She saw white picket fences around lush backyards, pies cooling on the counter, and mischievous young boys getting into innocuous trouble. The more she watched, the more she believed that it was not just possible, but commonplace outside of the Bronx.

In *The Munsters*, she found comfort and understanding. If you don't recall, the show is about a family of monsters with one completely normal-looking, pretty, blond daughter. The running joke of the show is that this daughter, who is beautiful by society's standards, is the ugly duckling of a monster family. Even though my mother had dark-brown hair and tan skin, she felt a kinship with Marilyn. Although others in her community thought she was strange for wanting more than a boyfriend from the neighborhood, she believed her desires were normal for who she authentically was.

For my mom, being misunderstood and standing out was proof that she was destined for more.

Thankfully, she ran into adults along the way who saw her potential and took an interest in her. She had an art teacher who acted like a kind aunt for her at school and went out of her way to nurture her. She even brought my mom to her family's beach house for a weekend out on Long Island. If that didn't plant a seed that made moving to Florida a reality ten years into the future, I don't know what else could have.

At the end of the day, the way to thrive in a world that builds systemic barriers to someone's success—either through systemic oppression or family trauma—is exposure to anyone who shows you it cannot and will not deter you from reaching your own success.

Systemic oppression boils down to traumatic experiences like everything my mother lived through. The fewer people and resources available, the more important role models and media become.

And as you achieve success, it becomes *even more* important for you to connect with people who experience systemic oppression. The more people they know who weren't held back—especially if those people are members of the same populations—the easier it becomes for them to believe they can beat the system.

Show Me the Money (Magic)

- **Role models show you what's possible.** Your brain can't tell the difference between inspiration gathered from a real person versus a fictional character or celebrity. You can take advantage of that circuitry by consuming media or following heroes who already have what you want. The more you relate to them, the better.
- **Rest is money.** Because we've been bombarded with messaging that we must be productive to receive money, resting can feel blasphemous when you're actively trying to manifest money. However, resting is a necessary part of the process! It shows your subconscious that you have all the time in the world at your disposal. And if time is money, then you have all the *money* in the world at your disposal, too.
- **The dark side of manifestation.** Systemic oppression is unfortunately a by-product of the world's collective shadow and subconscious beliefs that *want* to keep many people exploited and suffering. That shadow is woven into the framework of society, which makes it *that much more important* for members of oppressed populations to see examples of people who have beat the system. So, if you're currently feeling the pressure of oppression, collect those role models from *anywhere* you can. If you have found success, find ways to connect with people so you can help raise them out of oppression.

ACTIVITIES

- Off the top of your head, name a few people (real or fictional) who have shown you that you can have your manifestation.
- What kind of qualities or personality traits do you want to incorporate into your financial life? Can you find a deity who encompasses them?
- Have you ever been a superfan of someone? What about them were you drawn to? How could those qualities tell you more about the kind of person you want to be or the type of life you want to live?
- Plan your week based on what you *want* to do versus what you *need* to do. How do you feel about your week now? Are you surprised at what made this list or didn't?

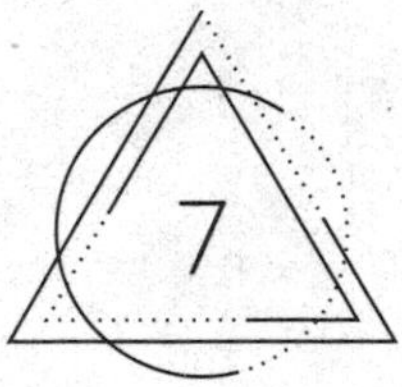

Take Inspired Action Daily

If I haven't made clear my stance that practical approaches are magic in the past six chapters, hopefully this list of shouty statements sets the record straight:

1. You cannot think your way to wealth!
2. Spells alone will not work!
3. Thinking positive is not magic or manifestation!
4. Crystals, readings, or healings cannot replace shadow work!
5. Magical/spiritual shortcuts do not exist!

Phew! OK, I'm sure I have more, but since those are the top nuggets of misinformation I see, I wanted to get them out in the open.

The reason why I feel so compelled to kick off this chapter with shouting is because I've witnessed some problematic thinking in a lot of spiritual, magic, and manifestation circles of the internet. And while I'll likely be debunking a whole lotta them for the entire book, I'm going to start with the crown jewel of problematic spiritual thinking as it directly relates to the topic of this chapter.

If you haven't received your manifestation yet, it's because you are not healed enough.

My dear, sweet, angelic readers. If you take anything away from this book, I hope it's this quote I've adapted from Shakespeare.

Doubt thou the stars are fire;

Doubt that the sun doth move;

Doubt truth to be a liar;

But never doubt that unethical internet psychics, healers, and spiritual coaches will always try to capitalize on fear and desperation to make a buck.

The truth of the matter is that life is a healing journey. You will never be fully healed and whole. You will have more bad days. You will experience more trauma. You will uncover more repressed memories and layers of wounds from childhood that you thought you had processed. You will do this work until you die.

If you need to be *more* healed to receive what you want, then what would that milestone be? Who would judge that? Could you even tell if you reached it?

Rather than believing you need more healing anytime a manifestation seems to take the scenic route into your life, I would rather you ask yourself, "What *actions* will make me feel more deserving *as the person I am right now* to receive my manifestations?"

At the end of the day, you don't need to be two steps shy of reaching nirvana to manifest a dream job, a chunk of money, or a successful business. What you need to do is *take daily action* in line with the new set of beliefs you've established. Because if you are indeed a new person with new beliefs, then you also need to be someone who takes a different approach.

What Is Inspired Action?

Everyone who pursues magic or manifestation seems to want a shortcut. And to be clear, I'm no different.

I started manifestation because *everything else I tried didn't work.* I wanted to become a life coach, an author, a speaker, and a thought leader. The only problem was that I kept trying to manifest those things without taking on coaching clients, writing a book, writing and delivering a speech, or sharing my thoughts.

It sure felt like I was taking action, though, because I was busy AF. I did a lot of researching and reading. I spoke to a lot of people about what I wanted to do. But at no point before manifestation work did it ever occur to me to, you know, *do* any of the stuff required to actually reach the goals I wrote on my manifestation list.

So, when I discovered that a necessary step of magic is to go forth from a spell and live like the spell already worked, I realized where the massive gap between manifestation and materialization had been in my life.

I couldn't just *think* and *feel* like I was that bitch. I had to show up *every day* and take *actions* like I was that bitch. In other words, I needed *inspired* action. That meant not just taking action for the sake of proving you tried. It's about taking action based on a moment of inspiration that shows you how to connect the dots from where you are to where you want to be.

This could sound like a stroke of genius that's completely logical. For example, "Wow, I've been saying I want to feel financially stable, but I never check my bank account and I don't budget so I keep forgetting when money is leaving my account and overdrafting. If I'm going to be a financially stable bitch, then I need to use some budgeting basics."

It can also sound like something that doesn't make sense, such as, "I don't know why, but I can't shake the feeling that I need to send an email to that old coworker and see how they're doing" or "Something is telling me to go hit up my favorite thrift shop today."

It's less about taking a ton of action that keeps you busy and more about zeroing in on specific actions that come from a place of inspiration and intuition. Remember, your brain wants to solve problems. If it senses that you're living a new set of beliefs but your external surroundings don't match what you believe, it will automatically try to close the gap between where you are and where you want to be. Those magical moments of inspiration are quite literally how your brain is guiding you to your manifestations using your intuition.

When you begin to intentionally search for direction from your intuition, it can be really tricky to figure out if the nagging feeling that you have to do something is from your intuition or fear. After all, the brain doesn't like change. It's easy to confuse a warning signal based on unfounded fear with an intuitive hunch or nudge to take action.

Thankfully, there's a simple trick to identify which is which when you start to pay attention. Your intuition will never give you directions that make you feel small, ashamed, or stuck. That means you wouldn't feel embarrassed to tell someone whose opinion you value that you took the action. It means you'll likely feel proud of yourself for making that choice. If it doesn't feel like that, there's a good chance it's sprouting from fear.

Tuning In to Your Intuition

About eight months into running my business, I had made enough money to just cover my bills, but the floodgates still hadn't burst open. I didn't understand why when I had a ton of interest in my work and I regularly had people booking calls to ask about my offers.

I felt frustrated and confused. I had a whole list of ideas of what might be wrong or how I could fix things, but none of them felt particularly compelling. Until I realized that it was because I was trying to solve the problem from my conscious thoughts, rather than trusting my intuition. Those rational, business-consultant ideas floating around in my mind were drowning out the quiet wisdom of my intuition, and I needed to find a way to tune in again.

I wrote about a few calls that left me feeling particularly stung when the person didn't choose to work with me. I wrote the judgments I had about myself and the potential clients who rejected me along with the emotions that came up in response. Then, I wrote about how I *wanted* to feel on my calls, along with the thoughts I *wanted* to have about myself and my potential clients.

Once I could see the clear difference in how I was feeling versus how I *wanted* to feel, I sat in my shit. I felt all those yucky feelings—rejected, angry, insignificant, and everything else. While I leaned into that pain, I remembered the first experience I had being bullied in middle school. I asked myself, "What did I need from this experience to become the type of person who has the emotions and thoughts I *want* on my calls?"

I saw my adult self show up at school and intervene. She took every nasty preteen down *several* notches before taking my middle-school self somewhere to talk. They began to talk with my adult self asking my child self questions that were designed to help her *think*, rather than telling her how to feel:

"Why do you think those mean girls treat you like this?"

"*I don't know. Mom and Dad say they're jealous of me.*"

"They're probably right, but does that feel true to you?"

"*No.*"

"If you don't think they're jealous, why do you think they bully you?"

"*I don't know. They just don't like me. Brittany hasn't liked me since first grade, and Tiffany is her best friend, so I guess she doesn't like me because Brittany doesn't. I'm a nerd and they're more popular. That's just how it is.*"

"Did you do or say anything that caused Brittany to dislike you in first grade?"

"*No! I literally have no idea why she doesn't like me. She's just always been mean to me.*"

"So, if you didn't do or say anything to make her not like you, is it possible that it has nothing to do with *you*?"

"*What do you mean?*"

"Well, if you didn't do or say anything that made her dislike you, then there's no way you could have acted or said anything differently to make her like you, right?"

"*Right.*"

"And there weren't popular kids and nerds in the first grade yet, right?"

"*Right.*"

"So, you had no way for you to change it. It was totally outside your control. That means she picked you because of how *she* feels inside. What do you think Brittany and Tiffany don't like about themselves?"

"*Nothing. They seem fine.*"

"Take a wild guess. Make it up."

"*Well, they're taller than a lot of the guys in our grade. And they have a few friends, but I don't think many other people actually like them. Actually, everyone is kind of afraid of them.*"

"Is there anything about you that might remind them of what they don't like about themselves?"

"*Well, I'm short, but I don't think that has to do with anything. And I'm not popular, but I'm mostly nice to everyone. No one really dislikes me except for them.*"

"So, if you remind them about some of the things they don't like about themselves, why do you think they treat you this way?"

"*I guess it's because pushing me down makes me less threatening.*"

"And is that anything you can change or control?"

"*No.*"

Finally, I asked if she wanted me to do anything else like help her talk to a teacher, but she declined. Instead, she went straight back into her life and anytime one of those bullies or the ones that would come later in high school tried to put her down, she responded with a mix of pity and compassion.

"*I know you're only doing this because you think I'm better than you, but you should know that nothing you say is going to make me believe I'm any less beautiful, intelligent, funny, or kind. So, if you really need to keep harassing me to feel better about yourself, I guess you can because it doesn't bother me. But you'll probably have more success telling the guidance counselor how you feel. Do you want me to go with you?*"

From there, I watched her grow up with Teflon confidence that saw her go after her goals with ease and conviction, knowing that naysayers were just people who shot down her dreams in an attempt to feel better about not pursuing their own.

When she reached the age I was at the moment I was in meditation, I imagined how her life looked: what she wore, how she engaged with people, where she lived, and anything else that made her vivid in my mind. Then, I imagined she stood in front of me and I asked her, "Why am I struggling to get interested people to become paying clients?" And she answered:

"*Because you don't know how to deliver a confident sales call. You don't know how to adequately describe what you do, which leaves both of you feeling unclear on whether you can actually help them or not. And because you're not sure, they're not sure. Learn how to sell so you can have more effective conversations. It's not about getting them to always say yes, but to know that when they say no, it has nothing to do with you.*"

I came out of that meditation clear that I needed to invest in a sales course that wouldn't just hand me a script or teach me how to manipulate people. Instead, I needed a course that would teach me effective sales communication. A few days later, one of my favorite business coaches announced a course on exactly that topic for $1,200, and even though I charged that to a credit card, I did it with total peace of mind. The following month after binge learning about sales, I cracked $10,000 in my business for the very first time.

Why Things Go to Shit When You're Manifesting

While there's absolutely a difference between busy action and inspired action, that doesn't mean the road to wealth is free from bumps, debris, or rain.

In fact, it's pretty common that the moment you start listening to your intuition and taking new, sometimes scary actions is the moment that your life seems like it's starting to fall apart.

I hate to say it, but this is part of the process.

See, you've essentially announced to the universe, "I am ready to be a rich bitch! I'm done with my broke-bitch thoughts and behaviors and I'm ready to receive my blessings!"

Now, if you've ever had an ex try to win you back saying they've changed, let me ask you something. Did their words matter as much as their actions? It's easy to say you've changed. It's a lot harder to *show* you've changed.

Up until now, you've been the fuckboi ex to yourself and your bank account. You've asked the Spirit of Money for more, more, more, without making any effort to be the partner Money deserves. You haven't checked in on Money by ignoring your bank account. You didn't spend quality time with Money by not taking an active role in managing your funds. You constantly believed Money would leave you. No matter how much Money provided, you told Money it wasn't enough for you.

Now you want Money to believe you've changed?

Well, just like we might entertain an ex for a while to see how they react to new or similar issues from our past relationship, Money wants to make sure you're not going to fall back into your old habits, too.

So, you'll encounter shitty situations that Money uses as a test to see if you've changed. These could look like bills or unforeseen expenses. You could have fights with your partner or family members. It might even be you experiencing a negative emotional reaction like anger, anxiety, defensiveness, judgment, or more.

Money sends you these situations to test you and see if you're ready for what you said you wanted. However, that doesn't mean you can *fail* these tests. Money loves you *unconditionally*. It will *always* take you back. Think of it less like a test in school and more like a cholesterol test. It's about determining your level of self-worth so Money can determine *when* you're ready for your manifestations.

It's as if Money is saying, "Oh, so you've changed, huh? Let's see what happens when I don't give as much as you want. Are you going to bitch about it or are you going to appreciate me for every small thing I do for you? It's fine if you don't, but if you can't say thank you for $20, don't expect me to put a rush order on that request for $20,000."

Even though the tests might technically be a surprise, they aren't *always* a surprise.

Often, these tests follow a set of patterns that vary based on the individual. For example, anytime I manifested a huge opportunity or a payout of some sort, I always seemed to get the same sequence of tests.

First, I would get a bill or unforeseen expense around $1,000. That could be a surprise unpaid medical bill, car repairs, or a missed credit card payment where the auto draft didn't process because some small charge put the balance too low for withdrawal.

About a week later, I would get another bill around $100 to $300. One time it was learning that my utility company hadn't been on autopay for a few months and my lights were about to get shut off. Another time, it was a yearly insurance bill I forgot was coming up. You get the picture.

Then, about a week *after that*, I would get a *third bill* for some laughably small amount like seven dollars. While it was small, it was usually crushing enough to make me feel like I would never make another dollar as long as I lived.

Two weeks later, luck would turn. I would wind up with a small, usually physical manifestation. One time it was a Le Creuset enameled Dutch oven in turquoise that I had been eyeing for years, but never saw drop below a *sale price* of $299. The few times I prepped myself to spend that on Black Friday or a Labor Day sale, I was too late. The turquoise had long since sold out and it was the only color I liked.

Then on a random June morning, I checked my email *less than five minutes* after receiving a promo announcing a sale at my favorite recipe and kitchenware website for *the exact pot* at $99.

My eyes nearly popped out of my head.

Without hesitation, I clicked over to the website, logged in, and added that turquoise baby to my cart, only to find I had $20 credit in my account! Even with shipping and tax, my final payment was $93.28. I was floored. I thought that was the final manifestation after my tests, but an even bigger one came.

Two weeks later, I debuted a small program that made me $12,500 in cash.

The first couple of times I lived through this round of tests, I really struggled. I got angry, I cried, I felt hopeless. However, it also had the effect of forcing me to surrender and stop worrying. It was almost as if I couldn't stop worrying about money until I reached what felt like financial rock bottom. Once I had nothing left to lose and cried it all out, I could stop obsessing about losing it because it was gone. At that point, I could only *make* money.

It wasn't until around the fifth time this cycle kicked off that I even realized it *was* a cycle. I had a moment of frustration with another big money snafu that made me whine, "Why does this keep happening to meeeeeee?" I had put so much effort into managing my money and learning new financial habits. I felt like I was being punished. That's when I had a spark of inspiration. If this was something that *kept* happening, was it possible that I could predict *when* it would happen?

I sat down and wrote out all the times I had huge manifestations come through, especially big paychecks. I wrote about what was happening in my life in the two to three months preceding the manifestation, including highs and lows. That's when I saw the pattern emerge: three financial tests, each about a week apart; a small physical manifestation; and then the Big Manifestation.

It came before big payouts, media features, and really cool opportunities. Just like that, my thinking flipped. I looked at this new, massive bill with *excitement*. Rather than panicking about how I would afford whatever financial problem came up, I would get hyped instead. That feeling only grew with each surprise bill as I waited with anticipation to see what awaited me on the other side.

Even now, when I face a big, unplanned expense, I get giddy. Big bills mean big blessings for me. And let me say, that's a *much* better feeling to have around surprise expenses than what I had before.

The Most Important Step in Manifestation You'll Ever Take

I'm sure by now you're starting to wonder, "Hey, I thought this chapter was about *action*. Why haven't you told me *what to do* to manifest money? Where are the herbs, spells, and crystals? Where's the financial advice? How am I supposed to create an action plan from *this*?"

To which I'll initially reply: *Don't worry, young padawan. All in due time.*

A.k.a. the next two chapters.

But if I'm being honest, it's because no plan I give you is going to be as good as the one you create yourself.

The issue with plans—whether they're for your finances, diet, exercise, mindset, whatever—is that they cater to a common denominator. It's about teaching what will work for *the most* people possible, not everyone. That's not necessarily what will work for you as an individual.

It's kinda like buying running shoes. You can drop $200 or more on a good pair, but you still might experience discomfort if you don't *also* buy supportive inserts. It doesn't mean the shoes are bogus. It's because everyone's arches, feet, and knee bends vary *so much* that a shoe company can't afford to make a bunch of different pairs to fit everyone's needs. Instead, they make a great shoe that comes with a sole insert that will work for as many people as possible, knowing that there are entire companies and doctors from which you can buy a custom insert to make the shoe *even better*.

That's why I'm explaining how you can create your own plan. If you know how to build an action plan for yourself, (a) you can feel empowered because you won't need to rely on someone else's judgment, and (b) my email won't get clogged with bitchy witches complaining that my spells don't work. It truly is a win-win approach.

Anyway, so far, you've learned about what inspired action is, where it comes from, and how to identify your personal manifestation pattern. The last piece of creating your action plan is, funnily enough, how to not obsess about whether your plan is working.

When people ask questions about when their spells will work, when their manifestations will happen, or how to tell if it's working, they're often met with another asinine statement from internet gurus.

"You need to release attachment to the outcome," says the thin, pretty white woman through her blond curtain bangs, probably while sitting cross-legged on a hand-woven cushion she bought from Anthropologie.

Just like the phrase that kicked off this book, "Money is energy," this concept is another one nobody seems to understand enough to explain beyond a knowing look. Thankfully, this one is a lot simpler.

It's akin to the adage, "A watched pot never boils."

The meaning is plain in that if you sit and stare at a pot of still water, waiting for it to boil, it will feel like it takes *forever* to get there. If you spent that staring time on something else like loading the dishwasher, chopping up vegetables, or playing a game on your phone, the time will feel like it's passing faster.

That's because time is relative. There's a whole scientific explanation to what that means, but instead of getting into it, I'll share this quote attributed to Albert Einstein instead:

"Put your hand on a hot stove for a minute, and it seems like an hour. Sit with a pretty girl for an hour, and it seems like a minute. That's relativity."

We don't experience time in the same way all the time. Time seems to pass according to what we do during it.

So, when people say, "Release attachment to the outcome," they're basically saying, "Stop staring at the pot."

When you obsess about whether your plan is working or when your manifestation is arriving, not only are you staring at the pot, but you're also adjusting the dials, removing the pot to make sure the burner is hot, adding more and more salt, and so on. Just like you *know* that pot of water is going to boil, you need to trust that your manifestation is on its way and find a way to make the time pass. And what's the best way to make time pass faster?

Have some fucking fun.

Yup! Everyone seems to forget that magic and manifestation aren't all about meditation and crystals and shadow work. They're also about hobbies, trying new things, deep belly laughs with friends, and movie marathons.

Think about it. I want you to remember the last time someone made a joke so good you snorted, did a spit take, or shot water out of your nose. When you were laughing and in the moment, were you worrying about money? Nope. You were fully living in the moment, unattached to whether your manifestation was on its way.

A shortcut I like to use when wanting to manifest money quickly is to think of a time when I received some easy money. It could be on a birthday or holiday, finding it in the washing machine, or a client who came out of the blue. Once I have that memory in mind, I list out at least three emotions I felt when I got the money, such as relieved, validated, and motivated.

Then, I ask myself, "What do I need to do to feel relieved, validated, and motivated today?" I write down whatever comes to mind and that becomes my action list for the day.

After going through that process enough days in a row, some sort of money manifestation will come through that gives me hope and confidence to keep moving forward.

So, no matter what action plan you create for yourself, make sure that it includes plenty of time for fun and rest. Having fun is one of the most magnetic and attractive activities we can do in magic.

Show Me the Money (Magic)

- **Lights, camera, action!** Inspired action is the trust you have in your unique plan of action. When you start listening to your intuition, you'll find that the actions you take will bring you to your results in a faster and more efficient way.
- **Ground control to Intuition.** If you're not accustomed to listening to your intuition, know that it will never make you feel ashamed, afraid, or stuck. Fear-based decisions usually leave you feeling embarrassed to tell people about your actions, afraid of what will happen, or as if you have no other choice.
- **Darkness before dawn.** When you start getting your financials together, you'll likely experience a series of annoying money events. That's normal. Money tests you to see if you're ready to commit to your new level. The best way to react is to keep calm and carry on. There's always a learning curve in the beginning. You're on the right track!
- **All work and no play makes Jessie a dull gal.** The best way to surrender in your money manifestation journey is to have fun! Fun is a form of surrender because you naturally live in the moment, free of any money worries for the moment.

ACTIVITIES

- Have you ever had a random idea or urge to do something that didn't make sense at the time, but paid off later? Have you ever ignored an idea or urge and had it backfire?
- Take a situation that's been making you feel shitty lately and list out all the negative emotions that have come up because of it. How would you prefer to feel and think in this situation? Can you describe the version of you who *does* feel and think that way? What advice might they give you?
- Think about the biggest manifestations you've had in your life. What highs and lows preceded those manifestations within three to six months before they appeared? What highs and lows have you been experiencing recently? Do you see any patterns?
- What are three emotions you felt the last time you received money with ease? What can you do today or tomorrow to experience those feelings again?

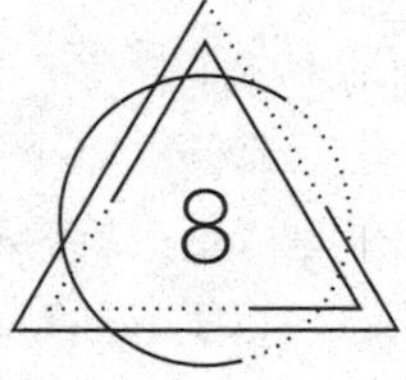

Practical Magic for Manifesting Money

Plenty of people misunderstand spells as an activity that's over once you're done with the ritual. As I've said before, the ritual is just the *first* step you take in a series of actions to bring your manifestations to fruition.

When it comes to money magic and manifestation, you only have two categories of methods for improving your financial life:

1. Make more money.
2. Reduce your spending.

At the end of the day, that's it! When you cast a money magic spell, you don't just sit and twiddle your thumbs. You need to leave the spell like you're a new person with new thoughts, new habits, and *new actions*.

Think of manifesting money as dining at a restaurant where you need to bring your own plate. I doubt these exist, but hear me out, 'k?

When you claim your money manifestations, you're essentially telling the server exactly what you want to eat. If you forgot to bring a plate, you can still get what you ordered, but it's probably going to take a while because it will need to go from the chef's pans directly onto the table in multiple trips. If you remembered your plate, the meal would come to you faster, look nicer on the table, and arrive all at once.

The plates you supply are the practical tools you use to manage your money and financial life. It's the budget, the job hunt, the business plan, the side gig. Those are the *vehicles* for you to receive money.

Can you get money without them? Yeah, sure.

Will it be easier and faster to improve your financial life if you use them? Absolutely.

That's why you need this chapter. Because the magic doesn't stop when the ritual is over. The magic provides the energy that attaches to all the actions you take in pursuit of your goals.

So, let's start with increasing your income.

Get a Better Job

I have a confession to make.

Despite being a life coach, an empath, and a super loving and compassionate friend, I am *the worst* person to complain to about your job or career.

It's a little awkward to admit, considering I help people curate their dream careers for a living, but I've had friends tell me I can be callous about their work situations. Apparently, saying, "Just get a new job" can be seen as mean or dismissive. Who'd've thunk it?

In all seriousness, if I set aside the frustration that comes from people not wanting advice on their careers even though I'm an *expert* job hunter, I know the main friction comes from a difference in our perspective.

More often than not, people *hate* job hunting. They hate feeling desperate to leave a job, sending in applications, finding excuses to interview during the workday, potentially never hearing back, and restarting the process dozens of times until something eventually comes through. Then they start their new gig only to wind up with the same desperate-to-leave energy a couple years later, if not sooner.

That hasn't been my experience in so long that I sometimes forget what it was like to feel like leaving a job was risky. In my more recent experience, it's always been a (mostly) enjoyable and easy process finding a great opportunity.

Not to mention that switching jobs is usually the best way to increase your salary. Some studies show that people who stay at the same job longer than two years decrease their lifetime earnings by 50 percent.[1] That's because a typical raise in a job that you're already in is typically about 3 percent. Meanwhile, moving jobs can skyrocket your income. Almost one-third of people who changed jobs in 2022 reported earning *more than* 30 percent of their old job's income.[2] Another 20 percent reported a salary increase of 10 to 20 percent!

Those figures alone are convincing enough for me to *always* leave a job when I suspect I'm being underpaid or underappreciated.

It all comes down to *how* you find a job.

Generally, people go hunting for opportunities via online job boards, which I loathe. Not only are some of the jobs not truly available (because they're going to internal hires or personal recommendations) but they're often jobs nobody wants.

These can be positions with high turnover due to low pay, a terrible boss, too much responsibility, a catty team, a company that doesn't give raises, or something else.

I'm not saying you can't find a job using cold applications sent in online. But if what you're really looking for is a *dream* job—something you love, that fulfills you, pays you a *thriveable* wage, comes with your ideal boss, and offers a perfect work schedule—well, that's a bit like hoping to find Mr. Darcy on Tinder. Impossible? No. Difficult and time-consuming? Absolutely.

Call me crazy, but the idea of sending out hundreds of applications sounds like a drag. I would prefer to do a lot of research and legwork so that when it comes time for me to send in a résumé, I know it's not only going to get read, but also will be sitting on top of the pile.

That only happens when you approach your dream job hunt with the kind of strategy and dedication that others aren't willing to use. After all, if you want a different experience, you need a different approach.

What follows is part of the strategy I teach my clients that I developed over the course of my career, learning how to network in a way that would work for an introvert. And it worked! In one of my career transitions, I literally *doubled* my salary.

First, you need to know how to use LinkedIn jobs. Yes, I see the irony of starting my strategy off with looking at a job board, but that's because we're not going to use it to apply. Instead, it's all about researching *what* jobs are out there.

The biggest problem job hunters have is that they don't know what titles companies use for the cool jobs they might actually want. So, your first step is to investigate and figure that out.

Google search "LinkedIn industry list" to get a breakdown of all the categories jobs get filtered into on the website. It's not actually available on LinkedIn, so any complete list you find on another website will do.

Find an industry that's intriguing, such as "Professional Training & Coaching." Navigate to the jobs section of the LinkedIn website and type it into the search bar. Don't narrow down the results by anything. The point here isn't to apply to jobs, it's to *research*.

Scroll through all the listed jobs and click on anything remotely interesting and read the description of the job. If it sounds dull or stressful, forget about it and keep scrolling. If you read it and think, "Hey! I think I would like to do that! And I think I might be good at it!" then you can save it. In a document somewhere, make a note of the title, company, basic description, duties, and requirements. Again, don't worry if you're qualified. This is just research. No one else is going to look at this except you.

If you see similar job titles for the same type of role (meaning the description and duties), make a note in your document of similar titles. For example, "Career Coach" versus "Career Advisor." They're basically the same job, but with different titles.

Repeat this process until you have at least three to five separate roles you could be happy doing.

Now, it's time to research companies where you might want to do this work. It starts with clarity around what you want.

Generally, people leave a job for one or more of these three reasons: (1) more money, (2) more flexibility, (3) more fulfillment—potentially in a new field or career.

I want you to know that you *can* have all three of these from one job. However, knowing the order of your priorities will make it easier for you to research companies because it will guide what information you should look for.

Once you have that, decide what your ranges are for those priorities, ranging from "bare minimum" to "ecstatic." However, when you decide your bare minimums, I want you to assume that whatever you select for pay, flexibility, or duties **will not change for at least two years**. It's much easier to negotiate terms for a new job when you have all the leverage as a qualified applicant, but companies know job hunting is a bitch. So, they have a much lower incentive to change anything once you're already working for them.

Here's what those ranges might look like:

PRIORITIES	MINIMUM REQUIREMENTS	IDEAL REQUIREMENTS
Salary	$80,000	$100,000
Flexibility	• Hybrid work schedule with work from home one day a week • Two weeks paid vacation • One week paid sick leave	• Fully remote work • Unlimited paid time off
Fulfillment	• 80% of job duties • Industry is flexible • Title is flexible	• 100% of job duties • In X industry • Y job title

Now, if you're desperate to leave your job, go through your minimums and bump everything up a bit. We always tend to settle when we're desperate. That adjustment could look like:

PRIORITIES	MINIMUM REQUIREMENTS	IDEAL REQUIREMENTS
Salary	$85,000	$100,000
Flexibility	• Hybrid work schedule with work from home two days a week • Three weeks paid vacation • Ten days paid sick leave	• Fully remote work • Unlimited paid time off

PRIORITIES	MINIMUM REQUIREMENTS	IDEAL REQUIREMENTS
Fulfillment	• 100% of job duties • X, Y, and Z industries • Title is flexible	• 100% of job duties • In X industry • Y job title

Now that you have your priorities sorted out, you can prepare your list of companies. Take the job titles from your list and plug them into the jobs section of the website. Again, don't narrow them down; we're just researching. Look at what companies are hiring for that role and click on the company page. You can read more about them there to get a sense of their values to start, but it doesn't stop there.

Run a Google search on them and see what you can find. Chances are, Glassdoor probably has a profile for them where people can share their salaries, what it's like to work there, whether they approve of the CEO, and so on. If they don't have a profile on Glassdoor, just find what you can from other websites.

Now, this is where our list of priorities comes in handy. Use the list to determine whether the company already offers what you're looking for from a job. That means if you want to work remotely, you want to make sure the company has some remote workers. If you want lots of vacation time, look for that. If mentorship matters, look for mentions of it. It's much easier to find a company to match your values and priorities than it is to convince a company to share your values.

Like I said, you *can* find companies that have your ideal scenario in all areas, but keep in mind that everything is negotiable once there's a job offer on the table. It's OK to include companies that are *close* to everything you want.

However, the minimum requirements for your top priority are *non-negotiable*. Using the previous example, that means if someone offers me a job that is everything else I want on the list, but they can only offer $78,000 after negotiations, I'm going to turn it down. If after negotiations they offer me $80,000, I'm going to turn it down. If they offer me $84,999.99, you know what I'm gonna do? *I'm going to turn it down*. The $85,000 is the bare minimum on your top priority for a reason. Don't sell yourself short.

Any company that gets through these researching tasks goes on your list. You can add as many as you want to your list, but I find it easier to get started with three. After all, the goal here is quality over quantity. Also, I know we didn't narrow down the organizations by geography, so this would be the time to do so. If they don't have an office near you, you don't want to move, you're not comfortable with remote work, or they don't offer it, don't put them down on your list.

Once that list is finalized with at least three companies that you know hire for the role you want and provide the type of pay and circumstances that matter to you, it's time for *dramatic drum roll*—

Networking.

Yep, you're going to network instead of just sending in your application. The best way to do this is to find someone at the company who works in the specific department. If you can't find anyone from the company website, this is where you can go back to the LinkedIn company profile and look at all the employees who have it listed as their current employer.

The goal is to find someone who isn't so senior that they wouldn't respond to an email or so junior that they won't have any sway or intel on the position. If you can find someone you have something in common with—such as an alma mater, a career path, or hobby—even better. If you have a friend in common with your desired contact, you've hit the jackpot. Ask your friend to introduce you to that contact so you can pick their brain about the company.

However, if you don't have any mutual contacts, you'll send a cold email. Generally, you can find employee's emails on the company website, but if they're not, try to find *anyone's* email address. All you need to know is the configuration used at the company and someone's name to take an educated guess on an email that will likely go through. My favorite places to check are on press releases in the media or news section of the website or on pages for conferences and events. Those generally have specific contacts available.

PS: if you can't find *anything*, here's my trick:

Guess their email address.

You've sent enough emails in your life to know that there are only a handful of first and last name combinations an organization can use. And you've met enough people with nicknames to guess alternatives they might use in that configuration. From there, use the bounce backs to indicate whether you've cracked the email address.

Once you have an address, you'll send a cold email that sounds something like this one I sent years ago when I was looking for a legal nonprofit job:

> Subject: Coffee invite from criminal justice reporter/lawyer
>
> Hi [Name],
>
> I came across your name while I was researching legal nonprofits that litigate criminal cases, so I hope you don't mind that I contacted you.
>
> I found your background as a federal public defender and nonprofit litigator/reform advocate really interesting, as I've spent the past few years reading and writing about the inner workings of the system as a criminal justice reporter for Bloomberg Law.
>
> I'm a former criminal appeals attorney looking to transition into either a nonprofit or government attorney position

working on criminal justice reform. I sent you a connection request on LinkedIn so you have a better idea of my background.

You seem to have had a similar career trajectory, so I would love it if you could lend me the benefit of your knowledge on nonprofit-versus-government work over a cup of coffee (my treat).

I could come by your office or meet you anywhere at your convenience. If not, I wouldn't mind a quick phone call. Any chance you're free this Thursday at 1:00 p.m. EST?

Thank you in advance for any time or advice you can offer.

Jessie DaSilva

Now, I have plenty of explanations behind the formula I use for cold emails, but I want to point out the most absolute, crucial part of the entire email.

I *never* say that I'm looking for a job.

In fact, I never even use the word *job*. Ironically, the j-word is probably the most toxic word you can use in job hunting, so avoid it at all costs. Try this phrase instead, "I'm looking to transition from [current job title] to [desired job title]." It comes with far less pressure for the person you're talking to. Asking contacts if they know of any jobs or can forward your résumé often puts them on the spot and makes them feel helpless if they can't think of anything off the top of their heads.

But advice or other contacts? People are happy to help with that! I would even say contacts are the most valuable results you can get from networking. Think about it: if you start out emailing three strangers and each one of them introduces you to three other people, you went from having zero industry contacts to having *twelve*. If they each introduce you to three more people? That's *thirty* total industry contacts. And you will have done it by sending *three emails*.

Say goodbye to awkward happy hour events with name tags and cheap wine because you're on your way to a new level.

When you meet up with people, ask them questions about their career, how they like working for the company, what their average day is like, and for any advice they might have for someone looking to transition into a similar role. You can even ask if they could provide feedback on your résumé. No matter what you ask, make sure you don't leave without asking, "Is there anyone else you think I should talk to?" If so, ask if they would be willing to send a connection email.

Now, I know you only found this person because you saw a job listed at their company that you're interested in applying for. If they didn't bring it up, that's OK. Instead, send a follow-up email to say thank you for meeting and inquire about it then. Keep it simple and broad with language like, "I saw that [your company] is hiring for [title]. Do you have any information about the opening?"

That question alone often pays off. If the job is promised to an internal hire or it's a shit position, well, now you've just saved yourself a ton of time by not applying.

If it *is* open, there's no harm in asking your new contact if they could forward your résumé. If not, ask if you can use their name in your cover letter. An opening line that kicks off with "I'm writing at the recommendation of X, [title]" usually gets noticed. Trust me when I say a name can go a long way!

Of course, plenty more goes into landing the ideal dream job, but I'll trust that you can take it from the interview and onward. Most of the time, the key to getting the dream job is knowing someone. Thankfully, it's really easy to know people if you learn how and where to connect with them.

Ask for a Salary Adjustment

If you read that headline and wondered to yourself, "What is a salary adjustment, and how is it different from a raise?" you'll be happy to know there's no difference.

Just as the word *job* creates a feeling of being put on the spot and not being sure if they can help, so can the word *raise* with your boss.

I'm not saying it's true, right, or fair that employees need to linguistically pussyfoot around their right to compensation—because it's not—but this is the reality we live in. Until the world is a different place where companies shower their employees with money, time off, and anniversary gifts that don't involve a company logo, you might as well learn how to get what you want.

Asking for a salary adjustment is an easier way to get the pay you deserve because it takes the responsibility off your shoulders to prove your performance deserves a meritorious increase. Instead, it forces the company and your supervisor to reevaluate your title, duties, and salary.

This is especially important for anyone who has taken on far more duties than what their job description entails, especially if they're duties belonging to your supervisor. If you're going to do work for two people or on the level of your boss, you should be getting compensated accordingly.

(Also, just in case anyone needs a reminder, if your boss goes on vacation, their job should not be the responsibility of those *below* them on the chain of command. Their work should be covered by someone at the same level or higher.)

Anyway, just like we needed to do some research before jumping into a job hunt, we want to find some information before we bitch-slap our supervisor with some truth.

To start, make a list of everything you do in your job and highlight or circle anything that *technically* isn't part of your job description. Research similar titles to the job you have now and titles that are a step or two above. Look at the duties and determine whether the job you're doing now is appropriately titled.

Once you have a solid title in mind, start researching what other people in this role are getting paid. You can look at Glassdoor or Payscale.com and compare a ton of factors, including company size, years of experience, similarly sized markets, and more.

If you find that you're getting paid what the average is, see if those details change if you add terms like *senior* or *lead* to the job title.

Another way to gather some research is to talk to your coworkers, especially those with similar job titles, responsibilities, or years of experience. I know it can be awkward to talk about pay in the workplace, but trust me when I say this benefits *everyone*. A lot of places get away with pay disparities just from a lack of communication between workers, so start talking! If you're anyone other than a white, heterosexual cis-male, start by asking your white, heterosexual cis-male peers. And if the person you ask bristles at the question and doesn't want to disclose what they make, play the "over-under" game.

To play, you start by asking, "Do you make over [your salary] or under?" Based on their response, change the number and ask the same question until you have a pretty good idea of what they're taking home.

Oh, and? Your employer is not legally permitted to stop you from discussing salaries with your coworkers. If they try to tell you that, feel free to let them know that's illegal.

Finally, consider reaching out to Human Resources. They often have job descriptions on file and sometimes they can provide internal salary tables. Of course, this is assuming you work at a company that has an HR *department* rather than, like, one woman named Deb on the brink of retirement who seems to commit the most HR offenses of the whole office. Maybe don't reach out if that's what you're dealing with.

When you have all of your data compiled, turn it into a presentation! It doesn't need to be over-the-top. Have one slide about what your job description is versus what it's become. Then have a summary slide explaining the findings on what your job title and average salary should be, based on your duties. If you have information from coworkers or HR, you can include those figures on the same slide or the next one.

Then, have about three slides of examples at other companies. Make sure to be transparent with everything. If the information from Glassdoor is marked as old or untrustworthy, disclose that! You can talk about how reliable it likely is based on the context of the other examples you use. All you need to show are screenshots. You can talk your way through them.

I know once you've created this masterpiece, you'll be tempted to run off and show it to your boss immediately, but instead I want you to ask them for a good time to meet about this. Since I'm a lawyer who's had "get it in writing" drilled into my head for over a decade, I'm going to say you should send them an email. Something like:

> Hello Boss,
>
> Now that the busy season is over, I wanted to set up a time to get your opinion on my work in the [title] role the past few months. Are you free [day] at [time] by any chance?
>
> Thanks!

Jessie

When that chat comes around, you're going to go into the conversation with the mindset that this is going to be a win-win conversation. You're either about to get a promotion and/or a raise or your job is about to get a whole lot easier. Let me explain how this conversation is going to go:

You: Thank you so much for meeting me today. I know you're busy.

Boss: Of course. Now, what did you want to talk about regarding your work?

You: I wanted to discuss my performance and my role here at the company. I've loved working here since starting back in [month/year] and I feel like I've grown so much since then. I've gone from XYZ to ABC and I'm really proud of the progress I've made. A big part of that is because of the feedback I get from you, so I trust your opinion. I was hoping I could get your advice on a recent discovery I've made.

Boss: I'm glad you feel that way. I try to be a good supervisor. What did you discover?

You: Well, as I've been growing in this role, I've obviously thought about my future here. I like working for [name] and I appreciate the experience I'm getting. So, I started looking at what the next step would be for me on this track at the company. I was really surprised because I realized I'm already doing about 50 percent of the job description for [higher job title]. That inspired me to revisit my job description, and I realized I've been doing work that's higher than at the level I'm currently employed.

Boss: Well, that tends to happen here. We work as a team and pitch in when needed. I'm sure that I've done some work that's technically below my level. Remember that time you were out for a valid reason that I approved? I wound up doing some of your work then.

You: I do remember and I'm grateful you did. However, stepping down to fill in your team's gaps is part of a manager's role. My position should only really encompass X, Y, and Z. I'm not bringing it up because I want to do less work. It's the opposite, in fact. I would love an opportunity to do more of this work under a more appropriate title and salary to match. Can I show you some of the research I found?

Boss: Sure.

That's when you'll whip out your presentation and talk about your findings. Remember, you want this to be informative for your boss, rather than accusatory. Most of the time, your boss probably has no idea that you're being underpaid compared to your coworkers or other companies. If they do know and they don't want to give you a raise, this is going to be the moment they reveal their hand.

Your supervisor is likely going to respond to the information in one of two ways:

1. "Wow, I had no idea your role had changed so much over time. You're absolutely right. Can you send me this research so I can take it to my higher-ups and see what I can do?"

or

2. "I understand where you're coming from, but unfortunately we don't have any money to promote you. I mean, I haven't even gotten a raise in five years. If we had money, we would be able to hire the help that we need and you wouldn't need to take on those extra duties."

If it's the first, congratulations! You're on your way to a promotion.

If it's the second, you're going to respond with a respectful amount of disappointment, thank your supervisor for their time, and go brush up your résumé. You know everything you need to know about your future at the company—you don't have one.

While you begin a job hunt, you're going to immediately cease the job duties that are outside your job description. If your boss asks you to continue with them, you're going to set a professional but firm boundary that you're not comfortable regularly performing those duties with your current job title, especially because they interfere with your ability to get your work done.

I worked with a client who had been doing some of her manager's work for a few months without any extra pay or recognition. She had no desire for a promotion and simply wanted to get out of the job or get paid more money. So, I told her to start saying no to taking on her boss's work with that exact explanation.

A week later, he told her he created a new job title for her through HR and asked her to apply. She did and wound up getting a $20,000 raise the week after her interview.

Now, even though she still doesn't necessarily *like* her job, she at least feels she's being compensated fairly. More money goes a long way when it comes to working a shit job.

Start a Business (or Side Hustle)

Plenty of times people don't want to find a new job or pursue a salary adjustment because they're just not interested in traditional employment anymore.

I feel that. I always joke that I tried every type of job available in the legal field before I gave it up. It took me the better part of a decade, but I just realized that working for others wasn't for me.

My first job out of law school was making $40,000 a year as the second attorney in a solo practice. I was paid twice a month, rather than biweekly, which means my bills were always at risk of overdrafting my account or bouncing altogether. I had no benefits. My commute was a solid thirty minutes on the highway on a good day. To afford health insurance, I had to keep working *at the mall* for $8.15 an hour after work and on weekends (and my insurance didn't even cover my inhaler or birth control because this was before the Affordable Care Act).

After nine months, I was laid off and replaced with a secretary who was my boss's wife's best friend *who didn't know how to use Microsoft Word.*

I've also been fired or pushed out of more jobs than anyone I know. I was fired from Books-A-Million in college because I refused to work shifts *during my classes* and rather than getting a better schedule, I was told that BAM should be my main commitment.

I was laid off from a legal internship at a law firm where my "office" was literally a table next to a printer in the storage room because the firm realized they were losing money.

I had an office manager literally lie to a firm owner, saying I was unprofessional and refused work, just so she could fire me. When the attorney I regularly worked for found out, she called the office manager into a meeting with the firm owner to tell the truth about my work ethic, called her out for lying, and made the firm owner extend another employment offer to me. I turned it down.

I was pushed out of my mall job at LOFT when the manager who liked me left.

And, finally, I was fired from my last legal job at a nonprofit.

Needless to say, I don't view traditional employment as stable. After all, companies are owned by people, and people make mistakes, lie, cheat, and do plenty of other things that can harm employees. But you know whom I do trust?

Myself.

I might have made some questionable decisions in my past, but I've never let myself stay down for long. I've run out of money plenty of times, but I've made it back every time after that. In the eternal words of Our

Lady of the Bronx, Cardi B, "Knock me down nine times, but I get up ten, bitch."

I share all of this because so many people crave the freedom of working for themselves, but don't ever attempt to start out of fear that it's too risky.

Of course it's risky. So is trusting a billion-dollar company or a non-profit that powers itself on the bleeding hearts of its employees to have your best interests in mind.

The only way your risk won't pay off is if you go into it blind. In other words, if you don't try it out first to make sure you love it, then deciding to make it your full-time commitment runs a much higher risk that you wind up with a business you can't stand.

Listen, I was the *queen* of side hustles before I went full-time in my business. When I began crocheting, I immediately thought about monetizing it. One flower headband later and I was over the idea. I couldn't imagine making a second, much less a twenty-second.

Years later, I tried my hand at it again with my art. I found a few images I liked and painted some ink-wash pictures, including a massive undertaking of Jack Skellington and Sally in the places of the farmer and his daughter in *American Gothic*. It was dope AF and took me *hours* to do. I uploaded everything to Etsy, promoted it to my network, and then...nothing. Not only was it crickets, but I was also exhausted. I spent multiple weekends producing incredible art that I enjoyed and then I was starting to feel down about it. I didn't like that.

I realized not all hobbies are meant to be monetized, and that's OK. My art was for *me*, not anyone else. Despite my love of money and working, not everything needed to turn a profit. Sometimes, relaxation and enjoyment are profit enough.

And then came network marketing with Beachbody. Despite the orthorexia I developed, I realized I loved everything that went along with the coaching industry. I loved social media strategy, talking to people, and helping people reach their goals. What I didn't like was helping people with exercise and nutrition—and it showed. It seemed like I coached my clients on anything *but* that.

So, when I decided to give life coaching and consulting a go, I wanted to make sure I knew I would love it first. After all, I hadn't done that before going to law school, and all I got was a miserable career and $280,000 of student loan debt. I wasn't about to do that again.

Before ever charging a single penny, I took on two pro bono clients. One was an acquaintance who said she was looking for a life coach. The other was a young woman who had just graduated from college and was looking for a job in her industry. She posted in a group about looking for a mentor. So, I started with them both and explained I would give them free biweekly coaching for three months to see if I could help them.

And I did! Not only did they feel more empowered in their lives and begin taking action they were always afraid to take, but I was more impassioned than I had ever been. Up until then, I had basically been forcing advice on my younger siblings. Having two people who actively sought my advice? It felt like a dream!

Once you've volunteered to make sure you love what you do, you'll feel *so* much more confident about taking the plunge.

The Easy Formula for Starting an Online Business

The benefit of living in the Internet Age is that the vast majority of people are accustomed to doing everything online. Like, I started a return to Walmart for a bottle brush and straw cleaner that have been sitting on my countertop for over a week purely because I would need to go *inside the store* to drop it off. Frankly, I would rather eat the $3.47.

Everyone wants to do everything from home, and I don't blame anyone for it. And the good news is, if you have a business idea, chances are you can probably do it online for considerably fewer start-up costs than you think.

After several years consulting, I can help just about anyone's business regardless of industry or size. But before I got *here*, I worked at the start of the COVID-19 pandemic with tons of laid off employees and brick-and-mortar business owners who needed a way to make money from home fast. So, I taught them how to start an online, service-based business or bring their existing business to Al Gore's internet.

And, boy, did they run the gamut.

I worked with the standard online business owners like coaches, social media managers, graphic designers, copywriters, and readers/energy healers. But I also worked with businesses that were accustomed to conducting business in person, such as attorneys, artists, therapists, consultants, and even a chef!

I truly believe that everyone has the ability to earn money online as long as they (1) have knowledge they can teach or a service to provide, (2) know how to build an offer, (3) know how to price their offer, and (4) start finding clients.

Inevitably, people will come back at me, "But I don't have any skills or knowledge people will pay for!" Trust me when I say you do. You probably don't value it enough to see it as marketable because it comes easily to you.

Take writing, for example. Thanks to careers in journalism and law, I've amassed a broad network of people who are talented writers. Many of them already had a natural aptitude for writing before studying and practicing it in their college major. Then they went off to further hone their writing skills in either a writing-based career or a graduate program where writing would prominently feature.

All along the way, they would have met and befriended *other* writers. They probably read each other's writing, shared book recommendations by talented writers, and generally marinated in language.

Yet whenever I see a writer think about leaving traditional writing careers like journalism, law, or academia, it's always with an air of premature defeat and hopelessness. They wonder what other job they could do, whether they could actually improve their pay, or if they could even find any openings, all because they *only* know how to write. It's always couched in that kind of phrasing, as if good writing is as common a skill as digestion.

In reality, clear and concise writing is one of the most valuable skills you can have! The National Association of Colleges and Employers reported in 2021 that 73.3 percent of employers across all industries favored writing skills in job applicants.[3] In fact, employers listed written communication as the fourth-most desired skill from job applicants—an increase from fifth place the year before.

Thanks to decades of emphasizing the importance of STEM education (science, technology, engineering, and math), there's a glut of brainiacs who don't know how to explain what they do to anyone else.[4] The same goes for those in business and finance fields and plenty others.

Yet the reason writers take their skill for granted is because they live in a bubble of other writers for whom writing is both *easy* and *enjoyable*. And if you grew up in a capitalist society, you generally don't believe skills that are easy and enjoyable can amount to wealth.

Meanwhile, ghostwriters and copywriters are, quite literally, raking in millions working for themselves.

So, when I say you have a skill you can teach, *I mean it*. It doesn't matter what it is. Someone out there probably needs it.

If that doesn't convince you, remember these two facts:

1. The first sale *ever* on eBay was a broken laser pointer.[5] At the time, fully functional laser pointers cost about $100 and buyer Mark Fraser, who had been doing a ton of

presentations on the road, knew his company wouldn't buy him one. He bought the broken laser pointer because he's a self-proclaimed electronics geek and thought he could get it to work. He didn't, but he kept it anyway.

2. Jewelry company Tiffany & Co. sells a tin can made from sterling silver and vermeil for $1,135.[6] It literally looks exactly like a tin can, except it's super shiny and has a Tiffany's blue stripe down the seam. *And it's currently sold out.*

Someone, somewhere (and probably way more than one) will be *excited* to buy what you sell.

So, once you have a skill or knowledge to teach, follow this process to build and price out your first online offer. I'm going to use an example for start-up coaching since that's what we're talking about anyway.

First, you need to get in the head of your potential client. What is their desired outcome from what you can teach, and how long will it take for them to get there? Ideally, you want something in the range of three months, so think about a goal they could reach in that amount of time. For my sample offer, I'm going to say that in three months, they will have three paying clients.

Next, how are they *feeling* before they work with you for those three months? Use www.feelingswheel.com if you need help getting descriptive.

Overwhelmed by everything they need to learn.	*Insecure* over whether they could actually do this.	*Frustrated* by their financial circumstances.
Pressured to make money to build savings or get out of debt.	*Worried* about what people will think of them for starting a business.	*Hungry* for freedom to work from anywhere, set their own prices, and enjoy life.

Bitter over having been in a low-paying career for so long.	*Confused* about what steps they should be taking.	*Ready and committed* to do what it takes to get there.

Now imagine how they'll feel once they reach their three-month goal.

Energetic because they're doing something they love.	*Eager* to see what else they can do in their lives.	*Confident* in their ability to continue making money.
Amazed at how far they've come in three months.	*Joyful* to be doing something they love.	*Optimistic* about the future and their earning ability.
Grateful that they can spend more time enjoying life.	*Peaceful* because they can stop worrying about money.	*Valued* for their skills and expertise.

Second, let's figure out your offer structure. Keeping in mind where they started and where they'll end up, list out everything your client needs to learn to go from Day 1 to Day 90.

How to identify their ideal client.	Matching their branding to their personality.
How to create an offer.	Time management.
How to price out their offers.	Principles of money manifestation.
Where to find clients.	How to use their intuition.
Best practices for social media platforms.	How to do a sales call.

I stopped my list with ten lessons, but I want you to make sure that you really do get down every single piece of information someone would need to make the full transformation. You won't get any benefit from cutting your list short.

Now that you know *what* your clients need to learn, you need to go through each lesson and ask yourself two questions: (1) Is there a way I would prefer to teach this lesson? (2) Is there a way that my client would prefer to learn this lesson?

For example, some lessons are specific to the individual, so you'll need to talk to them one-on-one, such as for "matching your branding to your personality" in the preceding chart. Other lessons will remain the same for every client you have, like "best practices for social media platforms," which could be taught using a prerecorded video, ebook, or flow chart.

As you go through each lesson, check it off the list so you don't lose track. At the end, you should have a list of features for your offer that looks something like this:

- Biweekly, one-hour, one-on-one calls (6)
- Text and voice memo support (12 weeks)
- Worksheet for identifying the ideal client
- Video on how to create an offer
- Video on how to price out an offer
- Social-media best practices videos for TikTok, Instagram, Facebook, and Pinterest (4)
- Blank planner/calendar sheet your client can print out (2 pages)
- Pinterest mood board for branding
- Videos on manifesting money (5)
- Recorded audio of a meditation for getting in touch with your intuition

- Sales ebook
- Sample sales presentation
- Recording of a successful sales call

Before we move on to pricing, ask yourself one more question: Is there anything that isn't necessary for the change but would be nice to have? If there is, such as a money manifestation reading or an abundance meditation for the preceding example, you'll add it to the list. We'll count these as bonuses.

Now you're ready to add prices! However, keep in mind we're going to go through this process *twice*. First, we're going to set prices as if *each item on this list were sold separately at full price*. This is called the value. We generally want to give an incentive for people buying a package by giving them a slight discount on most (if not all) of the components of the package, so we'll calculate that in Round 2.

Business gurus argue over pricing methodology all the time, but frankly I don't think any of the methods really save you time. Research is often a pit of quicksand for entrepreneurs, keeping them from ever taking any real action. Instead, I tell my clients to spit out the first number that comes to them for each item. We'll check our work at the end to make sure we like the numbers we picked.

Here's how it should look in your first round:

FEATURE	VALUE
Biweekly, one-hour, one-on-one calls (6)	$200/hour ($1,200)
Text and voice memo support (12 weeks)	$95/week ($1,140)

FEATURE	VALUE
Worksheet for identifying the ideal client	$15
Video on how to create an offer	$40
Video on how to price out offer	$40
Social media best practices videos for TikTok, Instagram, Facebook, and Pinterest (4)	$50/video ($200)
Blank planner/calendar sheet they can print out (2 pages)	$10
Pinterest mood board for branding	$100
Videos on manifesting money (5)	$40/video ($200)
Recorded audio of a meditation for getting in touch with your intuition	$30
Sales ebook	$50
Sample sales presentation	$250
Recording of a successful sales call	$250
Money manifestation reading for 1 hour	$200
Money manifestation meditation	$30
Total Value:	**$3,755.00**

Now, this isn't what we're actually going to charge for this package.

We want to give people some savings to incentivize the package. That means we're going to (a) give a small discount on every item in the package and (b) set the bonuses as free. At the end, it will look something like this:

FEATURE	VALUE	PRICE
Bi-weekly, one-hour, one-on-one calls (6)	$200/hour ($1,200)	$175/hour ($1,050)
Text and voice memo support (12 weeks)	$95/week ($1,140)	$83/week ($996)
Worksheet for identifying their ideal client	$15	$12
Video on how to create an offer	$40	$30
Video on how to price out offer	$40	$30
Social media best practices videos for TikTok, Instagram, Facebook, and Pinterest (4)	$50/video ($200)	$40/video ($160)
Blank planner/calendar sheet they can print out (2 pages)	$10	$0
Pinterest mood board for branding	$100	$85
Videos on manifesting money (5)	$40/video ($200)	$35/video ($175)

FEATURE	VALUE	PRICE
Recorded audio of a meditation for getting in touch with your intuition	$30	$20
Sales ebook	$50	$40
Sample sales presentation	$250	$200
Recording of a successful sales call	$250	$200
Money manifestation reading for 1 hour	$200	$0
Money manifestation meditation	$30	$0
Totals:	**$3,755**	**$2,998**

So, once all is said and done, the total value is $3,755 but the actual price someone will pay is $2,998. This is the pay-in-full price. Some people will need a flexible option for paying, such as a monthly or weekly plan. This price should be less in the breakdown, but more overall. That's because we add a little interest as security. You always take a risk when you accept less than the pay-in-full amount. Someone could disappear after paying you the first installment, leaving you without the guaranteed income. You would be surprised how useless a contract is if you don't plan to sue. The same goes for filing for collections.

Because this is a three-month container, we're going to assume three split payments. We won't go over that because once you've delivered all the content, it becomes even harder to persuade someone to pay if they're determined not to. Since it's a shorter term, we'll use the low end of the range for interest at 10 percent. The longer it is, the higher you'll go, but don't charge more than 25 percent or else the numbers just get silly.

In case you forgot how to calculate percentages, here we go:

$2,998 × .10 = $299.80

We add this to the total payment: $2,998 + $299.80 = $3,297.80

Now, take the total price and divide it by three. $3,297.80/3 = $1,099.27.

I'm generally not a fan of decimal points in prices, so I would probably drop that 27 cents at the end, which leaves us with three payments of $1,099.

Et voilà! There are your initial prices.

I say "initial" because before we move on, we want to make sure we like the actual prices and that they work for us. We'll use a few different rubrics for this.

First, ask yourself, "Would it feel *good* for someone to pay me this for three months of work?" If your answer is anything but "Fuck yes!" then start the process over with some new numbers. Also, ask yourself, "Should I round up or down?"

Let's say at the end of your process, you come up with $2,500 even. You always have the choice to round that up to something like $2,999 or down to something like $1,997. It doesn't matter which way you round it as long as it feels good for you. (PS: Why do we like to end prices with sevens and nines? It's because we read those numbers from left to right. Our brain only registers the first digit and makes us believe it's cheaper than it actually is.)

Now, calculate how much of a discount you're giving. After all, when you sell someone into this package, you'll need to explain that if you were to charge full price for everything inside the package separately, it would be way more expensive.

If you forgot how to calculate percentages, here's your reminder. Divide the value by the price, multiple the answer by 100, then take *that* result and subtract it from 100.

$2,998 / $3,755 = .798

If we round up to .8 and multiply times 100, that's 80 percent. That means the *discount* is what's left after subtracting from 100 percent. That's 20 percent savings when someone pays full price.

So, you can confidently tell someone, "This is a discount of 20 percent off my regular package!"

If you don't think that's a sexy enough discount, then go through the process and bump up the original numbers in the values list.

Finally, make sure you can hit your income goals with the number you picked.

Let's say that you want to replace your income of $80,000. Depending on what country or state you live in, you would need to bring in a total income slightly above six figures. I'm going to go with $107,000. That means you would need to make about $8,916 a month.

Using the prices you have now, you would need to sign about three clients a month. That means on average, you would need to have nine to ten one-on-one clients at any given time. If that sounds manageable, you're good! But if that sounds like too many, it might be better for you to increase your prices and play around with the math.

I know it's a lot to take in, but the reason why I'm forcing you to do middle-school math is because it will save you *so much trouble* in the long run. There are only so many hours in the day that you can use to market your business and take client calls—even fewer if you're balancing it with a full-time job. When you're forced to make decisions on what you realistically need to earn, you won't have any room for self-doubt on what you need to charge.

You don't start a business so you can work longer hours for less pay.

You start a business to have more freedom and control over your income. If you give that to yourself from the very beginning, it will be harder for you to burn out or doubt whether you can find success.

The Strategic Spending Plan

When I'm getting started with clients, the immediate question I ask after hearing about their income goals is, "What are your total monthly expenditures?" Nine times out of ten, I get a sheepish "I don't know."

So many people want to believe that all they need to manifest more money is a mindset shift and an action plan to increase their income. Those are *parts* of the full equation, but structure in managing your money is equally important. It keeps us on track toward our goals and speeds up the process because we're better able to understand where we are versus where we want to go.

Remember that story I told you about how I pivoted into start-up coaching and made more than $10,000 in a month? Well, would you be surprised to hear that the money I made *didn't* change my life overnight?

The reason was because I didn't have any management system in place for tracking my spending. In my head, I had more than enough money to take care of my needs. I doubled my payments on my highest credit card debt, hired an online business manager to help me in my business, and bought a handful of new clothes for summer since I didn't have anything that fit me. In my mind, I was set. Now that I cracked $10,000, I would be able to do it every month thereafter. I had finally arrived!

July went off without a hitch, and I was feeling great. I kept up with the payments without any issue. Then I *didn't* make what I needed to in August. I launched a program that flopped. I wound up putting my online business manager's payment on that credit card I'd paid double toward just two months before. I paid rent late. It felt like I was on the cusp of winning a game of Chutes and Ladders only to land on the longest slide that sent me back to the first row of the board.

It all came from not having a financial management system in place. Because I wasn't intimately involved in managing my money, I wasn't looking at what I needed in reserves every month to make sure I could have the stability I needed to prevent feeling desperate with my income. Later, I realized that even the actions I believed I took from abundance and financial responsibility—like paying double toward my credit card—were still based on a feeling of lack.

I paid double toward that bill because some part of me worried that I wouldn't have that much liquid cash again, so I needed to get ahead on my payments while I could. That's when I realized that I didn't feel comfortable keeping high amounts of money in my account. I was so accustomed to shit going wrong in my life after a bout of good luck that I created that result for myself. I put myself in a position where I couldn't perform so I could lose everything and feel the peace that came with being broke again.

This wasn't conscious, of course. I *hate* being broke. However, that's what I've been accustomed to for the majority of my life. Being broke was my security blanket. So, when I finally made impressive money, I immediately spent it down so I could stop feeling the fear of losing everything—by losing everything. After all, once you hit the bottom, the only way to go is up. I felt much more comfortable as an underdog than a repeat champion.

This is the challenge that naturally comes with money manifestation. We are so focused on building wealth and abundance first that we forget the first step on the way to those feelings is *safety*.

You cannot manifest consistent riches if—on some deep, subconscious level—you're afraid to have money. That's why we did so much journaling in the beginning. Finding out where those fears are shows you what mindset work you need to begin feeling safety around money.

The other half of that is to use a system of money management that honors where you are as well.

Often, people struggle with budgeting for the same reasons they struggle with healthy eating and exercise.

They think of a goal they want to reach—usually around a number on the scale, a pant size, or some other sort of measurement—and decide to reach it *no matter what*. They're sick of feeling sluggish, not fitting into their clothes, or are panicking over some upcoming event like a wedding or high school reunion, so they find a method that will get them the results as fast as possible like the keto diet, paleo diet, intermittent fasting, or Whole30.

And they do it! They crush it for like three weeks or a month, maybe even six months. They drop more than 20 pounds, get rid of their larger clothes, and then...the day comes when they slip up. That slipup becomes a gateway to loosening up on the entire diet, and the next thing they know, they gained back the 20 pounds, plus 20 more. They feel ashamed and less motivated to change than ever.

The reason fad diets don't work is the same reason why so many financial strategies don't work for most people: They're all based on restriction.

To succeed at keto and all the rest, you must have the mindset that you're never going to eat another full-carb bakery brownie or birthday cake for as long as you live.

Similarly, to succeed with a Dave Ramsey money management plan, you need to adopt a mindset that you will not spend a penny on anything other than your bills and debt until you are completely debt-free *and* have six months of expenses saved in your account.

That's an unreasonable way of living for most people.

It requires you to deny yourself joy and fun for the foreseeable future. If you're already struggling to believe that we'll have a future worth living what with massive civil unrest, COVID-19 variations, and melting ice caps, then what incentive do you have to deny yourself the small pleasures of the present in the hope that you'll enjoy spending money in a smog-filled, dystopian future?

What you need is a balanced approach to your finances, including debt repayment, bills, and treating yourself.

I've been a huge fan of Ramit Sethi, author of *I Will Teach You to Be Rich*, for years because of his approach to cutting back on what you don't really care about so you can spend lavishly on things you *do* love.

Yet even Ramit says his program is only for those who have already paid off their debt, pointing them to either the snowball method or APR method to get there.

If you haven't heard of those debt repayment methods or need a quick recap, I gotchu. First, you save up an emergency fund of $1,000 to $1,500. Then you make a list of all your debts, including the balances and APRs or "annual percentage rates."

The snowball method tells you to take all your extra income and throw it at the debt with the smallest balance while paying the minimum on your other debts. Once you pay off the smallest debt, you start throwing all your extra money at the *next* smallest debt. You even think of the minimum payment on that second debt as its required payment *plus* the minimum of the debt you just paid off. The idea is that it builds your motivation and momentum, encouraging you to pay off your debt faster.

The APR method is similar, except you pay in order of largest APR to lowest. This one will get you out of debt faster by saving you more money in the long term, but it can be harder to build motivation since the higher APRs could be on higher balances, which means it might take longer to see the payoff.

No method is better than any other. The best one is the one that works for you. However, I think before you select one of those methods, you need an even simpler plan.

Learn how to spend all your money without actually spending it to build a feeling of safety with having money.

That means using some budgeting software or creating a spreadsheet that allows you to track your spending every month. Give it a name that doesn't make you cringe when you hear it. I call mine a "strategic spending plan" because I prefer to *spend* money than save it.

For the first month, *don't change your spending habits*.

The biggest mistake people make when budgeting is to set lofty goals they can't keep. When they don't meet them, they get frustrated and quit before ever seeing any progress.

Instead, work on logging all your expenses for the month and observing how you naturally spend money. Once you see where you spend and how much you spend, it will be much easier to set goals.

The first time I did this, I literally watched myself spend $500 on DoorDash *in addition* to my standard groceries and I didn't take any action to stop myself.

Seeing that pattern allowed me to realize I was planning meals that I was too tired to cook. I was planning meals based on an energy level I didn't have any more, and I needed to adjust.

So, when I set my goals for the following month, I decided to see if I could cut my DoorDash spending in half to $250 by planning easier meals and letting myself order some freezer-ready dinners for the days I was too tired.

While I didn't hit my goal of $250, I *did* reduce that category to $300, which I celebrated. After all, that was a decrease of $200! That alone took care of one credit card payment!

After your month of tracking, set some reasonable goals for the next month. Then, whenever you get paid, spend all your money.

But not in the way you think!

To quote my favorite budgeting software and company, You Need a Budget (a.k.a. YNAB), "Every dollar needs a job."

That means you will divvy up every single dollar that comes into your account based on what you learned about yourself last month and the new goals you set in response to your tracking.

This ensures that you're taking care of your bills and necessary expenses without engaging in the type of extreme restriction that will make spending money more tempting. Small steps to shift your thinking and spending will take you so much farther than any extreme financial plan ever could.

The other part of finding success with a budget is knowing that *you will fall off the wagon*. Usually around month three, you'll get really sick of tracking everything and not seeing the progress you would like.

Yet no matter when it is, a day will come when you fall behind on your plan or get frustrated with realizing how little money you bring in and you'll snap. You'll say, "Fuck this! I'm sick of doing this shit! It doesn't even work because I'm *still* broke! I'm not doing it *any more*. If I'm in debt, then I'm in debt. How am I supposed to give a shit about paying back creditors when I'm basically living in a feudalistic society? J. P. Morgan can go *fuck* himself. Hashtag eat the rich!"

That reaction is *also* a normal part of the process.

Everyone goes through that when learning to manage their money. It doesn't matter how many times you fall off the wagon. What matters is how many times you get back on. If you expect yourself to fuck up now and then, it's a lot easier to restart every time. You're completely removing shame from the equation.

And in case you think financial gurus aren't just as at risk of this, know that it's July and I haven't looked at my budget since May—and it's not because I'm so rich I don't have to anymore. I had a busy couple months between writing a book, taking a vacation, witnessing society crumble around me, and watching my electricity bill double during a record heat wave on top of a standard North Florida summer.

I'll probably restart this week and just wipe my previous budget clean and begin the process over from scratch. And I won't even bat an eye at the months I skipped. I'm so far past the point of judging myself for imperfection in financial matters. Instead, I celebrate any and all progress I make. Starting with a clean spending plan will be reason enough for me to feel proud of myself.

Imagine how much further you could get if you decided to celebrate your progress instead of flogging yourself over your imperfections. If you can use a budget for even *six months*, imagine how much further along you could be this time next year.

So, *assume* you will fuck it all up. Then assume you'll figure it out again.

Show Me the Money (Magic)

- **Dare to dream again.** Could there be a job out there with both the duties and salary of your dreams? Poke around on LinkedIn and take note of new or interesting job titles you've never heard of before. Look up what kinds of companies are hiring for those roles. Once you find an organization that makes your heart flutter, try sending an email to one of their employees so you can get information on what it's like to work there. This is your first step in building relationships with people already working in your desired industry.
- **Make more money.** Are you making the right salary for your role? Do you have the appropriate title? Collect some research from LinkedIn, Glassdoor, or even your colleagues to see if there's room for a salary adjustment. If there is, make a PowerPoint and an appointment with your supervisor to ask about a salary adjustment.
- **You've got skills.** What knowledge or services could you monetize by taking on clients? Set some prices and give it a try. After all, you can always quit or change directions if you don't like it.
- **Everyone needs a budget.** Bite the bullet and set up a spending plan. And instead of beating yourself up anytime you mess up, embrace the lesson learned. Celebrate your progress at the end of the first month, no matter how big or small it is!

ACTIVITIES

- How do you plan to bring more income into your life? Follow the steps from the chapter to start taking action toward those goals.
- Has judging yourself in the past sabotaged your ability to improve your financial situation? What small steps can you take this week to better engage with your money?
- If you're in debt, read up on the two repayment methods. Which one sounds like it would be more motivational for you?
- Reading this book alone is a step toward financial freedom. How will you celebrate for making it this far already?

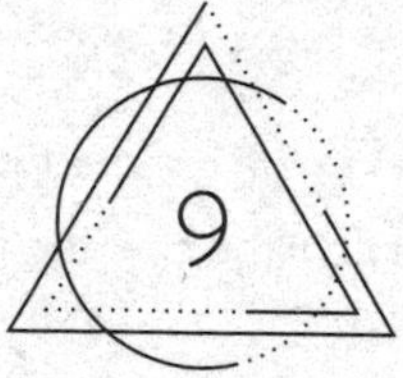

Wrichcraft Practices and Resources for Manifesting Money

You're finally ready! The time has come to share with you some of my favorite resources and rituals for the beginning of your money magic and manifestation journey.

Keep in mind that anything I say here is merely my thoughts and suggestions. This information is designed as a jumping-off point for you, which means you can customize to your heart's content! When in doubt, your intuition takes priority over mine *every* time. Putting your personal spin on something will only make it more effective.

So, let's get into it!

Prepping for Spells

I know you're itching for some real, actual magic spells, but if you want them to actually *work* and work *safely*, you need to understand basic protection and how to channel energy into them. Magic will naturally attract some psychic energies from the other side, which can be totally harmless, but we don't necessarily want to start a block party for all your neighbors' ancestors. Meanwhile, skipping energy building means that your spells will either flop because they have no juice or you'll wipe yourself out using your own energy.

Thankfully, protecting your space is easy peasy. Grab four open containers of any sort and pour into each a mixture of white salt, black pepper, and a bay leaf. There's no specific ratio, but salt should be the dominant ingredient. Now, fuse them with your intent.

Rub your hands together for a few seconds and pull them a few inches apart. Close your eyes so you can tune in to the sensation. When it feels like there's a little swirling ball of energy between your palms, turn your hands down over your bowls and imagine that ball of energy going into your containers. Imagine them glowing with a repellant force field.

Now, place them as close to the four corners of your home as you can—and make sure they're safe from pets and curious kiddos. If you live on multiple stories, you'll want to do this for each floor. Don't worry about attics or basements if they're just for storage.

Say a little something to set your intention. I'm casual about it, so I normally say something like, "Let this protect my home from any unwanted energy, bad vibes, or surprise guests. Please and thank you!"

That's it! Just make sure you change them out every so often, but you can use your intuition on that one.

Now that you're protected, you're ready to build up that spell energy!

Before you get started, you'll want to make sure that you drum up some of your natural energy to power up your spell. You can do this in three ways: (1) meditation, (2) channeling powerful emotions, or (3) moving your body and making music.

Just as you can't drive a car without gas in it, you can't expect your spell to go anywhere without some sort of energy source. Remember that the third step of spell casting is to take inspired action. If the spell is the action, then the energy you create within you is the inspiration that powers it. Otherwise, there would be no way to distinguish actions taken as part of a spell from actions taken out of eccentricity.

When it comes to meditation, you want to focus on channeling energy from a greater source than you. The most accessible sources are the earth or the air around us.

If using the earth, place your bare feet on the floor and imagine roots growing out of your feet, down into the floor beneath you, and traveling deep into the earth. Then, you can visualize red light traveling up through the roots into your right leg, swirling around at the root of your spine (the root chakra) until it glows bright, then traveling down the left leg and returning any stagnant or negative energy to the earth.

Recreate this imagery for each chakra point on your body from the bottom up. I won't get into the meanings of each chakra because it's not relevant for this exercise. For now, use this list and graphic to aid in your visualization of light colors and which parts of the body your energy circuit will pause to clean and light up.

Root Chakra (Red): Base of the spine, genitals, and legs

Sacral Chakra (Orange): Right below the belly button

Solar Plexus Chakra (Yellow): Above your belly button and below your rib cage

Heart Chakra (Green): Center of your chest (you can also imagine the light flowing down your arms and into the smaller wrist chakras at this point)

Throat Chakra (Blue): Guess where (It's the throat.)

 **Third Eye Chakra (Purple):** Center of your forehead

 **Crown Chakra (Violet or White):** Top of your head where a crown would sit.

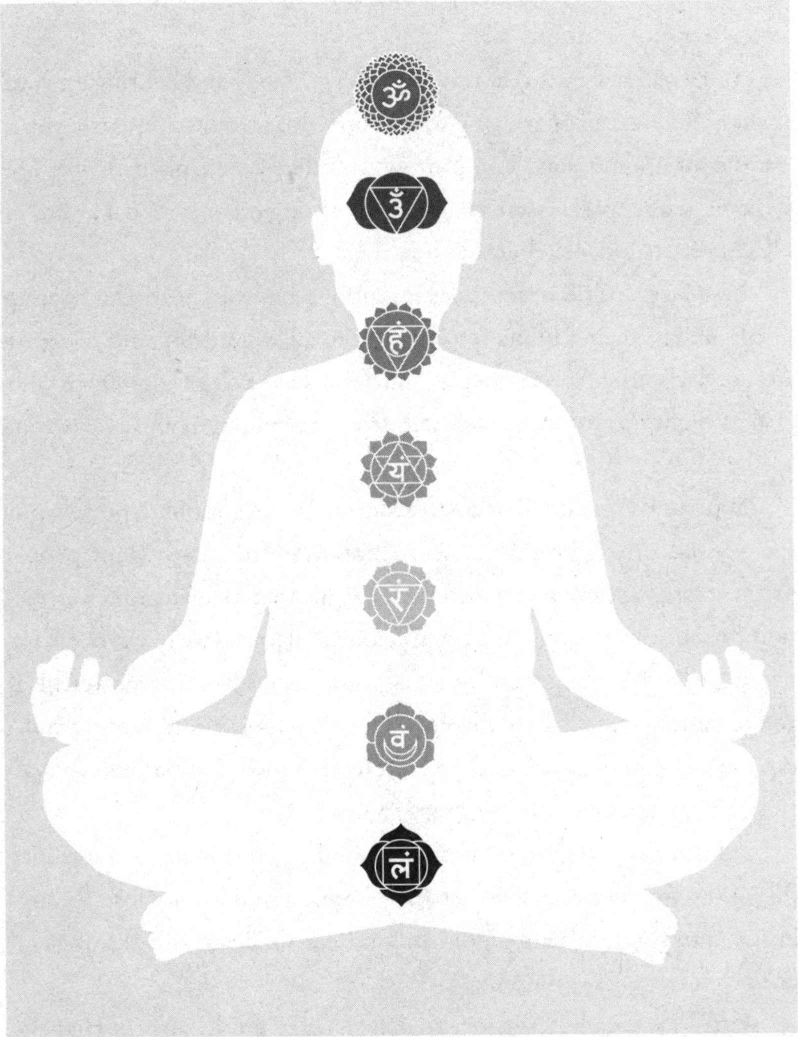

Meditate with each color traveling through the circuit you created with the earth. When you reach your crown, imagine white light shooting through the top of your head and traveling down your legs into the earth.

If this feels like too much work or you don't feel as strong a connection to the earth as you do the sky or the air around you, you can use the air as your source instead.

You'll still imagine light traveling up your body and lighting up your chakras, but instead of growing roots from your feet into the earth, you'll use the air around you. Think of yourself like an air plant or like Dr. Octopus from Spider-Man accidentally putting his suit on backward—whichever image works best for you.

Visualize tendrils or tentacles sprouting from your heart and floating in the air. See them pulling in energy from all around you and releasing any stuck or negative energy back into the air for cleansing. Once your chakras light up, you can come out of your meditation and begin your spellwork.

You can also use meditation to evoke specific emotions to power your spells—and keep in mind that *any* emotion is fair game. Many people prefer to use happiness or gratitude for spells that involve money attraction for obvious reasons. We often manifest because we're experiencing a type of lack. Yet anger and grief can sometimes be more powerful. If you're casting a spell that involves shedding limitations, for example, experiencing the anger or grief you felt toward those limitations can generate energy and give you a feeling of release.

All you need to do is to think of something, someone, or a memory that gives you a strong sense of that emotion and hold those feelings inside until you feel them bloom and pulsate. Once they feel strong and vivid, you can start your spell.

Finally, you can set a timer to dance, make music, and/or chant to create an energy flow inside your body. Just make sure you don't use anyone else's music for this. Consent in magic is a real thing, so it's best for you to do your own thing here.

You can do a clapping pattern, make up a song, rap, scat, beatbox—it doesn't matter. All that matters is that you're making music to dance to.

Dances don't matter either. I'm a big fan of twerking before a spell because it feels like I'm shaking the cobwebs off my butt that's normally placed decidedly in an office chair all day.

Once you feel energy pulsing throughout your body, you're ready to begin.

Note: After finishing a ritual, don't forget to take a moment to close down your energy channel. It doesn't need to take as long as the opening. Simply close your eyes and imagine all the rainbow chakra centers going dim from head to feet. If you grew any roots, tendrils, or tentacles, pull them back into your body. Now, you can go about your business.

Beginner Spells I Didn't Invent but I Will Tell You About

When it comes to actual spells, beginner rituals can seem a little disappointing because they're just *so simple*. I tell people about these and see them trying to hide the disappointment on their faces, thinking, "Wait, no cauldron? No eye of newt? I'm not slicing my hand open to use my own blood for ink? Am I even gonna set anything on *fire*?"

I mean, you *could* include those things. I won't stop you. I'm all for adapting spells to put your personal, unique spin on them. If that's authentic for you, then go forth and do all the weird shit you want!

However, if you're a beginner, start with small rituals and focus on having some fun with them rather than taking the process super seriously. Remember: Fun is its own version of surrender.

I didn't invent these rituals, and I wish I knew who did so I could cite them, but the truth is that they've been around for so long, that info is lost to the ages. These are the standard introductory spells that witches share with baby witches who want to start their foray into money magic.

Water Cup Power-Ups

Wayyyy back in Chapter 3, I told you about how vibrations can change the properties of water. Before that, I explained how *everything* gives off a vibration of some sort.

The Glass of Water Method is predicated on the idea that you can intentionally change the vibration of water to carry the energy of the results you want to manifest, and it's honestly the easiest magic you can do.

Take a piece of paper or a sticky note and write what you want to manifest. That could be "Motivation to network," "Self-control on Black Friday," or "$5,000."

Pour yourself a glass of water—preferably in your favorite glass. Place the glass on top of the note. Rub your hands together and get that ball of energy swirling. Now, cradle the glass in your hands without removing it from the note. Visualize all the energy in your hands infusing the water with your intent.

You can repeat an affirmation or one of the money chants described in the next section, but it's not necessary. When you feel like the glass of water is fully charged up, drink it.

That's it! You can repeat this as often as you would like, even twice a day if you so choose.

The second method is called the Two-Cup Method, which doesn't vary by too much.

Take *two* sticky notes or pieces of paper. On one, write about your current financial situation in as much detail as you can fit, including how it makes you feel. On the second, write about your *ideal* financial situation, including how you *want* to feel.

Place one cup on top of each paper. Pour water into the one sitting over the note about your current financial situation. Place your hands around the cup and imagine releasing all the emotions around your current finances into the water.

When you feel done, pour the water from the first cup into the second one sitting atop the note about your dream financial life. Rub your hands together to create that ball of energy and cradle the second cup without removing it from the paper. Imagine the energy infusing it with all the emotions, habits, and thoughts from your dream financial life.

Once the water feels sufficiently charged, drink the water and tear up the note describing your unwanted financial life. Toss it in the trash 'cuz that ain't your reality anymore.

You can also do this ritual as much as you want!

Money Jar

Creating a money jar is an easy way to use all the materials I covered earlier in this chapter or those listed in later ones.

All you need is a jar of any size with a lid. It can be an old marinara sauce jar, a pickle jar, or those cute, small jars you can buy with corks on them. Size only plays a role based on how you want to use the jar. If you want to tie it to a string to wear around your neck, you might not want to select a pickle jar, unless you want to look like Flava Flav starring in *Hocus Pocus 3*.

Once you have your jar, collect the materials you plan to put in it, like crystals, herbs, spices, money, or anything else that you want to include.

Grab a piece of paper and a writing utensil. Find either a green, gold, or white candle. Candles don't need to be fancy. You can get a three-dollar Glade candle from the grocery store.

Lay out everything you plan to use, rub your hands together to activate the ball of energy, then turn your palms facedown over your supplies and imagine infusing them with the energy of your intent.

When you're done, write down the results you both *want* and *believe you can achieve* within the next moon cycle (28 days) on a piece of paper. If you need to fold the paper so it can fit in the jar, make sure to fold it *toward* you, as you want to bring the results into your life. Place the paper in the jar, along with the other materials you chose. You can repeat an affirmation or money chant as you do this if you feel so called, but it's optional.

Close the jar, light the candle, and drip wax over the top to figuratively or literally seal it. Place it wherever you feel called. For example, on your desk, next to your bed, on your altar, or in another chosen place. If it's small, you can carry it with you in a purse.

When you feel like the energy of everything is used up, you can discard the materials or cleanse them with the smoke from incense or dried herbs for reuse.

Money Chants

Have you ever wondered why spells in movies or plays always seem to rhyme and sometimes sound musical?

It's for the same reasons lullabies do. Rhyming makes lullabies easy to remember, and the singsong cadence soothes babies to sleep.

Spells also rhyme because it makes them easier to remember. They sound like chants or poetry because the rhyming captures an element of sound healing.

The idea behind spoken spells is the same. By saying the verses, we use the sound waves from our chanting to emit a vibration that can impact our bodies, minds, and the environment around us.

Here's what's probably the most commonly used money chant—whose origins I can't trace because it's so widely used:

Money, money, come to me
In abundance, three times three!
May I be enriched in the best of ways,
Harming none, on its way.
This I accept, so mote it be.
Bring me money—three times three!

This will work as a default spell in any of the rituals mentioned earlier or if you decide to create your own.

If this doesn't do it for you, you can always find some great money chants on social media where witches and spiritual people love to share their creations for everyone's benefit.

As long as the chant encourages people to use their work, feel free to use it. Remember: Magic is like sex; we want *enthusiastic* consent from all participants.

Getting to Know You(rself)

I think by now you can guess that I believe self-knowledge is one of the most powerful resources we have when it comes to creating the realities we desire.

To that end, this section will help you get crystal clear on both your strengths and weaknesses in money. That way, you can move forward armed with an intimate knowledge not only of how you arrived at this place, but how you can make more progress toward your goals.

Naturally, this means I'm starting with astrology.

However, I want to clarify that astrology is a *language,* and anything I share here will be a small piece of a vast picture of your life and personality.

Additionally, don't look at any of this information as some sort of divine prophecy about your life. God/the universe/evolution granted us free will as humans, which means there isn't *one* way for your life to turn out. Don't use any of this in an attempt to *predict* your future, but to *plan* it.

As you might know, astrology is a lot deeper than your sun sign, which is your sign based on the day you were born. We have a bajillion other points to analyze at the moment of our birth that make up our personalities, ambitions, values, and even some life experiences. You could quite literally spend your entire life learning about astrology and still probably not know everything.

The summary of those placements, which include planets, houses, mathematical points, and their relationships to each other, is called your "natal chart" or "birth chart." Plenty of websites generate these for free as long as you know your *exact* birth time and place. If you don't, you probably can't follow along with this activity, but you can search for a forensic astrologer who can likely piece together parts of your chart based on that person's advanced understanding of astrology.

Usually, you'll get two components with a birth chart. First, a wheel with a bunch of planetary symbols and lines connecting them. Second, a written report explaining the breakdown of your personality and life based on that chart, which is reminiscent of a toddler's wall art. Here's mine as an example:

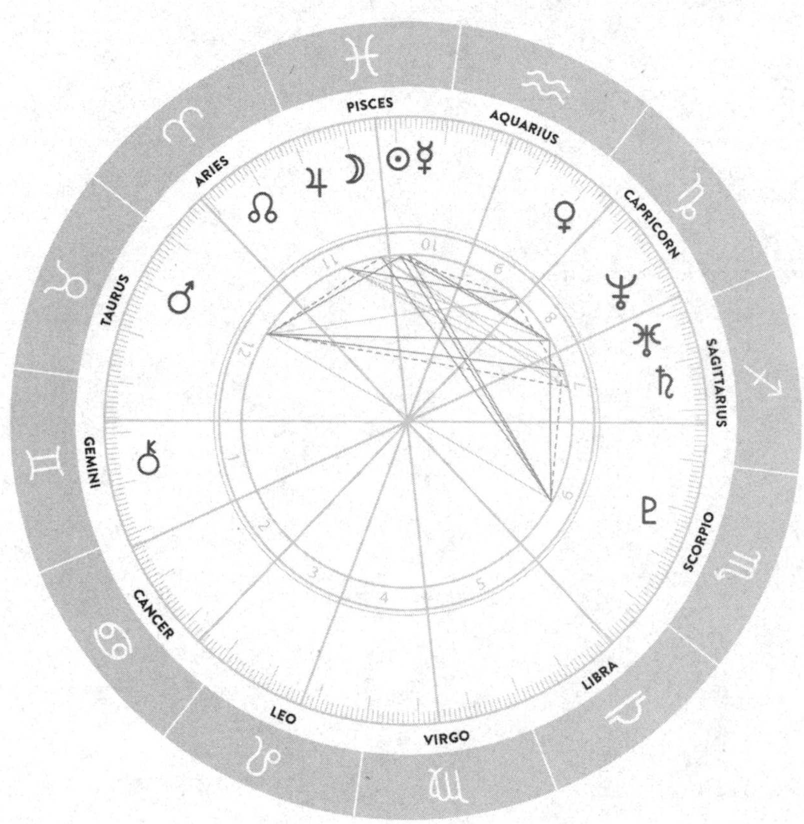

If you haven't seen one before, that probably looks like a satanic summoning circle, but I promise it's not as scary. You can read it once you know how the wheel is set up. For simplicity's sake, the next page shows a chart without all the connecting lines so you can better see the relevant information.

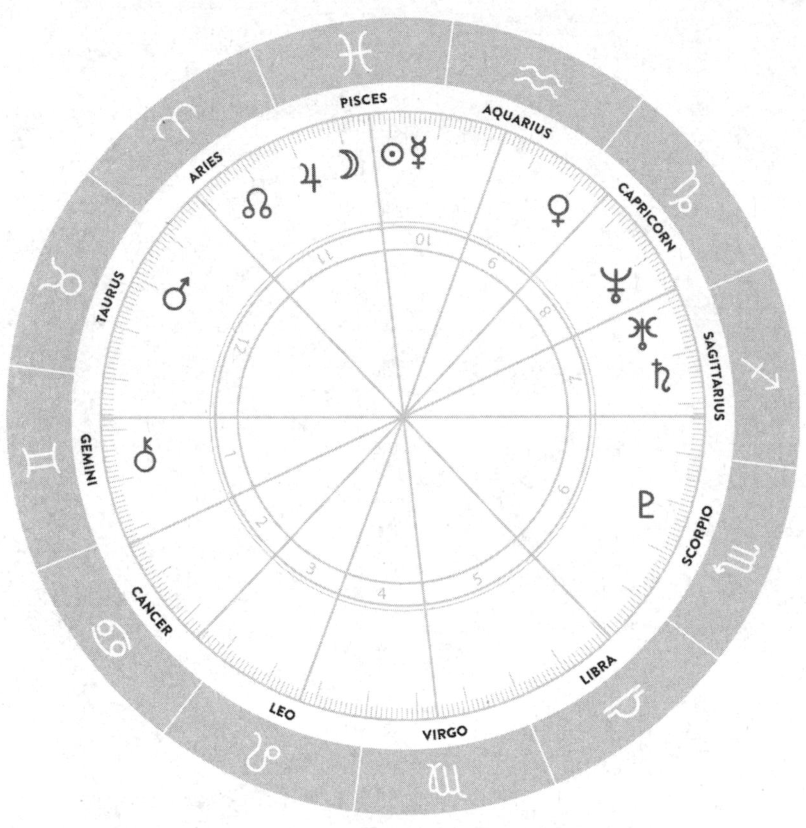

The outside wheel displays the symbols of all the zodiac signs in order. The symbols sprinkled across the wheel are the planets and comets. Whatever zodiac sign the symbol is in tells you what your sign is for that planet. Each planet corresponds to an aspect of your personality. The shorter a planet's trip around the sun, the more influential it is on your personality. That makes these the most important signs in your chart:

The Sun: The broadest version of your personality. Think of this as the umbrella over the rest of the planets in your chart.

The Moon: Your emotions and instincts. The part of you that reacts before you talk some sense into yourself.

Mercury: How you communicate (usually, but not always the same as your sun sign).

Venus: Your values and how you show up in love and relationships. It also dictates your money personality.

Mars: Polite people describe this as the planet of "physical energy," but, really, it describes how you fight and fuck.

Jupiter: Known as the planet of luck, Jupiter shows you how to grow, what you believe in, and what lights you up.

Saturn: You'll mostly notice this one from the ages of twenty-seven to thirty when it makes its return to the place it was in when you were born and fucks up an area of your life until it's fixed. "The taskmaster planet" is basically here to show you where your main challenges are in life and how to overcome them.

The three other planets don't really have much of an impact because they mostly define *generations* rather than individuals, but here's what they rule:

Uranus: Innovation, science, technology. Can you see how that takes on more importance in a generational aspect?

Neptune: Ideals, dreams, and drugs, which we also see more affected within generations than individuals.

Pluto: Named for the Roman god of the underworld, the non-planet planet affects death and rebirth, transformation, and the unconscious. It's easier to see Pluto's impact on countries and their (r)evolutions, rather than people.

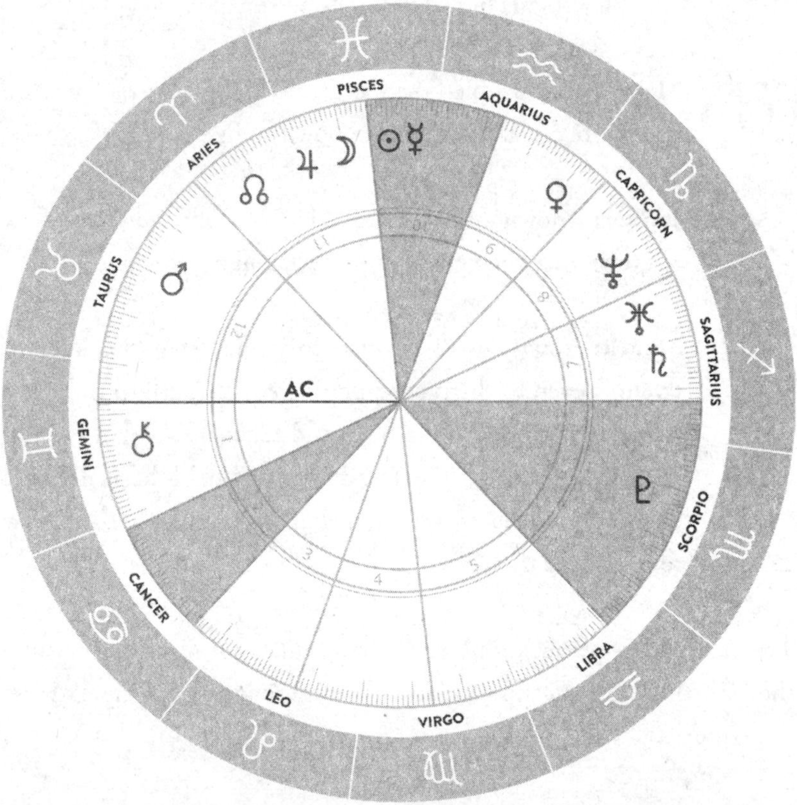

Returning to the chart, the pie slices with numbers in the center are the houses. The houses describe areas of your life. In this section, we'll focus on the Second House, which rules your financial life; the Sixth House, which explains how we serve others; and the Tenth House, which rules your career. I've highlighted them in my chart on page 210.

Whichever sign the first line of each pie slice lands in is the sign for that house. The line always starts with the slightly bolded horizontal line marked with "AC," which stands for "ascendant." From there, follow the lines counterclockwise.

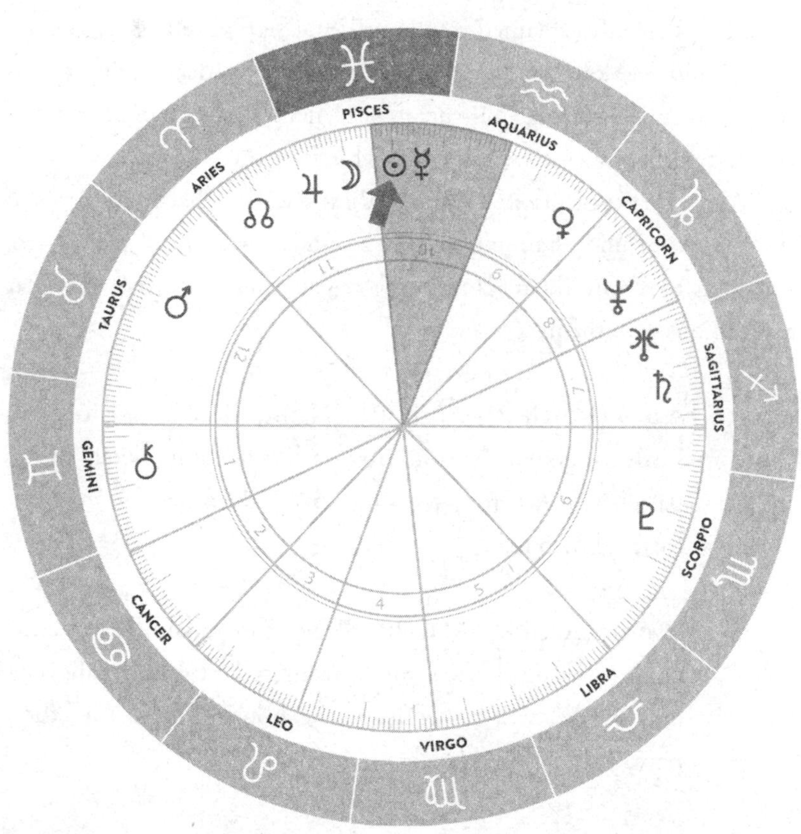

So, for example, I was born on February 28, which is in Pisces season. The symbol for the sun is a circle with a smaller circle in the center. In the chart on page 211, you can see it's in the sign of Pisces and the Tenth House slice, which I've indicated for you.

Don't worry about what the symbol means just yet; you just need to know how to locate it.

Money Placements in Your Chart

When it comes to money, the initial placements we want to focus on are Venus, the Second House, the Sixth House, and the Tenth House.

Now, I already explained that your Venus sign governs how you are in love and relationships in addition to money. Understanding this is similar to understanding your sun sign. Generally, each sign has a set of characteristics often seen with people who share them.

Although we mentioned some of these back in Chapter 2, it was in the context of understanding themes around new and full moons. So, I'm going to reprint them below and give you some of the most popular associations with them:

Aries (March 21–April 19): Natural leader, self-focused, easily angered, "shoot first, ask questions later," little patience, down for anything, loves adventures, more comfortable with risk.

Taurus (April 20–May 20): Bougie, loves comfort, foodie, appreciates aesthetics, super grounded, stubborn, appreciates nature, will never leave the house after taking their pants off

Gemini (May 21–June 20): Creative, funny, witty, talkative, constantly contradicting themselves, personality changes day to day, inconsistent, loves gossip, often accused of being nuts

Cancer (June 21–July 22): Nurturing, emotional, buries their feelings, the Mom friend, ride-or-die loyalty, very sweet with the capacity to murder like a cat

Leo (July 23–August 22): Loves attention and being recognized, great hair, takes pride in their appearance, courageous, loyal, sometimes vain, phone is full of selfies

Virgo (August 23–September 22): Organized, truth-teller, deep emotions they don't show, selective with their trust, uptight, "If you didn't want to know, you shouldn't have asked"

Libra (September 23–October 22): Charming AF, genuinely loving, loves art almost as much as they love arguing, craves connection and relationships, overly flirtatious, indecisive

Scorpio (October 23–November 21): Depth of emotions they'll never show, already a witch, intense gaze, human lie detector, doesn't need to take revenge because karma will get you first

Sagittarius (November 22–December 21): Travel lover, scholar, laughs easily, hot temper, no filter on their mouths, can't lie because their faces give it away

Capricorn (December 22–January 20): Ambitious, loves making money, traditional, likes structure, stick-in-the-mud, stable, loyal, probably thinks you're not reaching your potential

Aquarius (January 21–February 18): Deeply cares about humanity, loves politics, weird interests/habits, probably an alien, wishes they could turn off their emotions and become robots

Pisces (February 19–March 20): Idealistic, too trusting, dreamer, indecisive, creative, art as expression, philosophical, interested in religion and the occult, sensitive, glorifies suffering

Of course, plenty of people have their own associations with the signs and not everything will fit everyone. That's the point of looking at all the different aspects of your personality and life. You're made up of most if not all the signs of the zodiac in different ways.

So, if Venus is the sign for money, then you can become more aware about the way you naturally tend to think about money.

Using my chart as an example again (page 215), you can see that I have Venus in Capricorn.

While Pisces is dreamy, artistic, philosophical, and more, Capricorn is more practical, financially focused, and ambitious.

That means that my personality might generally come off more like a hippie dreamer, but when it comes to love, I tend to be more traditional.

And that happens to be true! While I understand, *theoretically*, that marriage isn't much more than a piece of paper, an institution traditionally used to keep women subjugated, and doesn't really mean anything except entitlement to some tax breaks... I've always valued it and wanted it for myself. I don't know why. I just have.

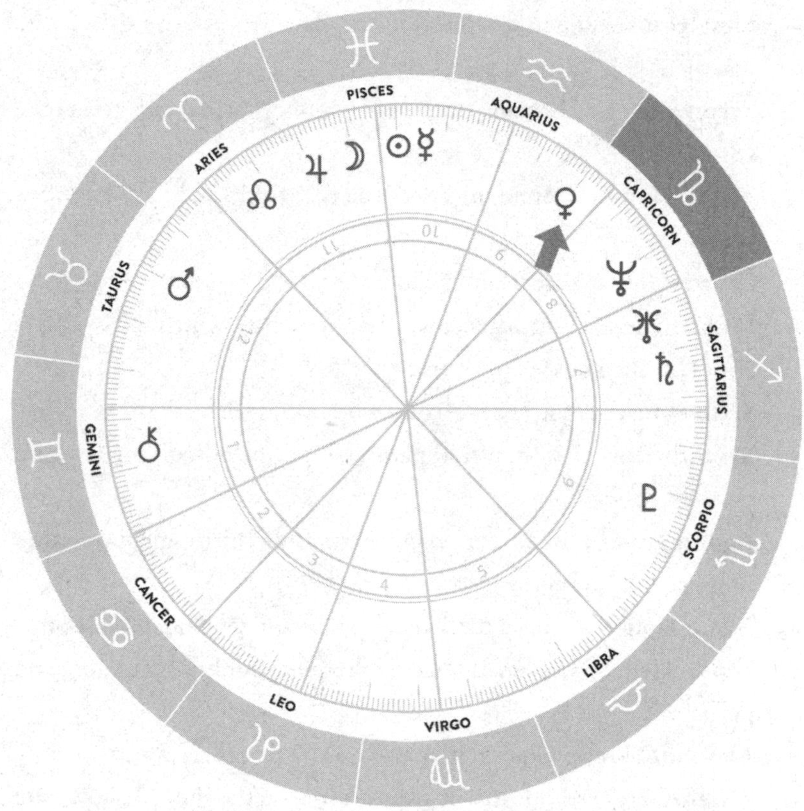

When it comes to how I view and handle money, it's with reverence and a desire for more of it. I love work and earning money, and I'm ambitious when it comes to my money goals.

So, you can see how these other planets can explain why you don't fit *every* quality associated with your sun sign.

If you want to take it a step further, look for the house in which Venus resides. That will tell you even more information about yourself. Once you do, check the following list to see what area of your life that house governs:

- **First House:** Identity, appearance, what powers you and lights you up
- **Second House:** Earning and losing money, assets and resources, self-worth
- **Third House:** Communication, daily habits, siblings, extended family
- **Fourth House:** Parents, home life, childhood
- **Fifth House:** Sex, children, and creative energy, which is why this is known as the house of pleasure!
- **Sixth House:** Physical health and work
- **Seventh House:** Committed partnerships, including romantic and business
- **Eighth House:** Transformation, death and rebirth, mental health, other people's resources
- **Ninth House:** Travel, education, publication, religion, philosophy
- **Tenth House:** Career, fame and honors, public reputation and perception
- **Eleventh House:** Community and how the world receives you
- **Twelfth House:** Spirituality, dreams, secrets, your shadow and subconscious

As with the quick-hit list of sign descriptions I provided, the houses can speak to more than just these subjects. However, these general subjects work as a decent enough jumping-off point.

So, now you know when I say that I have Venus in Capricorn that it means when it comes to love and money, I tend to have more Capricorn traits. Knowing the house gives me more information on Venus, so let's find it.

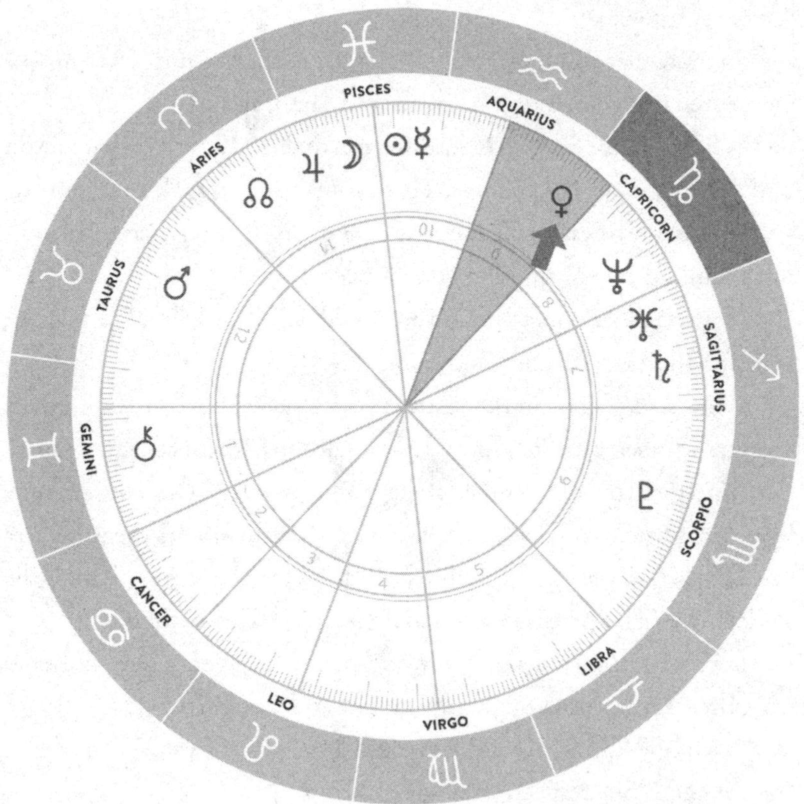

When we add in the placement of the Ninth House, that tells us *where* in my life I will likely find love and money.

It's no surprise, then, that I feel most comfortable making money through teaching and coaching others, writing this book (and hopefully more!), traveling (remember how I said I always make money when or right after I go on vacation?), and basing my coaching around spiritual practices.

I think it's also worth noting that I met my fiancé because a mutual friend taught with him at the same school and thought to set us up. He's a poet and an English and creative writing professor.

Isn't that wild?

So, now that you understand Venus, let's talk about the two houses most often related to money—the second, sixth, and tenth.

When I say the Second House dictates financial aspects, what I mean is that it's all about *liquid* assets. That means you can look here for ways it will naturally be easier for you to make money. It also governs expenditures, lending, borrowing, and other aspects.

However, that doesn't mean you would enjoy the work. For that, we look at both the Sixth and Tenth Houses.

Work as described in the Sixth House is about how we serve others and how they serve us. So, while it's not totally on point, it can give us some clues into the types of roles that might suit us in work. The Tenth House, however, is where you find evidence for your dream job. It's the work that you'll likely find the most fulfilling while bringing you success. This is the work you both become known for and *want* to be known for doing.

Let's return, once again, to my birth chart (page 219) to understand what these houses reveal about my money and career.

Starting with the Second and Sixth Houses, you can see they're in Cancer and Libra, respectively.

Right off the bat, this tells us that emotions probably govern my money—and that's not wrong. I'm prone to invest from my heart instead of my brain and can sometimes use spending money as a way to make myself feel better. It also hints at earning money that comes from nurturing, which I would definitely say I do with my clients. They always say that they feel better after talking to me because I'm able to really hear what they're saying and communicate advice in a way that's gentle and kind. Don't get me wrong, I'll kick their ass when they need it, but they know it's always done with love.

Having my Sixth House in Libra can mean that I'm often in a mediator role or helping people seek justice. Because I tend to be a peacemaker,

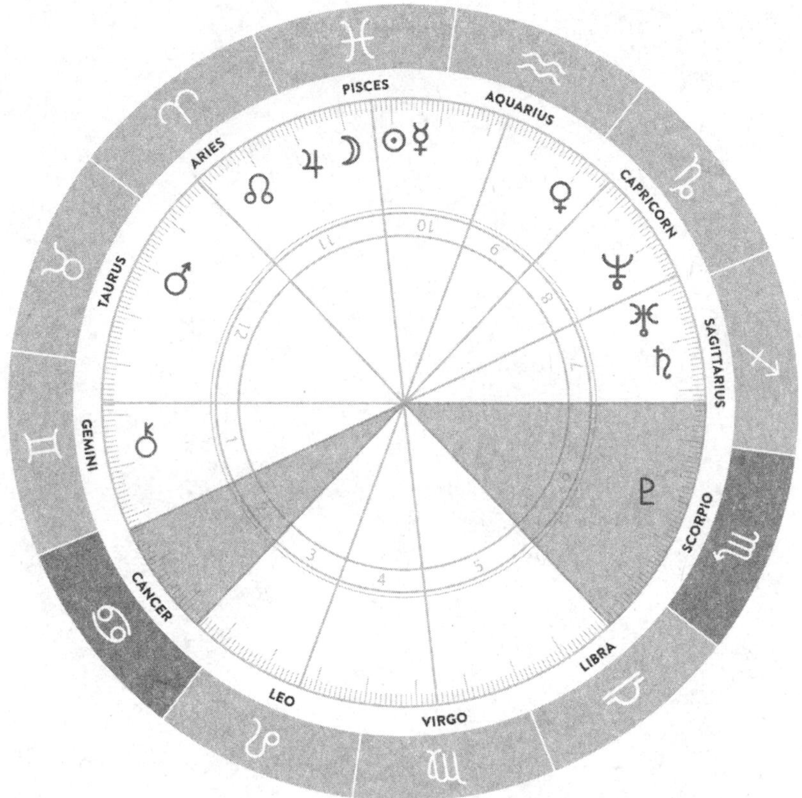

it means I might also be at risk of people pleasing and ignoring my own needs in work. Now, unlike my Second House, which doesn't have any planets, you can see that Pluto is in my Sixth House.

With Pluto governing death, rebirth, and the subconscious, it gives me a natural ability to see how others can grow and reach their potential. I'm also easily able to identify what subconscious beliefs hold them back or that they project on others.

Finally, let's unpack all the aspects of my Tenth House—and buckle up because we have quite a bit.

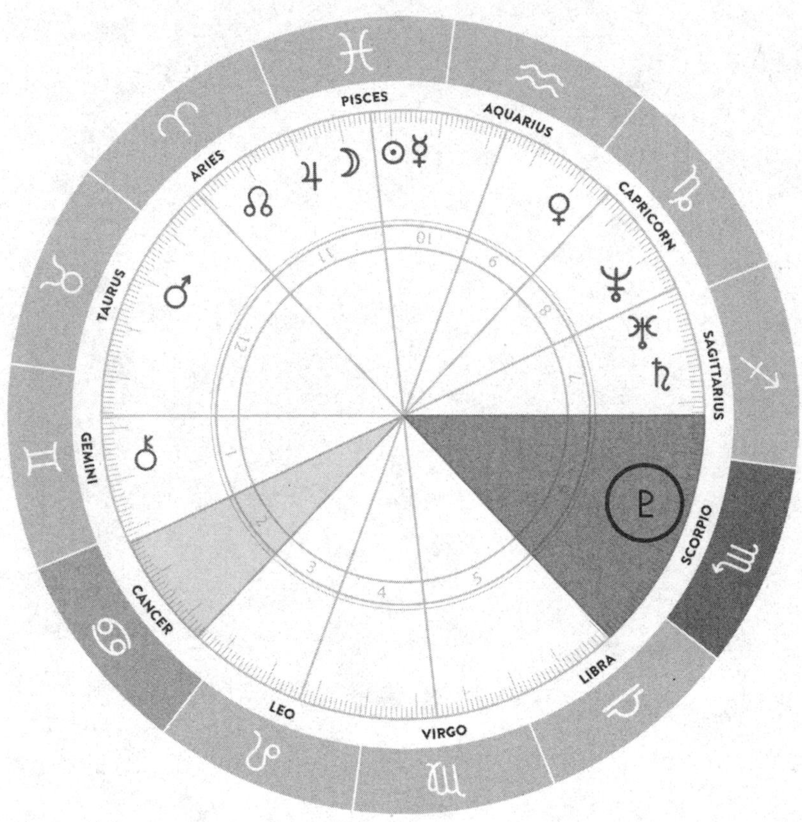

The fact that my Tenth House is in Aquarius (see page 221) means my career naturally tends toward humanity and the future. I want to do something that changes the world and makes it better for my fellow man. *Check!* It also generally indicates that I'm open to belonging to the world. I want my work featured, recognized, and appreciated by everyone. *Check!*

Two planets are also hanging out in my Tenth House: the Sun and Mercury.

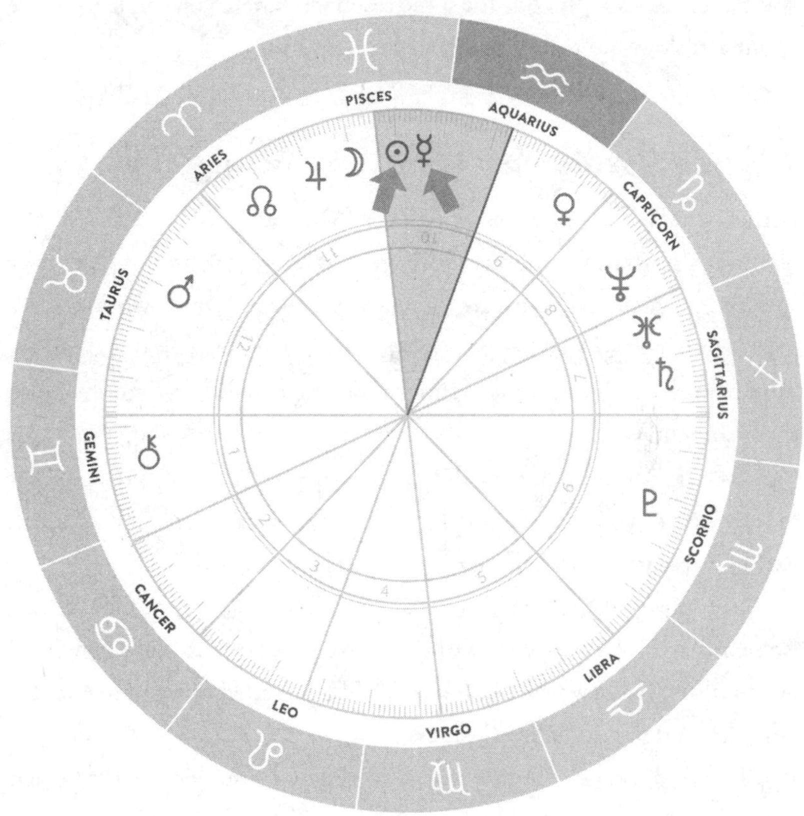

If the Sun is about our personality, then we can intuit that part of how I find success and accolades is going to be by sharing my personality with the world. Add in Mercury, which rules communication, and it's easy to see that I'll find fame and honors via communication.

Is it any surprise I wrote a book all about money where I openly share so much of my life and drop a lot of f-bombs? Probably not.

Like I said when we started this section, astrology is a language. So, just as with a language, it takes some learning and practice to get the hang of it. Thankfully, I've done the work for you. At the end of this chapter, you can check the QR code for some resources where you can learn more about astrology, no matter your fluency.

Money Deities for Your Everyday Life

Earlier, I talked about how deities can help serve as examples of the qualities you want to embody more when it comes to money. Generally speaking, when you want an increase in money, you'll work with a money deity who speaks to you—meaning they represent acquiring money in the way you want, within a specific timeline, or you relate to them somehow.

To start you off, I'm providing you with a short list of three popular money deities you can explore, but know that this is not an exhaustive list! Feel free to research deities you might connect with more.

You don't even need to use a deity specific to money either. Remember, I worked with Kore/Persephone, goddess of spring and queen of the underworld, because I felt like I needed more of her acceptance around duality in my business.

The only caveat I'll give you is to only choose deities from **open** practices.

Some witchcraft traditions are tied to cultural identities, which you can only practice if you're born into them or undergo a conversion process full of studying and rituals. Three closed practices that are absolute no-no's are voodoo, hoodoo, and Santeria. You can get readings from people who practice those belief systems, but you cannot start using their rituals or working with their deities if you're not an accepted member.

So, if you come across a deity not on this list who sounds like an absolute baller, make sure you Google the religion they belong to first.

All of the deities listed here are from open practices. I've given a little info about them and what they're associated with to make your deity work easier to start.

Lakshmi

- Hindu goddess of wealth, good fortune, youth, and beauty who has four arms

  Colors: Pink and blue

  Symbols: Lotus flowers, flower garlands, elephants spraying water from their trunks, coins, a bag of rice

  Days: Fridays and Diwali, the festival of lights, in late October/ early November

  OG myth: One time she traveled down to her temple on a Friday to see if anyone was worshiping her and only found a single, humble woman there. Lakshmi was so grateful, she decided to visit the worshiper's home for dinner. When she returned to her home inside the temple, her husband and brother-in-law berated her for dining with a member of a lower caste. So, she left and built a temple in the part of town with all the lower-caste members and went on strike. The two ding-dongs couldn't manage to successfully cook themselves meals or beg for food, so they eventually visited the new temple and begged for Lakshmi to come home. She agreed, but only if they first sat and dined with the lower-caste worshipers of her new temple. From that moment on, open dining and interacting among caste members was a requirement within all her temples.

Hermes/Mercury

- Known as Hermes in Greek mythology and Mercury in Roman, this deity was the messenger to all the gods and goddesses on Mount

Olympus. He is the god of money, business, travel, communication, artists, athletes, trickery, and thievery, oddly enough. You can recognize him as the guy with winged sandals and hat and wearing a money bag as a fanny pack in Red Bull commercials.

Color: Orange

Symbols: Money bag, cattle, dice, pairs of snakes, symbols of luck, lavender

Days: Wednesdays and May 15

OG myth: The day Hermes was born, he decided to leave his crib for an adventure. First, he picked up a tortoise shell, drilled two holes in it, threaded a string between them, and created the first lyre. After that, he decided to steal his brother Apollo's cattle and run off with them. After he'd eaten two, a mortal discovered him, but Hermes bribed him with one of the cows to keep silent. Apollo eventually ran off to their father and king of the gods, Zeus, who investigated the case. The mortal immediately ratted out Hermes. Zeus ordered that in exchange for stealing the cattle, Hermes had to give Apollo the lyre he invented. Once the two were satisfied, Hermes went back to the mortal and killed him. Snitches get stitches, I guess.

Caishen/Tsai Shen Yeh

◢ Chinese/Taoist god of wealth who is broken down into nine other smaller deities. It's similar to the Christian belief of one God broken into the three entities: God the Father, God the Son, and God the Holy Spirit.

Colors: Red and gold

Symbols: Incense, tigers, ripe bananas, dumplings, gold nuggets

Days: Chinese New Year

OG myth: Like all Taoist deities, Caishen was a person who became a deity after death. Although numerous stories about him abound, my favorite is that he originally lived as a very wealthy man named Bi Gan. Bi Gan's wife was aunt to King Zhou of Shang, known as Emperor Xin. Xin was essentially an angry, cruel fuckboi, and Bi Gan was the only relative who called him out on his behavior. Well, Xin didn't like that and had him executed. As they say, karma's a bitch and Xin was soon overthrown, putting an end to the Shang Dynasty. Bi Gan then became the god Caishen, who visits homes every Chinese New Year, traveling on the back of a black tiger with a magical cudgel in hand that can turn iron into gold. That dual imagery of the tiger and cudgel is important, though, says mythology expert Mike Greenberg. "Tigers symbolize many attributes and values in Chinese art. One of these, however, is persistence. Caishen may grant the favor of wealth, but by riding a tiger he shows that a god cannot be relied on alone to bring such fortune. Persistence, diligence, and hard work are just as important as Caishen's cudgel in attracting riches in the New Year and beyond."[1]

Now that you have a few solid choices for deities tied to wealth and success, how can you work with them?

The easiest thing to do is create an altar. It doesn't need to be anything intense or fancy—a windowsill or top of a dresser will do just fine. As long as it's something you can keep tidy and mostly undisturbed, you're good.

Once you have your space, place something to symbolize the deity on it. You can drop money on a statue or use a picture or figurine of one of their symbols as a stand-in. For example, if you're working with Lakshmi, you could use something with a lotus flower on it. If you're working with Caishen, you can find a toy tiger. Hell, you could even draw a picture if you want. Remember, it's the (literal) thought that counts with deities.

You'll use your altar to place offerings to your deity daily or weekly. That doesn't mean you need to spend money, though. You can pick flowers on your walk for Lakshmi, share a piece of banana with Caishen, or even pour a cup of water for your deity to enjoy.

From there, read about them. It can be academic research or fictional accounts, documentaries or movies, Wikipedia entries or webcomics—it doesn't matter.

If you come across a poem or song, such as an Orphic Hymn, you can read it or play it to them.

Finally, own some of their characteristics in your everyday life. Make yourself feel beautiful every day like Lakshmi. Play a harmless prank on your roommate like Hermes. Call out your debaucherous nephew like Caishen.

Whatever stands out to you about them that you could use within you, use this work to intentionally cultivate that characteristic.

Pretty Rocks

Crystals are one of those topics that naturally receive the most criticism when it comes to magic, witchcraft, and, honestly, femininity in general.

People love to hate on how expensive crystals are as if they don't find it totally normal to spend *one month's salary* on a diamond engagement ring. I hope you can feel the reverberation from how hard I rolled my eyes.

The way I feel about crystals is the way I feel about astrology, tarot cards, deities, and everything else in magic.

Who *the fuck* cares what works for you?

As long as you're not harming anyone, does it *matter* whether it was your spell or your networking strategy that got you the new job? It doesn't matter to me.

If you learn more about your relationship with money from astrology and manage it better because of that, do you care if astrology is real? I sure as hell don't.

It seeks to follow that if a sparkly, colorful, shiny rock makes you feel better when you hold it or look at it, who gives a flying fuck if it has magical properties?

It bears mentioning that before fidget toys were ever invented, people carried worry stones in their pockets. Literally, they carried rocks they could obsessively rub when stressed out to calm back down.

So, is it a crystal imbued with magical properties that will attract money and abundance to you or is it a pretty rock you can rub when you feel yourself worrying about money? It doesn't matter.

What matters is *how* to pick your crystal/pretty rock.

If you're in person, follow what naturally catches your eye and don't overthink it. The right crystal will call out to you. When you see something you like, pick up a piece and hold it in your left hand, closing around it in a fist. Close your eyes and tune in. You should feel...*something*.

Some people describe a subtle vibration. Others describe it as a feeling. Just know this isn't going to be like picking out your wand in *Harry Potter and the Sorcerer's Stone*. Don't expect a spotlight and whooshing or sparks bursting forth from your hand. There's a good chance you might not feel anything at all and that's OK, too. You can use a totally logical justification like "This one is on sale."

If you're not near a metaphysical store, go for the stone that carries properties you want to enhance. Crystals are less about magnetism and more about increasing or decreasing certain qualities or energies you already have inside.

Below, I've provided some wonderful beginner crystals to kick off your money magic journey.

Keep in mind that *all* of these stones are related to prosperity and money manifestation, so I'm not indicating those energies for each one. Instead, I'm focusing on the other qualities that *combine* with your desire to manifest money.

- **Pyrite, a.k.a. "Fool's Gold":** Mental clarity, willpower, confidence, vitality, and protection
- **Green Aventurine:** Creativity, independence, career success, inner peace, balance, optimism, gratitude, self-compassion
- **Jade:** Harmony, balance, good luck, self-love, authenticity, shedding limitations (fears, beliefs, habits, etc.)
- **Citrine, a.k.a. "The Happy Stone":** Playfulness, bliss, higher self-esteem and self-worth, reduced negative emotions, self-actualization of dreams
- **Peridot:** Leadership, self-growth, renewal, understanding your destiny, dissolving self-blame and guilt
- **Carnelian:** Power, ambition, drive, creativity, vitality, clear communication, agency
- **Andalusite:** Self-revelations, finding your true self, clarity in intention setting, meditation, releasing negative energy, protection
- **Lapis Lazuli, a.k.a. "The Stone of Truth":** Spiritual guidance, honesty, enlightenment, self-advocacy, fairness, confidence, intuition

Now that you have a crystal, what do you do with it?

Well, first, you need to energetically cleanse it, charge it, and set your intention with it. Up until it came home with you, that crystal has been sitting in a store, getting touched by god-knows-how-many people, and picking up *all* of their energies. It needs you to wipe its energetic slate clean.

You can cleanse your crystal in any of three ways: (1) Leave it in a cup of water overnight and pour the water down the sink or directly into the earth the next morning. (2) Bury it in a shallow bowl of mineral or sea salt overnight and discard the salt in the morning. (3) Move it around in the smoke from some lit incense or a bundle of dried herbs. That's it!

When choosing your method, first make sure to Google whether your crystal is porous or water soluble. Porous stones, which contain microscopic holes throughout them, can lose their shine if buried overnight in salt. Water-soluble crystals will literally dissolve if they're placed in water for too long, so you obviously won't want to cleanse with that method. Consider this one more example of how science and magic work together.

Charging it is just as easy. You can leave it in the sun for a day or in the moonlight overnight. If you're feeling impatient, you *can* charge it yourself. Close your eyes and rub your hands together for at least ten seconds. Pull your hands apart by about six inches to see if you can feel a ball of energy forming between your hands. If you don't, rub your hands together for longer and try again.

Once you have the energy ball, imagine it as a swirling ball of light. Turn your palms facedown over your crystal and imagine the ball of light infusing the crystal with energy, causing it to glow. When you're done, open your eyes. You're all done!

Finally, you need to set your intention for this crystal. It doesn't matter if it's a vague idea or a specific request. What matters is that you're giving your crystal some sort of instruction on where it can direct its energy. All you need to do is hold it in your left hand and focus on your goal for this crystal. You can do this silently or you can talk aloud—whatever feels natural. That's it. Your crystal is ready for use.

When it comes to crystal use, there are some general practices that work with every stone, but certain crystals have preferred activities. It's a bit like that saying, "Sex is like pizza—even when it's bad, it's still pretty good."

The most basic use for all crystals is in meditation. When you meditate or engage in other visualization practices, you can do so while holding your crystal.

The other most popular use is to wear it on your person. You could make a pendant from a crystal to use as a statement necklace or place your crystal in a pocket or purse. My best friend puts a crystal in her bra every day.

By keeping the crystal on you at all times, the idea is that it will naturally infuse *you* with the properties it promotes.

If you want to go deeper into the subject, you can always take to the internet to learn about crystal magic or specific rituals for the stone you selected. Just don't forget my previous words of caution: Google your crystal's properties to make sure that they're well-suited for any rituals involving water or salt.

Spices, Herbs, and What to Do with Them

The other major resource for easy, daily money magic is spices and herbs. It always sounds so intriguing to people who don't know much about money magic, but the coolest part of this is that you can probably find at least one of these in your home right now.

- **Basil:** Good for attracting money, luck, and love; promotes peace; cleanses energies

  Two of the simplest attraction rituals you can do with fresh basil: (1) Throw a few leaves in a bath and imagine yourself bathing in wealth. (2) Throw a few pieces on the floor before you sweep it all out the front door, imagining that the basil is taking with it all your bad luck and scarcity.

  And don't forget the Cheetos-dust witchcraft versions! If you don't have fresh basil, you can steep dried basil in a mug before pouring it into the bath or sprinkle the dried shit over the floor like it's an all-natural carpet powder.

- **Thyme:** Money, courage, healing, dreaming

  Remember how I mentioned cleansing your crystals with a bundle of dried herbs? Dried thyme sprigs are perfect for that. You can even burn them to cleanse the energy inside your home.

  Dried thyme can be made into a bath tea as well, except thyme will help you release any pain from the past and promote healing. To attract money, you can put a sprig of dried thyme in your wallet. And, while it can be a little messy, you can even put a sprig of thyme inside your pillowcase to promote peaceful dreams.

- **Cinnamon:** Money-drawing, passion, success, motivation, spirituality, psychic powers, energy cleansing

  Yes, our favorite fall spice is a money spice! That means any time you add it to *anything*, take a moment to do it with intent. Sprinkle some into your coffee in the morning and imagine that coffee not just wakes you up, but also gives you the motivation and passion you need to succeed in your business or career. You can also burn it to promote all of those feelings and enhancements as well! Sprinkling cinnamon around the threshold of your front door, especially if it's your business, is thought to attract money as well.

- **Allspice:** Business success, money attraction, healing, luck, relieving mental tension

  Listen up, friends, because I am a *slut* for allspice. Cinnamon is wonderful, but the second someone somewhere in the Northern Hemisphere gets a hint of autumn, I'm sprinkling allspice on everything

I eat and drink. It's my favorite not just because it tastes like a richer, earthier cinnamon, but because you can use it in any magic spell.

Allspice enhances whatever intent and energy you're using in a ritual. You can combine it with all of your cinnamon uses to amplify the energy. You can put a few dried berries in your purse or wallet to amplify the thyme. You can also use them on their own, carrying a small baggie of seven berries in your purse for a week before you burn them on the seventh day and make a wish. Whatever you want to do, allspice can help.

- **Cloves:** Clarity, prosperity, protection, shutting up gossips, clairvoyance, attracting friends, banishing evil

  You can channel all of the energies listed here just by keeping a bit of cloves out as a potpourri. They also work well for burning as an incense and adding more juju to spells that ask for cinnamon or other money-drawing spices and herbs. Carrying cloves in your pockets is said to keep you closer to your romantic partner.

- **Ginger:** Courage, energy, inspiration, passion, power, speed

  It was a common practice to chew a piece of ginger root before performing magic because it was thought to speed up the results of the spells. As someone who chewed a piece of raw ginger once, let me say it's not worth it. That being said, you can always sprinkle a little ginger powder in other rituals to hopefully, maybe, speed up your manifestations. You can even sprinkle a bit into your pockets or wallet for money attraction. Drinking ginger tea is thought to help attract money to you faster as well!

- **Nutmeg:** Health, money, fidelity, luck

  Gamblers used to carry a whole nutmeg in their pocket because it was thought to improve their luck fast. If it's good enough for old-timey bettors, it's good enough for you. Nutmeg oil is great for anointing candles for money spells. You can make your own by heating up a neutral oil on the stove, adding some ground nutmeg, and cooking it on medium-low until fragrant.

Show Me the Money (Magic)

- **Don't raw dog your spells.** If you want a peaceful home and an *effective* ritual, you need to lay down some protection and drum up your own personal energy. This keeps your home hidden from spiritual entities that might be drawn to the magic in your house while you really give your spell some *oomph*.
- **Keep beginner spells simple.** You don't need to add anything complex to your spell. Sometimes the most effective rituals are the simplest. If you want to put your own spin on spells, that's totally fine. Do whatever you feel called to do.
- **Inspire yourself.** Your natal chart reveals quite a bit about your financial life. It might not include *surprising* information, but it *will* help you find clarity on what might best serve you in ways to make and manage your money.
- **Get inspired.** Finding a wealth and success deity can not only add more power to your spells but also give you guidance on *how* you can show up in your day-to-day life to attract the money manifestations you're calling in.
- **Rock 'n' roll.** Plenty of crystals carry associations with money, success, and abundance. Whether you choose to use a crystal as a worry stone, a meditation tool, or decor, or place your full belief in its ability to attract your manifestation, all that matters is how *you* feel about it. Got it?
- **Become a spice girl.** Everyday kitchen spices carry spiritual properties. Even if all you do is imagine spices adding their spiritual properties to your food, that's enough to turn your regular cooking into kitchen witchcraft!

ACTIVITIES

- Set your salt protections. Even if you don't plan to do any magic, they still make an effective psychic barrier.
- Practice one of the intro spells and make a note of when you did it in your journal. Chart your progress.
- If you know your birth time, create your birth chart on either Astro.com or Cafe Astrology. Use the information here to journal about your Venus sign and house along with the Second, Sixth, and Tenth Houses and any planets that might be in them. Research those placements online to see how accurate your understanding was.
- Use your intuition to choose a crystal, whether in person or from an online vendor. Look up the meaning *after* you buy it to see what qualities your intuition chose for where you are right now.
- Take a moment to look up the spiritual properties of the spices in your next meal. Imagine taking on those qualities as you eat your food. That's magic!

PART 3

How to Keep Manifested Money

Why Manifesting Money and Keeping Manifested Money Are Different

If you've never attempted money manifestation or money magic before, you're probably confused over the labeling of this section. Isn't it *inherent* that if you're consciously manifesting money, you would want to keep it?

Yes, of course! But just as we can consciously want money and subconsciously push it away, so, too, can we simultaneously attract it and call in situations to sabotage our progress.

Plenty of times, people follow the activities outlined in Part 2, start making money, and never have an issue with keeping the money at all.

For me, personally? I was not one of those people. Not at first.

I seemed to live on a cycle where I would do a ton of mindset work and magic, make a nice chunk of moolah, and then encounter a bunch of bullshit that would eat up all the money I just made.

I didn't understand it, and it drove me *nuts*. How could I be out here helping clients make tons of money from careers and businesses on a permanent basis, but couldn't seem to do it for myself?

What I learned is that it's because all of us have a threshold for what kind of money feels *safe*.

The Money Manifestation Wave

Based on the experiences we had growing up, some of us feel safer with more money and some feel safer with less. Generally speaking, if you had a fairly comfortable and privileged upbringing, you'll get to that safe feeling much faster than someone who carries more financial trauma with them. In particular, if you grew up with *instability* around earning money, it might take you a while to trust that money is even capable of sticking around.

Several chapters ago, we learned how our brains don't like change, even if it's good. Those of us who struggle to *consistently* make more money will start by manifesting in waves. We make a ton of money, feast for a while, and then retreat to famine. Sometime later, we earn it back, then lose it again, and so on and so forth until one day it eventually evens out.

But why? Why, if all we want is financial peace, would we find ourselves in a loop where we constantly get our hopes up only to continuously break our own hearts? What benefit could that *possibly* give us?

The benefit is that **eventually** you'll stop feeling the fear of losing money.

If part of you feels pressure to perform—either because you were given too much responsibility as a kid or you're a former gifted child who experienced the crushing weight of others' expectations from a young age—chances are, you're more afraid of failing than anything else.

The only issue is that once you're finally out of a school environment, the only way to achieve radical success in your life is to *move toward failure*.

So, if your subconscious is worrying about whether you're going to get an A-plus in entrepreneurship, your job, or financial planning, you will avoid anything that makes you feel like you're getting an F. And what generally makes us feel like a failure? Things we have to work at because we're not naturally good at them.

That looks like not putting yourself out there enough in networking or promoting your business. It can be second-guessing every decision you make. Sometimes, it's self-sabotaging behavior that turns into a self-fulfilling prophecy.

Whatever it is, you do it because you're afraid of trying to give something your maximum effort and failing. *Trying* alone is enough to make us feel afraid. Since we don't want to feel fear or discomfort of any sort, we spend our time half-assing our efforts instead of giving our whole ass.

'Cuz if we use our whole ass and the effort doesn't pay off, then our asses will just be out there for everyone to laugh at. At least that's how it feels.

Cycling through money gain and money loss is our way of slowly getting accustomed to success. At first, the gaps between money manifestations will take longer than you like, but eventually they'll get shorter and shorter until they disappear.

The entire lesson is all about trusting ourselves enough to keep moving toward failure and trusting money enough to keep showing up.

Every time we make money after losing it, our brains trust a little more that it's safe to *try* and safe to *receive*—even if we fail first. Money stops feeling finite as our subconscious starts to realize that once it leaves, *it always comes back.*

It's a different way of learning the same level of trust that people who address their initial money fears and skyrocket straight into abundance do. Their brains learn that money is energy and click into the abundance setting from that alone. Our brains need to *live through* the gain-and-pain cycle to understand that money is energy.

It's a bitch, I know. It wasn't fun to live through it, but that's why I wrote these chapters. To make your detour an easier (and dare I say faster?) ride.

Drama Queen Supreme

Alright, buckle up, witches, because I'm about to blow your brain and make you hella sad at the same time. I promise it's for your own good—kinda like that cough medicine flavor they try to pass off as cherry. *You're not fooling anyone, Robitussin.*

If you find that you struggle *a lot* with keeping manifested money, there's a good chance you unknowingly suffer from an addiction.

An addiction to *drama and chaos.*

This can co-occur with actual addiction, but more often than not, it's powerful enough on its own to muck things up. You can always identify the drama and chaos addicts because they seem to have their shit together from the outside, but they're scrambling behind the scenes. They're like ducks, gracefully gliding across the water of a pond because their feet are furiously kicking below the surface.

The one thing they all have in common is the underlying fear that nothing gold can stay. They live in a perpetual cycle of anxiety and release. So much so that if something isn't going wrong, they're feeling anxious over the fact that everything seems *right*. That, of course, makes them anxious that they're anxious over nothing.

How do I know? Because I'm one of them. I've had an anxiety disorder my whole life that wasn't diagnosed until I was twenty-nine. I am *the* drama queen supreme. Here's the wild part about anxiety, though. While some people are predisposed to anxiety disorders and experience them from childhood, *everyone* is capable of developing an anxiety disorder.

Essentially, anxiety disorders are a malfunction in your brain where it defaults to sending out excess adrenaline and cortisol, the stress hormone.

That comes in super useful if you need to outrun a wild boar, but less so when you're trying to sleep and can't stop thinking about that time you farted during circle time in kindergarten and whether anyone remembers it.

And if you're *not* in any danger, your brain will find an explanation for the anxiety by looking for threats or *inventing* them.

If you lived through extended, ongoing trauma at any age—even mild verbal abuse or a bad job—your brain likely switched its default setting to an overproduction of adrenaline and cortisol. Once that switch is flipped, there's no way to flip it back off.

Even if you find yourself living in total safety and comfort, your brain is now wired for anxiety. That means it will either find justifications for the anxiety or create situations to explain it. The moment your brain experiences *chaos* that adequately justifies the anxiety, it can finally let your nervous system calm back down again.

You see this in animals all the time. Every time a dog gets spooked, starts barking at a stranger outside, or growls at noises behind the door, it releases its anxiety the moment the trigger is gone with a full-body shake.

But humans don't have that instinct to shake off anxiety once the trigger leaves. So, we manufacture situations that cause us to break down into a panic or anxiety attack, a crying fit, or violence so we can finally experience a physical release and hit that emotional zero. Only then can we finally relax from the pressure that's been slowly building inside us.

Two of the most common outlets for that emotional release are relationships and money—and I've used them both. "How?" you ask? To feed my addiction to *drama*.

Drama's Starring Role

I've noticed one main way drama addiction tends to present itself in people's lives.

Sometimes drama comes in the form of spending money to cope with the anxiety of stillness. So many people spend all their money and beat themselves up for being financially irresponsible. What they fail to realize is that it's a trauma response completely undeserving of such harsh judgment.

You get addicted to spending for the same reasons people become addicted to substances or porn. Even if it's not enough of a problem for you to consider it a full-blown addiction or compulsion, keep in mind that spending cash still releases dopamine in your brain. When you're depressed, anxious, or otherwise feeling shitty, a small hit of dopamine can feel like a sexy stranger checking you out after a year-long dry spell.

So, rather than judging yourself for spending money that's already left your bank account, maybe you can be grateful that you haven't sought out more destructive means. I say that with all sincerity, regardless of *what* you spend it on, too. You could give all your money to starving orphans or spend it on $600 bikinis and dildoes. There are worse ways to cope with trauma.

I was a criminal law attorney, Broseph. I don't judge people for getting hooked on substances that are *literally designed* to create dependence, so why would I judge people for falling victim to consumerism as a form of coping? Capitalism is *also* designed to create victims by getting us hooked on spending money.

Also, healing is never linear, logical, or perfect. Often, we latch onto spending money because we've given up another more destructive habit. To me, that's still progress worth celebrating.

Self-knowledge and new coping mechanisms are the keys to moving past our addictions to drama and spending money. If you have a recurring problem in your life, investigate the timing and triggers for those cycles just like I (unintentionally) did with my doctor regarding the fights with my fiancé.

If you feel like you don't necessarily have any repeating problems, let me assure you that you just haven't found the common denominator yet. Sit and think about the past twelve months. Write down the most memorable highs and lows from each one. Then look for patterns. Maybe every problem you have is different, but you're doing it on a four-month cycle. You won't know until you can map it out.

Once you have a full picture of the cycle you live on, mark it in your calendar. You're already living on a fuck-up cycle. You might as well give future you a heads-up on when you'll start fucking up your life again so you can plan accordingly.

Plus, knowing when you'll likely be more sensitive or reactive gives you a leg up. During those periods, ask yourself more questions around whether certain thoughts come from you or your trauma.

If you think about it, it's no different than tracking a menstrual cycle. If you know around your period you always crave white cheddar popcorn and Hershey's Extra Creamy Milk Chocolate Nuggets with Toffee and Almonds, you can set up an auto-delivery to arrive at your doorstep just as you expect the cravings to start back up.

The same goes for your cyclical money habits. If you know when you'll likely be jonesing for some drama, you can give it to yourself in more productive ways. This is actually how I started getting into horror movies and running. I found that when I'm in a heightened state of anxiety, my brain will accept both scary movies and running as acceptable explanations for adrenaline and cortisol.

Now, I'm not saying you need to sign up for a 5k with me. (Trust me, I will *never* be that friend.) But you *do* need to find your own outlets. A longtime client and friend of mine has a weekly emotional breakdown. She sits on her bed, rocks back and forth, and listens to a playlist of sad music until she starts sobbing. After about twenty minutes, the anxiety lets up and she feels much better. Whatever gets you your kicks.

If you enjoy meditation and visualization, you can create a safe space for yourself inside your mind, making it as vivid as possible. Think of it like Sherlock Holmes's mind palace where he stores memories and information. This is called resourcing, a tool used in addiction therapy.

You can invent the loveliest room, house, park, whatever imaginable, and call to mind the person who feels like the most comforting, accepting, least judgmental person in the world. You can let them hold and reassure you in this place until you feel centered.

They don't even need to be someone you personally know. You could hug and cry it out with Jonathan Van Ness while he does your hair and tells you in the mirror, "Let it out, you gorgeous queen. We love a sensitive Sally."

No matter what you do, if you learn to sit with difficult emotions, feel them, and experience a physical release, you won't feel the same pressure to seek out drama or a semiannual clearance sale to calm your nervous system. Instead, you'll just directly calm your nervous system.

Meet Yourself Where You Are

If you haven't figured it out yet, the main lesson you need to learn when you're struggling to hang on to manifested money is that you need to meet yourself wherever you are in your journey without denial or judgment.

What I mean by that is you need to accept that for whatever reason, you are not manifesting the full result of what you want and accept that, for the time being, you need to embrace that quote from *Mean Girls* and "stop trying to make fetch happen—it's not going to happen."

When you decide the universe isn't giving you that dream life right now for a reason, it frees you to set new intentions that feel more believable and take new actions that are more achievable. The funny part of all this, of course, is that by scaling back your goals and actions, you're more likely to reach *and surpass* them.

Before we get into how to do this, let's talk about why it's important.

The first truth you need to accept is that if the universe is withholding something from you, it's probably because you're not ready for it yet.

I mean that literally.

My very first coach asked me this question, and it's one I ask all my clients now.

"If someone gave you a check for $10,000, how would you feel after the excitement wore off?"

Generally speaking, people who are manifesting in these unpredictable waves usually feel some form of nervousness or self-doubt. Their immediate thoughts are around a fear of losing the physical check, spending it all in one place, or that they don't deserve it.

Those are all thoughts of someone who isn't ready to receive huge amounts of money.

Someone who feels ready and deserving of receiving big payments isn't intimidated by those big numbers. They know with certainty how to manage it and trust themselves to do so responsibly.

Think about it: People for whom those amounts of money are not unusual are accustomed to spending and receiving those figures. And most of the time, those levels of transactions became commonplace because those people got really good at managing whatever money they started out with.

Some people can feel that level of self-trust right away. Others need to work their way up in waves of money manifestation so they don't overwhelm their nervous systems.

Working your way up is also important because those who are caught in the manifest-and-bust cycle tend to make decisions based on unrealistic levels of best-case-scenario thinking. It sounds a little something like this:

"Now that I've manifested some money, I'm going to sign up for that coach/program/course. Yeah, I have some debt and my savings are pretty slim, but I *know* this is the answer to getting some viral success. I'm confident I'll make the money back fast enough to pay it off. You need to spend money to make money, right?"

"I really need an assistant/cleaner/whatever and I *love* [Name]. The monthly payment is a little steep, but I had a good month! I can at least afford enough to get started. Once they're working for me, I'll have so much free time, I can really devote myself to making more money. They'll pay for themselves."

"Wow! It feels so good to finally have a nice chunk of money in my bank account! Now that I have some disposable cash, I can afford to buy some new clothes, get a haircut, and update my running shoes. I'm manifesting the money I want, so I can ease up a bit and treat myself a little."

The problem with all of these examples is that the person is assuming that nothing will change. This upswing in income is here to stay. They've flicked on some magic switch and now their income is safe from fluctuation. "It's only up from here!" they think.

Except money doesn't work that way, even when you have a consistent paycheck. Life still happens, which means unexpected expenses *will* pop up and they *do* pop up every month. Like Murphy's Law says, "Anything that can go wrong will go wrong, and at the worst possible moment."

I know that sounds depressing to the people stuck in the have-it-and-lose-it wave. No one wants to have their bubble of optimism popped. Being realistic feels like a needle big enough to vaccinate a hippo. Isn't manifestation all about believing in magic and that great things are on their way? How could it possibly be beneficial to assume you're not going to keep manifesting this much money?

It's beneficial because for those natural optimists, thinking like a pessimist *works* when it comes to finding balance and stabilizing your finances.

If you've lost the money in the past after manifesting a big chunk of cash, you know there's a pretty solid chance you're going to lose it again—whether on purpose or not. When you plan like *you know* you're going to lose your money, your plans will probably reduce either the *chances* of losing it or the *effects* of losing it.

The truth is that your highest, best, most stable month is not your average—just like your lowest month isn't your average either.

Your average is the amount that exists somewhere between your highs and lows. That's literally the definition of the average. So, it's common sense that if you can keep your expenses lower than your average income, you can start building and getting accustomed to financial stability.

In my favorite budgeting software, YNAB (pronounced WHY-nab, short for "You Need a Budget"), they automatically give you an expense category called "Stuff I Didn't Budget For." That's because they know that while you might not have an expensive emergency every month, you *will* have stuff you didn't budget for.

That could look like setting aside money for a haircut and color only to have it come out $60 more expensive than you planned. You could budget for an Uber to an event only for it to be a rainy day that has them in demand, so you wind up paying $40 instead of $25. These aren't huge emergencies, but they add up over the course of the month. Assuming that you'll have unforeseen expenses or that you'll make mistakes—and that those expenses or mistakes could eat up all your extra income—is how you protect yourself *from yourself*.

If you fail to account for your perfectly normal human behavior to overestimate how long extra money will last you, you're setting yourself up for a sharp ride down that money manifestation wave.

When I lived in my wishful planning manifestation wave, more money meant more wiggle room. I could finally buy a new bottle of my expensive moisturizer or pay a little extra to my credit card debt. The issue is that I would always have shit I forgot to budget for or unforeseen expenses that would ruin even my best, most carefully calculated plans.

I remember sitting at my desk in total shock a few months after I made the most money I ever had in one month of my business—$26,000 in sales and $14,000 in cash. I took the opportunity to buy a desk, invest in a new coach, and sign up with an expensive financing company to make my services more affordable for potential clients. You gotta spend money to make money, right?

Well, I couldn't keep up with the payments with that coach so we had to suspend our sessions for a while, and *none* of the potential clients who needed financing could qualify for it. I wound up canceling the financer four months later and eating the $495 "setup" fee and four installments of the $49.95 monthly membership fee.

Once I accepted that I lived on this wave, I saw the big sale months as opportunities to create more of a cushion for myself. I learned to let my money sit in my account. If I still felt tempted, I would transfer it to an external savings or checking account so I could see a balance that made me feel broke without spending it to get there. Rather than reinvesting in all the courses, coaches, and certifications I was thirsty for, I prioritized the stabilization of my wave.

Even when I had big, pay-in-full clients come through, I didn't pay extra toward debt or spend much outside my monthly budget. Rather, I kept earmarking the money for future bills. Whenever deposits were slow from a holiday weekend or I went a month without signing a new client, the money already sitting in my account managed to cover all the bills until those deposits hit my account. Trust me when I say that nearly losing all your money right before a delayed deposit hits your account is a much smoother flavor of stress than when you run out of money thanks to overspending.

So, if there's a moral to the story, it would be this: The less time you spend shaming yourself over your inability to resist spending, the more time you have to create solutions for those habits.

Now, I'm not asking you to give up on your dreams for financial stability and overflowing wealth. I would never! After all, I had a book deal on my manifestation list for *five years* before someone gave me the chance to write it.

Instead, what you're doing is loosening your grip on the end-goal. By using shorter-term, bite-sized goals to help stabilize your wave, you're essentially following bread crumbs that lead to the candy house you imagined from the outset.

I've used a similar example before but it bears reusing in a new context.

Let's say you want to earn $150,000 in a year through a business. That would break down to about $14,000 before taxes each month. If you've only ever made $5,000, making that jump is going to feel *huge*. However, if you decide you want to try for $6,000—only $1,000 more—that will feel *much* easier. You might even overshoot that goal, which would really get you feeling confident. You might get such a confidence boost, in fact, that you feel comfortable setting a goal for $10,000 the month after.

Yet even if you didn't and only ever increased your monthly income goal by $2,000 a month, as long as you hit those goals, you would make $204,000 by December 31—crushing your goal for the year *and then some*.

Compare that to the crushing weight of needing to make $14,000 *right from the start* and running the risk of not hitting it. When you're in the make-it-and-break-it wave, I would always encourage you to set a lower, more achievable goal that you *actually reach*. You'll sail out of the mess so much faster.

The Iceberg to Your Money-Magic Titanic

Sometimes losing money happens in a way that runs the risk of creating such a deep sense of shame that it can throw you onto a seemingly unending detour on the road to manifesting wealth.

What could possibly pull so much weight?

Getting scammed.

Well, getting scammed and losing money, *literally*. As in you physically lost cash or a check that you can't replace.

Is there anything more awe-inspiringly embarrassing than those two experiences? Probably not. And that's exactly why they pose such a threat to your money magic and manifestation journey.

It's too easy to beat yourself up for getting scammed. You shame yourself for not knowing better, not doing your research, not listening to your intuition, or just being vulnerable enough that you let someone manipulate you.

If shame is one of the main cinder blocks our brains use to build prisons that prevent us from taking actions they perceive as risky, then a single scam or money loss could easily build the solitary confinement wing.

And if you get scammed or lose money while on a money manifestation journey or after performing some dedicated money magic? Oof, that's going to raise some questions in your mind, too. Mainly, "How—and why—the fuck did this happen?"

I hate to say it, but scams are basically just giant tests-slash-lessons. Think of them as massive neon signs from the universe, trying to get you to pay attention to one or more major ways you're not honoring yourself, living in alignment, or taking the right actions.

Yeah, it sounds like bullshit to me, too, but it's the best explanation I've got. Rest assured that most people get scammed or lose money one way or another in the course of their lives. You're far from alone. I've even been scammed before. I've paid $500 for bullshit psychic readings that were clear scams from the start but that I didn't clock in time. I've bought expensive products that seemed like a buy that would give me swagger and were of course garbage, immediately falling apart and, of course, nonrefundable. I've paid for expert advice I could have gotten from a fortune cookie, and I've bought courses that I could have written before I attended. It happens to the best of us. Losing money through careless action (theft, irresponsible spending, miscalculations in what commitments can cost) can feel just as triggering, but just as with scams, you're not alone.

It Happens to Everyone

Regardless of whether you've lost a bunch of money you just made, got scammed into buying fake Bitcoin, or accidentally returned a book to the library with your cash bookmark tucked into it, I want you to know that this kind of shit happens to everyone at some point in their lives.

In fact, some reports show that highly educated people like doctors and lawyers are some of the most common targets for fraudulent investment scams.[1] Why? It's because they literally think they're too smart to get scammed. When someone can successfully pass themselves off as an expert, smart people are just as likely to get conned as anyone else.

If you doubt it, just look at Bernie Madoff.[2] He ran the greatest Ponzi scheme in history, eventually pilfering *$68.4 billion*. The only reason he got found out is because he told his sons that his prestigious wealth management firm was actually a giant pyramid scheme. They almost immediately reported him to the FBI, who arrested Madoff the next day.

Madoff sat on the board of a *governing agency* that recommended policing policies within the financial industry. He was the chairman of *NASDAQ*. Does it get more legit than that? Apparently not for Kevin Bacon and Kyra Sedgwick, two of his more famous victims.

Not only did Madoff hold himself out as an expert, but he also manipulated people into joining and staying inside his investment firm.

He purposefully targeted golf clubs and Jewish congregations because he knew that people trust the judgment of their peers. If anyone asked questions about his investment strategies, he threatened to kick them out, thus creating massive amounts of FOMO.

That all sounds shady when you say it back-to-back like that, but most people didn't know about a fraction of what was going on. Plus, a few people *did* earn more money than they invested. It was all easy enough to dismiss.

So, if you can accept that smart people and celebrities can get scammed without looking down on them, maybe you can cut yourself some slack, too.

There's even a psychological benefit to that. People who forgive themselves for losing money are less prone to get scammed out of it again. It's only when you feel desperate to recoup losses fast and rebuild your reputation that you become *more* likely to invest in offers that make empty promises of big, quick returns.

I would venture to say that goes for all those coaches and business investments you want to make but can't afford as well. If you can forgive yourself for paying into coaches and courses that didn't get you the results you wanted, you're less likely to invest in any more of them out of desperation, which will naturally make your investments more intentional.

If you're not sure what it means to stop shaming yourself and move on from whatever experience caused you to lose money in the first place, move through these steps to see if it helps you get to the other side.

First, let yourself feel like shit. You can't move past the shame, grief, anger, or other emotions if you don't let yourself feel them. I once needed to sob and then weep for several hours over having money stolen from me before I could even think about cracking a smile. The longer you push away those emotions, the harder it will be to make real progress.

Second, talk about it to your least judgmental, most loving and supportive family members or friends. At the time of the $500 psychic scam, I confided in one of the friends who had gotten a reading that day only to find out the same psychic pulled that exact stunt on her! At the time, *both* of us were attorneys. My friend had planned to spend the money and changed her mind when I told her what happened. Not only did she comfort me, but she really drove home how believable the psychic made it all sound. Whether we were both suckers or whether it was convincing was beside the point. I felt better and so did she.

Third, give yourself some love. Self-care is often one of the best ways you can nourish yourself and provide comfort. If your mind and body are in a state of panic, you can meditate, rest, take a bath, journal, go on a walk, or anything else that will serve as an act of love toward yourself. Focus on creating a feeling of peace inside your body, and you'll find it much easier to look at yourself in a kinder light.

Fourth, ask for help when you need it. It's always better to process with someone if you feel yourself obsessing over negative self-talk. Don't be afraid to bring it up with a therapist. After all, they're literally paid to listen and *not* judge you. Whatever you've been through, it's probably not even the weirdest thing they've heard *that day*.

Fifth and finally, pay attention to your thinking and shift it whenever possible. For example, what if you looked at forgiving yourself for money lost as a form of abundant thinking? Money is energy. That means it can flow back into your life just as easily as you lost it. I've definitely made back the money I've lost in scams and carelessness multiple times over in the past decade. With time, you'll earn back whatever you lost, too. I promise.

Debt

The last mindset shift we need to move out of our wave-based manifestation results is around debt. I don't care how much of it you have or how you got it. By the end, you'll realize that no matter what, you are still worthy and deserving of having lots of money.

As of July 2022, the average debt per American adult is $58,604, and 77 percent of American households report owing some type of debt. [3]

The U.S. Federal Reserve reported that, collectively, Americans owe a total of $1.57 trillion in student loan debt and $787 billion of credit card debt alone. If you add in auto loans and mortgages, that adds up to just under $15 trillion in debt.

That doesn't even include the 100 million Americans with health care debt![4] A quarter of them owe more than $5,000, and one in five don't believe they'll ever repay it.

Owing money is widespread and deadly. Financial stress is one of the leading causes of suicide attempts.[5] Someone with a high debt-to-income ratio is *twenty times* more likely to attempt suicide.

That's why I need to address this issue—not only to keep debt from sabotaging your money magic but also to ensure that it never impacts your mental health to such a degree.

As I'm sure you know by this point, shame is the emotion that most often takes a financial situation and turns it into a big, ugly roadblock on the way to abundance. Hopefully by now you also understand that shame, while a completely valid emotion, is not exactly useful. I know it's easier to say than feel, so let me put your mind at rest.

First of all, I'm still in debt. Here I am, writing a book about how to magick your way to gobs of money, and I have $52,660.83 in consumer debt. I'm on a monthly repayment plan with the IRS for forgetting to pay $8,000 in taxes for my second year of business. I'm facing a little over $280,000 in student loans from a *now-defunct* law school. My credit score is just barely out of the toilet at 605.

Those numbers used to embarrass me. They made me feel like a fraud. How could I teach people about fiscal responsibility, increasing their income, and money magic when my debt-to-income ratio was that bad? Even if I made $20,000 every month, I wouldn't have much to show for it until I could dig myself out of that hole.

Unsurprisingly, that mode of thinking made me feel *less* motivated to figure it out. Instead, I focused on trying to increase my income as much as possible. As we now know, focusing on making lots of money *fast* often leaves you open to investment scams as you seek to recoup your losses. Well, I might not have been scammed, but that's part of the reasoning for how I wound up with that debt in the first place. I invested in coaches and courses to make my business successful.

It wasn't until I finally took the steps I needed to confront my debt and begin chipping away at it that it hit me: My debt made me *more* qualified to coach and consult on these topics.

Does anyone want to learn how to make money from a trust-fund baby? Doubtful. If you really want to learn how to manifest abundance, start a successful business, or get your finances in order, you want to do it from someone who started from a similar place as you.

It's just like hiring a personal trainer. I'm not signing up at LA Fitness to work with a twenty-two-year-old named Gabi whose waist is the same circumference as my left thigh. I want to find the trainer who birthed three kids, ran their first marathon after forty, and knows that past a certain age, hangovers last a week.

This is how I'm now able to bring this information to you, dear readers. Because I'm digging myself out of the hole I dug and I'm doing it without even the tiniest shred of shame. When I see how much debt I have, I'm reminded that I managed to pay it down by almost $8,000 in six months. When I see my "fair" credit score of 605, I remember when it was in the 550s at the start of the year.

All shame does is get in the way of action.

You know that saying, "What would you do if you knew you could not fail?" It's time to start asking yourself, "What would I do if I weren't ashamed of my debt?"

For me, the answer was to call my credit card companies and ask for help, call my friends who were good with money and ask them for help, book a call with a financial advisor and ask her for help, and hire a CPA to help me figure out my taxes...and ask her for help.

That's how I realized that my shame wasn't just blocking my belief that I could get out of debt. It was also blocking me from asking for the help I needed.

Deciding not to sit alone in that shame and be honest with people who were in positions to help me put me on a different path. It allowed me to at least *picture* the light at the end of the tunnel, even if I couldn't see it yet. In the end, all of that information made its way into this book.

So, if you've been beating yourself up about anything we've covered so far, now is your chance to make peace. Because the longer you cling to that shame, the harder it will be to see your way out.

Remember, spending money is often a coping mechanism. If you used debt to regulate your nervous system or process trauma instead of abusing substances or people, then you probably didn't do as much damage to your life as you could have. Can you find gratitude for using this method instead of something worse?

Maybe gratitude feels out of reach. That's understandable. It's all too easy for us to beat our past selves up for not knowing any better.

But if you can look at amassing debt as a phase of financial growth, it's easier to find compassion.

Do you shame yourself for falling down when you were learning to walk or ride a bicycle? How about beating yourself up for jerking a driver's ed teacher around your first time in a car? I'm guessing you probably don't even remember those moments. They were natural parts of growing up.

What if you looked at your debt as one of those moments you fell down while you learned a life skill? Could you find some self-compassion then?

Also, it's not like financial literacy is widely taught in schools. Many people learn about money from their caretakers or from, you know, living life and fucking it up.

Just because you're in an adult body doesn't mean you're expected to have equal expertise across the full spectrum of life skills.

Six months ago, I put a bunch of old soup down my garbage disposal and accidentally made enough rotten baby food to fill a kiddie pool. I had to panic-scoop it out of the sink before the maintenance staff showed up so I could lessen the embarrassment. Then I stood there feeling like a ding-dong while a guy named Justin with too much hair gel and a diamond earring explained that you can't put solids down the garbage disposal.

I look at my debt the same way. I didn't know how to handle my debt, so once I learned how, it was embarrassing to look back at all the cringey decisions I made. But I'm not going to make myself feel bad about it anymore because that's not productive and only hurts the progress I'm making. You, too, need to free yourself from your shame so you can grow, learn, and earn.

Show Me the Money (Magic)

- **Ride the wave.** Some people naturally manifest money in a wave because their fear of losing money is so deep that the only way to break it is to lose money over and over again until they realize it always comes back.
- **Chaos addiction.** Sometimes people feel so uncomfortable with safety and peacefulness that they become addicted to behaviors that ensure they're never stable. People who experienced trauma or developed anxiety disorders find chaos more predictable and safer than stability and success—because they've never experienced either for an extended period of time.
- **Spending as coping.** Addiction to chaos and drama can often manifest as overspending or avoiding finances altogether. Both are trauma responses. If you manifest money in waves, your best bet is to shift your goal from wealth to *stability*.
- **Stop trying to make fetch happen.** When you accept that you're manifesting on a wave, you can plan your expenses better. Rather than functioning from a place of hopefulness, you can plan realistically and feel pleasantly surprised if you overperform. This insulates you from mismanagement while strengthening your ability to believe that you can achieve your money goals.
- **Ditch the shame.** Whether you've been scammed out of money, lost money due to carelessness, or amassed a ton of debt, shame only keeps you distracted from taking action and finding solutions to create your greatest financial life yet.

ACTIVITIES

- If you've been caught in a cycle of making and losing money, break it down right now. List out the times when you lost money and the circumstances going on in the weeks before. Do you see any patterns?
- Review your last year. List out your high and low moments—regardless of whether they're financial. Do you see any patterns around timing?
- Look at your big money magic goals. Can you break them down into smaller goals to focus on that would be easier to achieve? How does it make you feel to focus on that instead of the original, loftier goal?
- What financial misfortunes have you been beating yourself up over? If you had to identify a lesson that came from them, what would that be?
- Anytime you feel tempted to shame yourself over your debt, remember that a past version of you dug that hole out of pain. Put your hand on your heart and send some love to that version of you right now. Close your eyes and tell them, "It's OK that you're coping in this way. I'm here now and I'll take care of us both. I love you even when you make mistakes because I can always fix them."

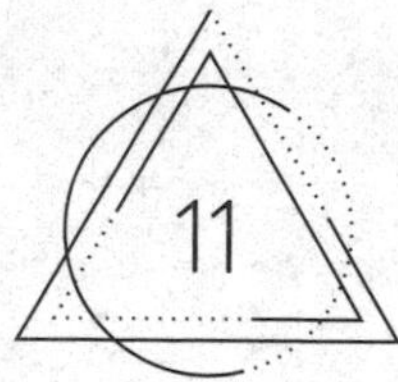

Strengthening Your Nervous System

Just as we broke our big goals down into milestone steps that would allow us to make progress toward the big vision we have for our dream life, we need to create an in-between step for embodiment.

For example, when you decide to become a runner, you don't jump off the couch and try to run a 5k right off the bat. You train your body for that over the course of a few months. You'll start with interval training where you mostly walk, but with one-minute bursts of running in between. Gradually, the running intervals increase while the walking decreases and eventually you're able to run that entire 5k with no problem.

Think of this chapter as your guide to interval training. If you're getting inconsistent results in your money magic or manifestation practice, scale it back. Focus instead on how you can test the limits of your nervous system so you can raise the baseline for the level of peace and blessings you can tolerate.

It will take some time, and you'll definitely have moments where it seems like you've reverted to old coping habits like self-sabotage, spending, or something else—but that's OK. It's all a part of the process. Just as a rubber band snaps back to its original size the first few times you stretch it to the max, so will you. Eventually, the rubber band will loosen up a bit and become capable of holding more. It's the same with people.

And to use the running example one more time, everyone has bad runs now and then—even seasoned runners and Olympic athletes. Sometimes you've slept like shit, you're menstruating, or your feet are sore from a pair of unsupportive work flats the day before. Sometimes we skip runs, even if it's not a rest day. It's all a part of running.

So, even when you feel like you failed or backslid into old habits, *you are still manifesting*.

If you're able to identify what you're doing and why, that's already a huge step up from the old version of you. That's worthy of celebration, in my opinion.

Energy Leaks

Often when people are riding their manifestation wave phase, they're confused and stressed. They've spent all this time reopening childhood wounds, journaling and crying, visualizing their next level, finding role models, casting spells, getting excited about initial results, and it feels like they're continuously winding up back at square one.

Naturally, they look back at everything they've done so far and wonder, "Did I do something wrong?" as if their chocolate soufflé didn't rise.

Well, money magic is a bit like baking soufflés. Some people have such natural confidence in the kitchen that their first soufflé comes out perfect. That doesn't make them better chefs. It makes them freaks of nature. Just kidding. *Kind of.*

It's easy for soufflés to fall flat because there are so many different scientific reasons for why they might not rise. But no amount of examination of the old soufflé will guarantee that the next one comes out perfect enough to appease Gordon Ramsey. The only solution is to keep making soufflés and learning from each one.

On the next attempt, you need to pay attention to the common fuck-up points that happen in the soufflé-making process and be brave enough to accept that your soufflé might collapse again anyway. To quote food writer James Beard, "The only thing that will make a soufflé fall is if it knows you're afraid of it."

The same goes for money magic and manifestation. Looking back at what you've done so far, searching for the misstep or where you didn't do something harder, faster, stronger, or for longer is not going to get you the answers you need. All you can do is keep moving forward and look for the fuck-up points.

I refer to these places as energy leaks. They're all these small ways that you're killing your own money manifestation boner without realizing it. You're literally leaking your magnetic energy through all these places where you're settling for less than you should.

In Part 2, we talked about hacking your environment to support your next level. This is basically another version of that, except it might not be as obvious as the first time you attempted it. It's the difference between noticing a pebble stuck inside your sneaker versus one stuck in the cracks of your soles.

You'll feel that internal pebble *right away*. With the other one, you might not notice it for a while because you're focusing on other stimuli like the beauty of nature around you, stimulating conversation with a friend, or the true-crime podcast keeping you hypervigilant every time you pass a fat tree. Only once those stimuli are gone will you realize, "Hey, wait a second, I'm feeling something *annoying* under my foot," and stop to check the bottom of your shoe.

For me, it was pens.

A few months after moving to DC, I realized I couldn't stand any of the pens in my apartment. They all seemed to come from hotels, conference swag bags, and law firms. You know the type. They're clickable ballpoints made of that cheap, light plastic, and you have to press so hard into the paper to write that you might as well carve your grocery list into the cardboard backing of your notepad.

I realized I *hated* them. I cringed inside every time I picked one up to write anything. Why did I even have them?

Because I always had. My parents didn't buy themselves nice pens. They collected free pens, too. When we needed pens for school, we would get the cheapest BIC ballpoints available during Florida's tax-free week at the Walmart back-to-school sale. Who gives a shit about *pens*?

Turns out, I do.

So, I rounded up every single crappy pen I couldn't stand and donated them. I went online and bought a pack of my then absolute favorite pens, Staples brand OptiFlow in blue ink. I put a couple in my work bag, a couple in my purse, a few in my pen cup, and left the remainder of the box in a kitchen drawer.

From that moment on, I never allowed a cheapo pen into my home again. When my pens ran out, I ordered more. When Staples discontinued my pens, I found equally good replacements. As it turns out, journaling and making to-do lists is a lot more enjoyable when you're not thinking about how much you hate your writing utensils.

The reason I didn't do this before was because I had much bigger issues than pens.

I lived with a hot-and-cold boyfriend whom I had to beg not to break up with me about every three to four months. I had a job that wasn't fulfilling in a super-conservative environment that didn't suit me. I drove a crappy car that kept breaking down and eating up all my money. Thanks to that, I didn't have enough money to actually do anything fun. The last thing on my mind was how it felt to write with the pens in my house.

Once I adjusted to a new normal with a job I loved in an apartment with a gorgeous view of my dream city, the smaller things I'd overlooked took on more weight. When I replaced all those small nuisances, I was in a more relaxed state that allowed me to better receive inspiration on what the next steps in my manifestation journey would be.

So, if it's been a while since you started your money manifestation journey, now would be a great time to reassess. What's low-key eating at you these days? Literally sit down and write a list. If any of it is within your control, this is your chance to change it. One small leak doesn't pose a threat to a ship, but *lots* of them do. *You'll be surprised at how much energy and inspiration you have when you plug up all the small ways that your energy is leaking through the cracks in your life.*

Sometimes our energetic ships aren't threatened by a ton of small holes we've learned to ignore, but one *massive* leak we failed to notice because it played into familiar dynamics and hid in plain sight.

For example, it could be a close friend who's slowly become a toxic presence in your life over time. It's always hard to come to terms with the fact that someone with whom you share a lot of memories and good times isn't worth keeping around anymore.

I know from experience. I had a close friend I made during my time in Tallahassee who took me in after I was dumped by my ex and had to move out of our apartment less than a week later. She rallied our small friend network to move my stuff into storage. Later, she sold my furniture for me while I looked for a job and apartment in DC.

Despite repaying the favor when she joined me in Washington and I housed her until she found a job and a place to live, I could never shake the feeling that I owed her closeness for coming to me in my hour of need.

And even though we had plenty of fun times, there was an increasing number of instances over three years where she would talk shit about me to our friends, set up situations to test my friendship, and be downright mean to my other close friends when she met them. If I didn't act the way she wanted me to, she would pick a fight over how I was being a bad friend. Meeting my now-fiancé made it even worse.

But when things were good, we had the *best* times—gut-busting laughter, ride-or-die loyalty, trashy bar outings, low-key leggings nights, deep conversations, and so many other shared interests that make a friendship worth keeping. When there's so much good in a relationship, how do you decide it's not worth trying to fix anymore?

For me, it came when I saw the headline on a news article that said something like, "Study shows that friendships lasting longer than seven years last a lifetime." In the split-second it took for me to read it, my first thought was, "I can't let this relationship reach seven years."

That shocked me. We had been in a good place. I wasn't actively hurt or angry. We had recently bought plane tickets to take a trip to Phoenix together. Why would that be my instinctual thought?

So, I began working it out with my therapist.

"Would you make friends with this woman if you met her today, knowing exactly how the relationship would be?" she started.

"No, definitely not. None of my other friendships are this difficult," I said.

"You told me that you kept her at arm's length until she helped you after your breakup. Why was that?"

"Well, she told me a couple stories about how two separate best friends of hers abandoned her once they met their now-husbands. It's kind of how I think of people talking about their exes. If they shit-talk them, I assume they were probably more at fault than they're letting on."

"What made you change your mind about that?"

"I don't know if I did. It's more like she swooped in and helped me so much, and I was really grateful. I feel like I owe it to her to be a good friend."

"But you let her stay with you, right? You already repaid her kindness. Why do you still feel like you owe her almost two years later?"

I had to stop and think about that. She never *said* anything to indicate that she believed I still owed her. Even if I had that impression, I had no evidence for it. When I said I didn't know, my therapist pushed ahead.

"Does this friendship remind you of a relationship you have with anyone else?"

I recalled the most common emotions that came up with this friend. After a moment, I told my therapist it reminded me of my dad. My dad would *not* stop treating me like a teenager, despite the fact that I was thirty years old and had changed so much over the years. Although we had managed to find a new respectful dynamic, that had only happened recently.

Before then, whenever I would make decisions he didn't agree with or try to set boundaries, he would immediately try to make me feel like I was being disrespectful or a bad daughter by listing out all the sacrifices he ever made for me and all the ways I had wronged him or caused him shame. Of course, all his go-to examples were over a decade old.

I felt as if I was always trying to get him to see that I was a good kid who didn't deserve everything he heaped on me—not then and definitely not now. Meanwhile, he seemed to think his consolation prize for sacrifice and love was the ability to treat me however he wanted.

I wasn't OK with that and decided that if he couldn't accept it, I just wouldn't play along anymore. I learned the power and freedom that came from not giving a fuck if you piss off your dad. If he tried to use decades-old stories to shame me, I would warn him that I was going to hang up the phone. And if he continued, I would hang up. Eventually, he learned to stop.

I explained all this to my therapist, who didn't miss a beat.

"What are you trying to prove to this friend?"

I thought for a second.

"I guess I'm trying to prove that I *am* a good friend."

"Why is it important for her to think you're a good friend?"

"Because I don't want people to think I'm a bad friend."

"Well, do your mutual friends believe her when she says you're not a good friend?"

"No. They all just tell me what she said to them and how messed up it was."

"So, who are you worried she's going to tell?"

That took me another moment to reflect.

"I guess other people? Maybe her other friends who don't know me or future people she meets."

"So, just to clarify, you're worried about what she's going to tell a bunch of strangers about you that you'll never meet? If you can stop worrying about what your dad thinks of you, why would you worry about what strangers think of you?"

It was the perspective shift I needed. I realized that it actually had nothing to do with my friend and everything to do with repeating a familiar dynamic leftover from my dad. I hadn't noticed that it had become toxic because I was used to having at least one relationship like that in my life. If it wasn't my dad, it would be a romantic partner. It was as if by ending the dynamic in those two major areas of my life, I needed to find a new person to step in.

I didn't notice the friendship was toxic because that dynamic was hidden in its familiarity like three raccoons in a trench coat.

While I had learned to identify warning signs of toxic relationships in dating, I couldn't yet identify them in friendships. It's not like my friend looked like my dad, agreed with him on anything, or shared any of his obvious qualities. The moment I saw it, though, I couldn't *unsee* it.

Just like I decided that I wouldn't let it bother me if my dad got upset when I set boundaries or expressed myself, I did the same with my friend. I had tried making my words as palatable as possible for long enough. Now, I would say them respectfully and naturally and let her react however she was going to react to them.

Of course, it didn't take long for her to have a strong reaction. A few days later, we got into a yelling match over the phone before calming down, talking it out, and discussing boundaries. But at that point, I couldn't see the friendship as a net positive anymore. I had come to see it for what it was, and with *no other friendships* in my life that difficult, I knew this wasn't worth salvaging.

About two weeks later, I sent a text after a tense night at a friend's going-away party to ask if we could take some time apart. She said if I needed time apart, then I could consider our friendship over. I didn't argue and I let her go.

I woke up the next day expecting to feel a sense of loss or grief, but it never came. Instead, I felt relief. A mutual friend told me that after a few days, my now ex-friend said she felt relieved not to have me as a friend anymore as well. We had both been caught in a toxic cycle that wasn't serving either of us anymore.

I had spent so long ignoring my own discomfort in that friendship because I was desensitized to the toxic dynamic we had. It took an outsider like my therapist to see the connection between two seemingly unrelated people in my life.

You might not have a dynamic on this level of toxicity, but sometimes the reason we're unable to connect with our greatest lives and money blessings is because we've been desensitized to living in constant discomfort or dissatisfaction. We simply don't realize how miserable we are.

What's even trickier is that me saying this might not even help you see if you have one of these relationships in your life. So, I'm going to advise that you ask someone whose opinion you care about if they can see any areas in your life where you're recreating unhealthy dynamics.

And keep in mind that if you feel an immediate urge to punch them in the face, they're probably right. Lizzo's right: truth hurts.

If you don't have someone like that, conduct an inventory of your relationships. Go through the people you spend the most time with or talk to most frequently and list the common emotions you experience after speaking with them.

Do you really want people in your life who often make you feel shitty?

Clearing the small and big energy leaks from my life made it much clearer to me the other ways I felt like my life wasn't aligned. Ending that friendship, especially, gave me time and space to reflect on my career. Soon, I realized I had also grown tolerant of a toxic boss and fallen out of love with my job.

When I was preoccupied with shitty pens and friends, it felt like I never had extra time or space to think about whether my job *still* felt fulfilling. Now that I wasn't distracted, I could see that the way I made money resembled the same feelings of settling I had with my pens and that friendship.

I began networking soon after, and by the end of the year, I was on the cusp of getting hired for a brand-new role at a nonprofit I loved. Plugging the energy leaks meant I could sail my ship to new waters *faster*.

You're Not the Average of Your Friends

While you're already reevaluating your relationships, you might as well take this opportunity to look extra closely at all the people you spend time with in your life.

I'm sure you've probably heard the saying, "You're the average of the eight people you spend the most time with." While I understand the point they're trying to make, I don't necessarily think that statement is true or fair.

It sounds a bit consumerist to me, as if the people around us should be useful rather than loving and accepting. Plus, if we put all our stock in that saying, we would be dumping friends and family left and right because they weren't inspiring us or helping us get ahead in life. That's just not how I roll.

Instead, I would say that you're the average of the eight *information sources* you expose yourself to the most.

That can include friends and family, of course, but it also includes your therapist, teachers, social media, the news, TV shows, movies, books, podcasts, and all other forms of information you can think of.

So, maybe you're a young adult in a phase of life where you and all your friends are still trying to figure out what your passions are and in what way you want to be successful. Just because your five closest friends are in the same position doesn't mean none of you will rise above. At least, not if you spend significant amounts of time gleaning inspiration from other resources.

My brother Joe is a fantastic example of this. When he was in high school, he fully planned on working in professional sports, an industry that can be difficult if not impossible to break into when you don't have any contacts—and believe me when I say we didn't have any.

But, like me, Joe has always been a dreamer and that never stopped him from thinking he could do it. Starting in the seventh grade, Joe began working part-time at the local minor league baseball team's stadium. He started by manning the pitching game and a bouncy castle outside the stadium on game days in the summer. When he got a little older, the manager hired him to clean up the locker room. Once he proved himself there, he was given a uniform and became an official bat boy.

All the while, he read—almost nonstop—books about the business and sports industries, including biographies of managers, businesspeople, athletes, and more. He filled his head with exposure, getting as close to his dream as possible from the beginning.

When he went to the University of Florida, he studied sports management and got involved with the university's Athletic Association, taking whatever gigs he possibly could. He volunteered to do fundraiser phone calls, he worked the parking lot during baseball season, anything that would get him noticed. When they posted opportunities for professional sporting events within Florida, he signed up for those, too. He worked stints at NASCAR and PGA events alike.

My parents, out of love and concern for a stable future, feared that he was unrealistic in his goal setting. They constantly begged him to take the LSAT, apply to law school, and consider becoming a sports agent because at least he would have a degree to fall back on. He's always been close with my parents, so the conflict weighed on him and he would call me to ask if he was doing the right thing by not listening to them. Since I was in law school at the time, it felt easy to validate that he was on the right path.

"Law schools will always be around. You can always go if sports don't work out," I would explain. "But if you go straight there, you'll always wonder what would have happened if you tried."

So, sophomore year of college, he hit the digital pavement. He began applying to every internship possible. He applied to almost every professional sports league, all of his favorite teams, teams in cities he was interested in exploring, and more. He cast a wide net, knowing at least part of getting one of these exclusive summer internships was a numbers game.

And his number got picked!

He was tapped for a summer internship with Major League Baseball in New York City. Between scholarship money and our generous aunt, he was able to spend three months at his dream job and he milked every moment. He met as many people as he could, always sending thank-you notes for any advice they were able to spare. When he left, he already had an offer to return the following summer and, later, another internship lined up after graduation.

He was able to move from that internship directly into his first job at the Washington Nationals where he started in special events and eventually moved into sponsorships. He was there when they won the 2019 World Series, qualifying him to buy his very own World Series ring at twenty-six years old.

After the pandemic, when he was ready to shake the dust off his cleats, he got a job in sales at the Miami Marlins that nearly doubled his salary. Now, he has the job of his dreams, driving an Audi, attending cool conferences, enjoying paid work travel, pitching multimillion-dollar deals, and more.

To others, he probably looks lucky, but I know better.

He's a money magic warlock whose belief is so powerful, he can literally manifest anything he wants. All he needs to do is find proof that he can have it, envision it happening for him, and put the work in to get it.

Yet if he *didn't* seek out that proof and his only influence had been small-town friends or my parents, it would be a different story. He might never have dared to think that he could make it into the industry. He would be another person who called it a dream and left it at that, assuming that without the industry contacts, he could never make it inside.

That's why I don't say you're the average of the eight people you spend your time with, but the eight information sources. Joe's friends were just *one* of those eight. My parents were a second. The other six were books, interviews, contacts, podcasts, and anything else he could expose himself to that showed him his dream was not only possible, but *inevitable*. That led him to experiences, which only strengthened the belief that he could do it.

So, if you feel like your money magic journey is sputtering, look to where your inspiration is coming from. If your friends don't show you that what you want is possible, it doesn't mean you need to ditch them. Rather, you need to identify *at least* seven other sources of inspiration to show you that what you want is not just possible but *inevitable*.

I mean it when I say your inspiration can come from anywhere.

After I submitted the proposal for this book, but before I knew if the publisher wanted to pick it up, I binge-watched all six seasons of *Younger* to make sure I would feel like the approval was a given.

If you're not familiar, *Younger* was a Freeform TV series about a young-looking fortysomething struggling to get back into her career in publishing after eighteen years as a stay-at-home parent. So, she passes herself off as twenty-six and gets hired in an entry-level job at a large fictional publishing house.

Obviously, the show is far-fetched, and not just because of the premise. It's a sensationalized and totally implausible depiction of the book publishing industry. Thankfully, your subconscious doesn't care about logic or realistic thinking. And the only reason I watched it was because almost every episode featured people getting unrealistically high book deals.

Unrealism aside, *Younger* showed me passionate editors who did everything they could to get the authors and books published if they loved them. It not only kept my anxiety at bay, but also left me with a rock-solid belief that my book deal and eventual success was *inevitable*.

So, if you're manifesting money as an entrepreneur, maybe you need to watch more *Shark Tank* or shows where investors help people make their businesses profitable. If you want a new career, see if you can find books or movies with characters working in your field or at least living the kind of life you want. Entertainment can be inspirational when you use it with *intention*.

That's the secret to finding your sources of inspiration. It doesn't matter if it's all serious industry experts or a cheesy sitcom. If it gives you a calm sense of "It's only a matter of time before I get this," then it's worth counting as one of your consistent sources of info and inspo.

If at First You Can't Receive, Try, Try Again

While we're talking about receiving money, we might as well talk about the downswings on your money waves.

Sometimes we get in our own way when it comes to manifesting money because we aren't comfortable receiving it.

I know that sounds *laughable*. Obviously if you're reading a book about manifesting money, you would be more than happy to receive it!

Receiving is more about an energy of openness in all areas of our life. When we're struggling with inconsistent results from our money magic, it's often because we're trying to control *how* money comes to us—and that's just not something we can do. All that's within our control is asking for it and *receiving* it.

For example, my client Courtney came to me because she hated her job and wanted to start a business, but wasn't sure what kind she should pursue. She spent three months playing around with creating different offers and doing market research, but still hadn't landed on anything that she felt was a "fuck yes."

Regardless, she told me and the others in my group program that she felt like she had the confidence she always needed to leave her job at the end of the month. We celebrated! Courtney had *arrived*! She felt motivated to make a change and to trust herself to figure everything out once she had the time.

Well, after a few months, I followed up with her to ask how she was. I hadn't noticed any social media about a business or anything else. I admit I was more than a little curious.

Courtney told me she was still at her job. I was surprised when she had been so excited about leaving. That's when she told me that within a week after our last call, her boss called her into a meeting, told her that he knew she had been covering the work of two people while they were short-staffed, thanked her for sticking it out, and *tripled her salary*.

"So, yeah, I decided I would stay on longer, build up my savings and pay down some debt. Since then, I've paid off $32,000 in credit card debt!" she said.

I could *hardly* contain my shock and excitement—and it must have shown. She jumped in to tell me that she never expected it, but she specifically remembered that I always said you can't predict *how* money would come to you, and you shouldn't have to. So, that's exactly what she did.

Even though she decided to stay with her job longer, the compensation suddenly made the work worthwhile again. Because of that, she said she knew that starting her business would be much easier once the time came for her to make that move.

What allowed that money to come through was Courtney releasing her attachment to *how* the money needed to show up. For so long she had been focused on knowing exactly what she needed to *do* to make money through a business. She obsessed over whether it was the right business idea or if anyone would buy it. When she stopped looking at *how* she could make money and instead focused on trust, the universe sent the money she asked for.

Another client of mine, Erin, experienced something eerily similar. Erin signed on in June 2021 to work with me for six months with the goal of quitting her full-time accounting job at a nonprofit by December.

Nearly two months in, she was severely struggling to balance a busy period at her job while scaling her business. She had issues with her boss, a coworker driving her nuts, people dumping work on her without warning, and then an annual event she needed to provide support for. Meanwhile, she was worrying about how she could keep up with the increasing demand in her business and what she could do to make more money without expending a ton more time.

Finally, she paused for me to respond.

"Why don't you just quit?" I asked.

"What?!" She definitely wasn't expecting that.

"You said you have savings to cover your expenses for like seven months, right?"

"Right."

"So, if your job is causing you *so* much stress that you're struggling to keep the passion alive for your business, and the only thing holding your business back right now is your lack of time, then why not quit? Give them your two weeks' notice."

"It's not really about the money *per se*. I would disappoint so many people. I would definitely be leaving them in a tight spot."

"Haven't they been leaving you in a tight spot for years?"

"Well, yes..."

"Then that sounds like the consequences of their own actions. Listen, if your business went tits up, would you want to go back there to work?"

"No."

"And do you have another colleague familiar with your work who could serve as a reference if you needed it?"

"Yes."

"Then why do you care if they get upset with you?"

She thought for a second. "I guess I don't."

By the end of that call, Erin had decided to sleep on it. After a couple days, she told me she was ripping off the Band-Aid. She would wait until after their big event to give her notice. She wouldn't have the full year's worth of expenses saved up that she wanted, but she felt calm about leaving if it meant choosing between the passion she saw as her career and just a nine-to-five job.

Except she never even had the chance to resign. Her boss was so appreciative of how hard she had been working that she surprised Erin with a raise and a $10,000 bonus—and just to remind you, this was a *nonprofit*. Erin had never gotten a bonus from her job *ever* before in the more than five years she worked there. She chose to stick it out until her original planned departure.

After our work together finished, Erin told me that when she eventually gave two months' notice to her boss, her boss was *ecstatic* for her and gave her a whole pep talk about how now was the time in Erin's life to take a chance on herself. It all worked out even better than she imagined. Now, her business is booming and she's living her best life. I just talked to her the other day and spent ten minutes complimenting how clear, dewy, and radiant her skin looked. She answered, "I guess that's what happens when you're living your authentic life!"

Erin tells this story whenever she talks about the process around leaving her career behind. She said the moment she realized she didn't need to follow the exact plan she had for *how* the money could flow in through her business was the moment she felt open to alternative money blessings.

Neither Courtney nor Erin expected to make the money they were manifesting through the full-time jobs they were planning to leave. But the reality is that we can't control *how* the money comes. Often, obsessing over *how* we will receive money is blocking the pathway for it to find us.

If you sit and think about everything you have control over in your financial life and money manifestation, generally your list will look something like this:

- How I spend my time
- What I think

- What information I consume
- My actions
- Setting my prices/negotiating my salary

Now, if you write a list of what is *not* within your control, that sounds more like:

- When my manifestations arrive
- How they come to me

When you think about the universe/Spirit/God as your partner in money magic and manifestation, you're essentially hiring the ancient, cosmic force to manage the list of what is *not* within your control. And you couldn't have picked anyone better for the job because the universe/Spirit/God is a timeless energy controlling the when and how of all reality since before it began. Which begs the question:

Why are you trying to micromanage a cosmic being?

You cannot do God's job better than they can. *Let it go, bro.*

Instead, use that critical eye to investigate yourself. Look for signs that you might struggle with being *truly* open to receiving money. I've noticed that people who find it difficult to receive have the following traits:

- **They can't take compliments.** They either get embarrassed or make derogatory comments about themselves in response like "Oh my god, *no*, I *hate* my voice! That's so funny that you like it." They need to learn how to say, "Thank you" with sincere gratitude and pride.
- **They can't accept help.** People who are ultra-independent don't have room for assistance from the universe. The universe doesn't show up on our doorsteps with a gift box. Instead, it sends people

to help us. When you turn away help, you're telling the universe, "I don't have needs because I can meet all of them myself."

- **They can't accept gifts, tips, or charity.** Early in my business, an old friend said she wanted to help me get started in my business and booked a job-hunt coaching session with me. For the entire hour, I felt like every suggestion I had, she responded with, "I've tried that." I felt like I wasn't helpful, so when she asked how much she owed me, I told her she didn't need to worry about it. But the entire reason she booked was so she could pay me. Even if it wasn't a mind-blowing call, I still gave her a solid hour of my time that I could have used for someone else. By turning down her offer, I communicated to the universe, "I do not need payment for my time."

  I've seen this happen with people when older relatives try to give them money and they turn it down. First of all, we always want to show the universe we are open to receiving money from anywhere. Second, and this is just a little personal advice for you, it's never about the money. Older relatives can't provide the same kind of care and usefulness they did when we were children. Sometimes giving you gas money when you visit is another way for them to say, "I love you."
- **They feel uncomfortable when their pleasure is prioritized.** Yes, I mean sexually, but not *exclusively* sexually. These are the people who struggle with questions like, "Where do you want to eat?" "What do you want to watch?" or "What do you want me to do to you?" They've become so accustomed to not prioritizing their own needs that it's almost too much when others want to center their pleasure in any way. When you can't receive consideration from someone else, you're telling the universe, "Please don't prioritize what I want. I'll take what I can get."

At the end of the day, all of these—compliments, help, gifts/tips/charity, consideration—are small manifestations from the universe. The universe uses small, nonmonetary blessings to gauge your level of self-worth in the same way it uses tests and triggers. And just as with those, your actions matter far more than your words do. The universe takes everything you do literally, so pay attention to what your actions are communicating.

If you ever read the children's book series Amelia Bedelia, you'll know what I'm talking about. Amelia was a terrible servant who had never heard standard terminology for chores, which seems like a severe failure for whatever sort of training program she attended. So, when the lady of the house asked Amelia to draw the drapes in the living room, Amelia would literally sit down with paper and pencil and draw the drapes.

Each book would detail all the ways Amelia failed at her job by taking everything as literally as possible. I know the whole point of the book was to teach those phrases to children, but even at seven years old, I felt bewildered that she was still gainfully employed.

My friend Corbie Mitleid, a professional psychic for over twenty years, likes to say, "The universe is a short-order cook with no imagination."

It always makes me laugh to think of the example.

Imagine you order a cheesy omelet, bacon, and orange juice. When you get your order, you see a plate with a cheesy omelet and bacon *drenched* in orange juice. Would you eat it? No way! You would send that shit back to the kitchen and ask for a cheesy omelet and bacon with orange juice on the side in a glass.

The universe is reading your order literally. It doesn't know if it got the order totally right unless you take action to send it back. It sees the new order and says, "Oh! They wanted the orange juice on the *side* in a *glass*? Well, how was I supposed to know that?"

Literal actions, babe. It's the name of the game.

Show Me the Money (Magic)

- **Life leaks.** Every low- or high-grade annoyance in your life pulls on your energy. Add them all up and you have a recipe for depletion. Plug up those energy leaks and watch how much energy you bring back into your life.
- **Average Joe.** You're not the average of the eight friends you spend the most time with, but of the eight information sources. Consider your friends and family as two sources. If you fill the rest of that list with media showing you that what you want is possible, it will be that much easier for you to get it.
- **Receive to believe.** If you want to speed up your money manifestation journey, make sure you're accepting whatever blessings *do* come your way, even if they are as small as a compliment or offer to help. The more willing you are to accept small manifestations, the better your chances to receive larger ones.

ACTIVITIES

- Take inventory of all the things in your life that are stressing you out. Can you make any immediate fixes? If you can't find them, try asking a friend or colleague you trust to tell you where they see you holding yourself back.
- What are your eight main information sources? How do they make you feel about your potential to reach your goals? Do you need to replace any?
- Do any of the common receiving blocks feel relevant to you? Where in your life can you open yourself up to more blessings?

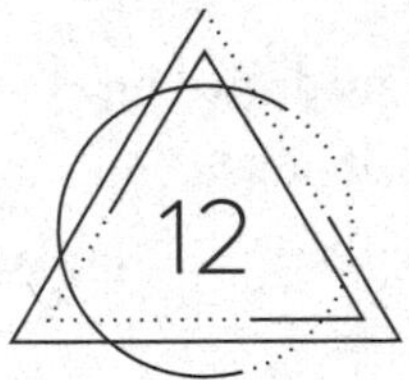

Holding Yourself Accountable

So far, we've been nice and comfy talking about how to blame external sources for your problems with manifesting consistently. But by now you know I love a little torture, so it's time to discuss the ways in which *you* are the source of all your problems.

Specifically, we're talking about the need for setting some boundaries with yourself.

Now, when personal development gurus discuss boundary setting, it's often in the context of other people—how to stop people pleasing, how to get your boss off your back, how to develop a less codependent relationship, and so on.

All of that is incredibly important, especially if it's impacting your money. You can't allow yourself to get pulled away from your personal finance goals to make everyone around you happy.

Rarely, however, do they talk about ground zero for boundary violation: yourself.

Am I the Drama?

How many times have you made promises to yourself and not followed through? I bet if you think about it, you could name at least five promises you've made to yourself that you broke this week. They probably sound like:

- I'll run tonight. I want to sleep for another hour. Plus, it's too hot this morning. I don't want to pass out.
- I'll log my work hours tomorrow. I want to beat rush hour traffic. Plus, I told my partner I would come home earlier.
- I'll stop reading in an hour. I can't leave off on a cliffhanger. Plus, I've been saying I wanted to read more.

You'll see that when we break promises to ourselves, we'll generally give two reasons for it: (1) The real reason why we're making our choice, which usually sounds like a great impression of a giant, whiny baby. (2) A perfectly logical, justifiable reason that anyone could agree with if you told it to them—and if they don't believe you, you would happily submit to a lie detector test because it's not like it's *un*true.

You and I both know the truth. You're never actually following through *solely* for that noble second reason. It's all about the first one. And the reason it sounds so much like a giant, whiny baby is because you *are being* a giant, whiny baby.

By now you know that your inner child is alive and well inside your psyche. Well, when you have these knee-jerk moments to break promises to yourself, it's no different than when you were a kid refusing to get up for school or eat all the broccoli on your plate.

The difference is that you don't have an external parent to remind you that all your friends are at school waiting to see you or that broccoli makes you grow big and strong. Instead, you have your adult-ass self. And your adult-ass self is *terrible* at self-parenting because it feels every pang that your inner child is experiencing. You are, after all, the exact same person.

That's why it's easier to enforce a bedtime for the kids in your life than it is to stop playing Level 118,233 of *Candy Crush*. When real kids whine, you have the perspective of the wise adult who knows that when they're well rested, they're less feral. When your inner child whines, you're the pushover who would rather be well liked, even if your inner child is an asshole the next day.

It makes sense. Like the ol' saying on procrastination goes, "Procrastination is like masturbation. It feels good, but in the end, you're only fucking yourself."

It's also why you continue to manifest money inconsistently—because you're inconsistent!

I understand this more than anyone else. Procrastination defined my entire life. I was the child who told her parents on a Sunday at 5:00 p.m. that the science fair was tomorrow. I saved all my college papers for the week they were due and pulled all-nighters until they were done. I never packed for a trip more than an hour before leaving for the airport.

So, when I tell you what you need, please know that this is Jessie-tested and Jessie-approved.

What you need is intentional rest and radical honesty.

Intentional rest is exactly what it sounds like. This is where you consciously indulge yourself. You purposefully do all the shit you guilt yourself over wanting to do—sleep in, eat crap, ignore your work, binge-watch TV, play on your phone, scroll on TikTok past the alerts that tell you to take a break, and so on.

The difference is that you *decide* to do it rather than mindlessly defaulting it to pass the time.

For example, I love playing *Settlers of Catan* on my phone. I could literally play that shit for hours *and I have*. The big difference, however, is that I do it consciously. Sometimes that looks like setting aside an hour or two to play without guilt. Sometimes it means when my fiancé asks what I want to watch, I'll say, "You pick, but pick something I don't need to stare at the whole time because I really want to play Catan on my phone."

The reality is that when you purposefully set aside time for things you crave, they stop becoming taboo. This is the same logic that psychologists have used to help people with binge eating disorder (BED). The only way to unlearn binge eating is to eat as much as you want of your so-called "bad" foods whenever you want until it finally clicks that you can have them anytime you want.

When I deconditioned myself from orthorexia and BED, I ate so many bags of white cheddar Cheetos, it was unreal. I literally bought four bags at the grocery store each week *just for myself*. I ate them all day, sometimes for breakfast, and I never forced myself to stop. If I ate an entire bag, then I ate an entire bag. I needed to truly learn that white cheddar Cheetos were *abundant* and could be a permanent fixture in my life.

If you think I got sick of them after a month, you would be incorrect. I *was* able to stop binge-eating them, but I still love them. The difference is that I'm able to snack on them—straight out of a family-size bag if I want—and stop after a couple fistfuls. One of those bags that I would eat in a sitting could last all week. I've even had them long enough to go stale.

I had to go through the same thing with all the other off-limit foods I had until I fully believed that I was allowed to have them whenever I wanted. The fact that I found about a quarter of a pint of ice cream in the back of my fridge with freezer burn would honestly have shocked me five years ago, but it literally just happened.

It's the same thing with the addictive activities we use to procrastinate on. You need to be willing to indulge yourself as much as you want until the activity loses its appeal. You need to recognize that it's not going anywhere and you can indulge in it anytime. When you *plan* for it, it naturally makes you more committed to doing the shit you initially didn't want to do. Your inner child has already been satisfied.

When it comes to radical honesty, that means you're going to stop using Very Reasonable Reasons to explain why you're breaking promises to yourself.

Now that your guilty pleasures no longer have guilt attached to them, you don't need to justify them. If you want to leave work instead of catching up on your time sheet, you're literally going to say to yourself, "That's not a priority for me right now. I would rather go home and scramble to get this done tomorrow."

And unlike all the other self-help gurus who want you to say it so you can shame yourself into getting things done, I'm telling you that it's OK. "I don't want to" is a perfectly justifiable reason to *not* do something.

However, if you say that and you realize that you *don't* actually want to scramble tomorrow and that sounds *worse* than going home right now, this would be a great opportunity to change your mind.

When you become more honest with yourself, it becomes a lot easier for you to be honest with other people.

Boundaries with others often sound like "no" or "maybe." Boundaries with yourself sound more like a delicious game of "Would you rather?" where both options sound enticing.

- Would I rather sleep for another hour and feel cozy for longer or work my body and feel strong and productive?
- Would I rather get home faster so I can take my pants off or finish my time sheet so I can leave earlier tomorrow?
- Would I rather keep reading and find out what happens now or save it to liven up my boring commute tomorrow morning?

This is a perfect example of how to romanticize your life. By making decisions about what to spend your time doing moment to moment, you turn your life into win-win situations. Everything suddenly takes on a more positive approach. How could making money ever feel rote or boring when life is so delectable?

What to Do When You Don't Wanna

Of course, sometimes we need to do things that we struggle to get excited about. Maybe it's doing the tax calculations for your business. Maybe it's cleaning the cat's litter box. Maybe it's writing a term paper. How do we turn those into deliciousness?

We don't. Rather than fighting it, we become intentional with our time. Put your phone on airplane mode, set a timer for twenty-five minutes, and for the entire duration, try to get as much of the shitty task accomplished as shittily as possible. Perfection be damned!

That means if you're writing, you aren't going to read what you've written, try to make it sound good, or fix typos. Instead, you work the entire time without stopping. If the timer goes off and your task isn't complete, set a timer for a ten-minute break. Once it's done, do another twenty-five minutes of nonstop work. Repeat until your task is done.

I know this one works because it's the only reason you're reading this book right now—not because I didn't enjoy writing it, but because I spent a long time hemming and hawing, worrying about how far I had to go and whether it would be any good. Eventually, I had to throw out the overthinking and perfectionism and just do the damn thing. That's what editors are for anyway, right?

When you're able to take that imperfect action to move yourself forward, it becomes more believable that you don't need to be perfect to receive money. Instead, you know that it's as simple as deciding *which way* you want to enjoy your life *or* taking messy action to get some pretty dang good results.

There's another saying among neurodivergents and psychologists that "anything worth doing is worth doing half-assed." That means if you don't have the will to shower, washing your face is better than not washing anything. If you can't bring yourself to brush your teeth, rinsing with mouthwash is better than skipping it altogether. If you can't make a sandwich, eating all the components of the sandwich separately is better than not eating.

It's the same thing with your money. If you're not ready to budget, checking your bank account once a week is better than ignoring it. If you can't bring yourself to apply for jobs, asking a friend to look over your résumé and cover letter is a perfectly acceptable start.

The same goes for when you've been putting off activities you need to do. You can always set a timer and send as many networking emails as possible in two twenty-five-minute sessions so your brain doesn't have time to talk you out of them. You're bound to surprise yourself at how much faster you can receive money when you prioritize action over perfection.

Gettin' Kinky wit' It

Have you ever considered the idea that maybe some part of you *likes it* when you fuck up your financial life?

That's the basic concept behind the premise of Carolyn Elliott's book *Existential Kink.*[1]

You might remember this book from Chapter 6 when I spoke about deity work and my personal journey with understanding Kore/Persephone, goddess of spring and queen of the underworld. That story of the duality of lightness and darkness in all of us sets the stage for the foundation of all Elliott's work, which she calls "existential kink."

Essentially, her theory is that there's a fucked-up part inside all of us that loves to suffer. Just like those in the BDSM community who get off on inflicting or receiving pain, she argues all human souls *desire* painful experiences.

The way I explain it to people is that our souls are essentially on earth to study abroad. We're not human bodies with souls; we are souls experiencing life in a human body. Because our meat-suit spaceship lasts a much shorter time than our cosmic, ageless soul, we want to experience *everything* we possibly can while we're on earth. We don't just want to visit! We want to ingratiate ourselves into the experience of what it means to be human.

Imagine if an alien asked you what it was like to *be human*. If you only spoke about love, bliss, orgasms, laughter, and tacos, would they get an accurate understanding of human culture? Would that even be an accurate description of your life? I'm guessing not. As much as we might not want to admit it, to be human is to also suffer. To fully convey the human experience, you would need to talk about a lot of unpleasant topics, too, like anxiety, systemic oppression, menstrual cramps, grief, and people who don't wear deodorant at outdoor music festivals.

Our souls crave those painful experiences because they make the high points so much sweeter and, according to Elliott, we're just kinky like that. We have a fetish for pain and our souls are just trying to get their fill.

Therein lies the magic of what she recommends.

Rather than avoiding the pain, she encourages you to relish in it. You must dive headfirst into a painful experience and let yourself feel it all over your body as if your lover were dripping hot wax onto your nether regions.

Only when you can wholly and willingly turn yourself over to the experience of that pain can you see exactly why you want to experience it.

The truth is that we all get some benefit out of the low points of a wave-based money manifestation journey. Plenty of benefits are attached to money loss and chronic brokeness.

If you're broke, people often pay for you if you can't afford to eat out with them. They give you money, they give you *stuff*, and, the most exquisite of all, they give you *attention*. Even if they're bitching at you for all the money you owe them or worrying about what you'll do to dig yourself out of the hole you dug, all the focus is on you. On some level, it can be a delicious, powerful feeling to know you wield so much influence over someone's thoughts and emotions.

When you pinpoint exactly what you're getting out of your pain, that's when you can finally let yourself enjoy it.

During one of the low points of a money manifestation cycle, I remember paying the last bill I had and seeing my bank account hit dangerously close to zero. Rather than crying or stressing as I had in the past, I exclaimed aloud to myself alone in my office, "Ah, yes! The *deliciousness* of being broke! People can feel *bad* for me. My sister might even buy me presents to make me feel *better*! Ahhhhh, I can finally relax. I have nothing left to lose."

I put my hand on my heart, closed my eyes, and imagined how upset my fiancé would be if I didn't make enough money fast enough to pay my bills next month. What if he left me? I let the feeling of white-hot shame and fear pulse through my body and zeroed in on exactly where I experienced sensations. And I just sat in that activation, feeling completely electric.

Rather than dragging my feet the next day, depressed about the money prospects in my business, I was able to show up with excitement. I felt like an underdog again who had to fight her way back to the top. Could anything feel more inspiring? I was going to do what felt impossible!

It reminded me of an anecdote I read once about Lady Gaga.

Apparently, whenever she gets ready to write and record a new album, she takes down all her platinum albums and hides all her awards in the closet. She gets rid of all evidence indicative of her music success and pretends she's starting all over again. She pretends that what will likely become another hit in an incomparable discography is *her very first album*.

If Gaga can lean into underdog energy and use it to power her empire, you can, too.

So, the next time it feels like your business or career is swirling around the toilet, tell yourself that you're just Gaga writing her next album. You've hidden your progress and accomplishments so you can get the push you need to write your next platinum album.

Show Me the Money (Magic)

- **Cut the crap.** It's OK to not do things you know you need to do. The more you prioritize intentional rest, the more energy you'll have for getting things done. The other secret to holding yourself accountable is to be honest with yourself about what results you want. There's nothing wrong with front-loading on rest, as long as you're honest about it with yourself.
- **Just do it.** When you can't drum up the desire to get something done that you *must* finish, set a timer on your phone and work nonstop for twenty-five minutes. If the task isn't done, take a ten-minute break and do another twenty-five-minute segment. Repeat this until your project is complete.
- **Don't kink-shame yourself.** There's a pretty good chance that you enjoy the fucked-up situations you keep getting yourself into. That's a normal part of being a human. If you can learn to embrace your lackluster money manifestation results as the manifestation of a subconscious desire, it's easier for you to feel like a powerful and successful witch.

ACTIVITIES

- What promises to yourself do you regularly break? How do you plan to be more honest with yourself about your priorities in the future?
- What guilty pleasures can you take the guilt out of by giving yourself full permission to enjoy them?
- How can you romanticize your life with either-or scenarios?
- What benefits do you get from the chaos in your financial life? How can you let yourself enjoy these fucked-up experiences?

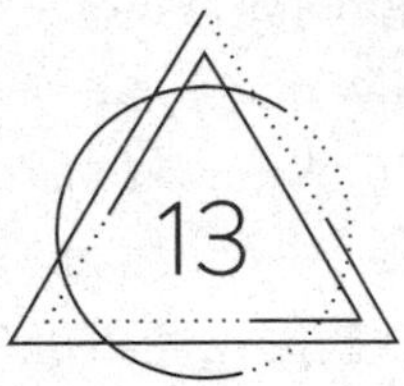

Practical Magic for Keeping Money

When it comes to finding ways out of your financial wave cycle, you need to accept that it requires you to truly engage with your finances in an active way. That means you need to have a plan for building stability that aligns with your goals.

Too many people think that building stability is all about woo-woo practices to calm your nervous system. By only focusing on spiritual practices, they wind up making their cycle worse by not building balance with how they use their money.

That's why the most important task for stabilizing your finances is breaking the paycheck-to-paycheck cycle.

You've probably heard the term before, but just in case, living paycheck to paycheck is when all of your income is eaten up by the time your next paycheck comes. One emergency that would use any money outside of what you already pay for is enough to put you in financial crisis.

Unfortunately, this is the way I would say most people live. I know I did until I got serious about breaking out of my feast-and-famine cycle.

But to do that, I needed a plan that was different from what so many of the financial gurus were describing as ideal.

It felt unrealistic to think that I could only spend 25 to 30 percent of my income on rent in the dystopian real estate landscape we live in. And does anyone *actually* have the discipline to set aside 10 percent from every paycheck into savings? I sure as hell didn't. I still don't.

So, instead of relying on my own self-discipline, which is next to nonexistent, I've learned to turn my financial strategy into a game by aging my money.

How Old Is Your Money?

"Aging your money" is a concept I learned about from using my favorite budgeting software, YNAB. (I swear they aren't paying me to name drop them. I just love them that much.) My absolute favorite feature of their software is a number in the top right-hand corner of the screen indicating how many days old my money is.

The idea is that when you spend less money than you make, your money ages. When you can pay your bills based on money that was left over from previous months, you're not actually paying your bills with your current income but with older money.

It's such a simple way to incentivize and explain budgeting. And because YNAB automatically tracks your income and spending, it's able to accurately calculate how old your money is based on that data.

How I do this is, at the end of the month, I take whatever money is left over and start dividing it up for the bills I expect to come through the following month.

For example, let's say it's the 28th of the month, all my expenses have been paid, and I'm not expecting to spend any money before the first day of the new month. I'll take whatever money is left and start earmarking it for the bills I know are due within the first two weeks of that new month.

As money comes in, I continue setting it aside for my expenses, which doesn't just cover bills, but spending money, too.

This takes a little while to build up, so be patient with yourself. I started this practice when I had less than $100 left at the end of the month. I would figure out what the next or most important bill would be in the next seven days and budget whatever money I had toward it.

Yes, this did involve a little bit of restriction for a month or two, but you'll be surprised at how much progress you can make when you decide to turn it into a game. I got competitive with myself and wanted to see how old my money could get.

If you're able to get your money to thirty days old, you'll officially be a month ahead on your expenses. If you get to ninety, that means you've officially built up three months of living expenses. By aging your money, you're saving it automatically without having to transfer anything out of your account. Rather than checking your bank balance, you learn to check your budgeting software instead.

However, if you find that it's difficult to remain disciplined when the money is accessible, for example in a checking account attached to a debit card, it's OK to transfer it out. In fact, I would rather you open five or more accounts at different banks to age your money by holding it in different places so you can remove the temptation to spend it altogether.

I'm sure some people will read this and pooh-pooh it, thinking to themselves, "That's great for *you*, but I don't have *anything* available at the end of the month. This will never work for me."

Well, I have some advice for you, too. It's time for you to KonMari your finances.

Yup, just like Marie Kondo taught us the life-changing magic of tidying up our homes by getting rid of anything that doesn't "spark joy," she can teach us the life-changing magic of tidying up our finances. I can almost guarantee that no matter who you are, there's at least one subscription you're paying for that you don't actually want or need.

Going through my subscriptions was how I once found that I was paying $16 twice a month on some mystery membership called "Great Sites." I still don't remember what it was. I just know that in six months, I spent almost $200 on it. I was just grateful my bank could remove most of the charges.

There are two ways you can go through your expenses to see if they're still sparking joy for you. One is literally making a spreadsheet and going through every one to decide whether it sparks joy or calculate how many times you need to use it to make the monthly fee worth paying.

The other one is to unsubscribe from *everything* and for thirty days, only pay piecemeal. So, rather than spending $50 on a gym membership, you would cancel it and pay for daily passes. Instead of listening to Spotify or Apple Music, you would either listen to the radio or pay for individual album or song downloads like it's the 2010s all over again. If you spend more on the reduced subscriptions, you can go back to subscribing for monthly access.

I will admit that while I like the *idea* of the second one, I shudder at the level of chaos it would likely inflict in my life. My ADHD brain could not handle the added time commitment of paying for things I use on a daily or weekly basis.

The good news is that once you have this figured out and you're able to end your month with a little additional cash, you can start putting it toward other bills to slowly age your money and build stability in your finances.

When it comes to how old you should age your money, that I can't really tell you. Most financial gurus argue for three months' worth of living expenses, but some say six. I know the idea of saving up for that much in living expenses doesn't exactly sound *fun* when there are so many things we want to spend money on to realize our dream lives, so let me explain its importance this way.

Don't think of it as a safety net. Think of it as a "Fuck-You Fund."

When you have several months of disposable income saved up, you are immediately catapulted into a level of not-give-a-fuckery that empowers you to live the life you want.

Got a toxic boss who berates you in front of your entire office? Say "fuck you" by quitting and living off your Fuck-You Fund until you get a new job or start a successful business.

Did your live-in partner cheat on you? Say "fuck you" by dumping them and using your FYF to put first and last month's rent down on a new apartment.

Regret taking on a difficult client? Say "fuck you" by firing them and paying back part of their investment with your FYF so you can save yourself the headache and find better clients.

I always find it much easier to get motivated by channeling rage, even if it's over a completely hypothetical scenario that might never happen. It's like pretending to argue with someone while in the shower, even though you know you'll never say any of it to them in real life. You get to be the attorney, judge, jury, and executioner without ever engaging in any real confrontation.

So, take any shit you're experiencing, experienced in the past, or could experience in the future and use it as fertilizer to help that FYF grow. Once you have enough to feel comfortable telling people to fuck off, then you can move on to some other goals.

What Money Goal Should Come First?

One of the funniest things I've noticed about anxiety is how differently it manifests in people.

For example, my fiancé is someone whose anxiety makes him the *most prepared human* on the planet. He turns in research papers *early*. His suitcase is always packed days—if not a full week—in advance of a trip. He's always at the airport *two hours* before takeoff when he travels. When he picks me up from the airport, he always seems to pull up right as I walk out the automatic doors.

Mine, on the other hand, is the exact opposite. I would stay up for twenty-four hours before a paper was due to finish writing it. Before we traveled together, I never packed more than an hour before leaving the house. And if I feel overwhelmed by what I need to do, I shut down and completely disassociate.

That can look like throwing myself into a hobby, cleaning the house from top to bottom, endlessly researching what I know I need to do, helping other people with their problems, playing on my phone, reading an entire book in one sitting... You get the idea.

So, naturally, if I'm not sure *where* to start because I have so many ideas, actions, or goals, it's incredibly easy for it to bring me to a complete standstill.

In my time as a coach, I have yet to meet someone like my fiancé. Everyone I've ever coached falls squarely within the "analysis paralysis" iteration of anxiety.

That's why I'm going to help you figure out which financial goals you're going to go after first in order to build your stability. If I can tell you what to focus on or, at least, *how* to decide what to focus on, you have a better chance of actually taking action on it.

The absolute, nonnegotiable first financial goal you need is to set aside *at least* $1,500 in a savings account. This is the one piece of advice that Dave Ramsey and I will always, forever agree upon. The most important part of building financial stability is knowing that emergency situations do not need to be the catastrophic financial events they've always been.

And when I say emergency, I mean a *true* emergency, such as a death in the family or an unplanned medical or dental issue for you, a family member, or your pet. The average vet bill alone is around $1,500, so by ensuring you always have that money set aside in a separate account, you'll make sure that you don't wind up in a situation where you need to use a credit card and go into debt for an emergency.

You want to get this money set up as soon as you can. Ramsey says to sell as many things in your house as possible—to the point that your kids will worry that they're next—and put all the earned cash into your savings fund. It's a solid practice not only because you'll literally be decluttering your home and creating physical space, but because you'll be building momentum toward your goals as well.

I'll add to that approach that side hustles or easy, temporary gigs you could find on Craigslist or other apps would be perfect for this, too. You don't *always* need to start a business to earn side money. Plenty of people in your city are probably looking for help with random tasks like running errands, organizing their home, or, hell, folding laundry.

A friend of mine in DC decided to earn money while getting in shape by delivering for UberEats on his bicycle. I've even heard of a service where you can hire "Karens" to be bitchy on your behalf if you struggle to advocate for yourself. I've been recommending that as a side gig to more than a few of my friends.

If you can gamify it to see how quickly you can set aside that $1,500, you'll be shocked at how fast you can do it. The first time I tried it at twenty-six, I made $1,000 in thirty days, despite not having a single spare penny outside my biweekly paychecks. To say I was proud of myself is an understatement.

Also, if you *do* wind up needing to use this money, make sure that you immediately put all other goals on hold until you replenish those funds. There's no guarantee that just because you had one emergency another won't follow on its tail. Remember: Murphy's Law! What can happen will happen—and at the worst possible time.

I know that's a massive downer, so hopefully you find the next part a little more fun.

Make a list of everything you want to buy or pay for along with an estimate for how much each thing will cost. That includes everything, no matter the price. It can be a nice $10 face mask or a $25,000 wedding. No one is going to see this but you, so go balls to the wall.

The figures don't need to be perfectly exact, but they should be within reason. So, if you want to take a trip to Thailand, don't just guess. Check the rates on the types of hotels where you would like to stay, find the average airfare from your city, estimate how much fun money you need, and so on. Make it an *informed* guess.

Then, write either an S, M, or L next to each item to denote whether it's a small, medium, or large goal. In your budget, list out all your goals with the amounts and letter designation. This way, you can see them front and center as you decide how to allot your money.

The best way to decide which goal to tackle first is to ask yourself: What will give me the most pride and motivation to stay committed to my financial stability?

It seems like a simple answer, but it's one that changes.

Sometimes what gives you pride and keeps you motivated is treating yourself to a designer bag or the trip of a lifetime. Sometimes it's an investment in education or making a massive donation to a cause you care about. Sometimes it's hoarding your money like a dragon just because you can.

I can't tell you what's going to hit that pride and motivation G-spot for you—only you can figure that out. The best I can do is encourage you to throw what you think you "should" pursue first out the window.

When you focus on pursuing the goals that will reinforce your desire to continue building stability, you can set aside any judgment you might have about how you use your money. This is about the *long* game. Choices that keep you on track matter far more than whether other people would be impressed by your goals.

When You're Drowning in Debt

While we're talking about throwing "should" out the window, this is a perfect time to discuss some alternative methods for debt repayment that no other finance books even *try* to touch.

Frankly, I'm not sure why they don't. Maybe because it's not a popular opinion, maybe because people feel like it's morally superior to repay your debt as fast as possible. I don't know. What I *do* know is that there isn't one solution that works for everyone, so I would rather arm you with information so you know what else is available to you.

But first, I want you to know that there is not a single solution to debt repayment out there that you should be ashamed of pursuing. Whether you decide to put everything you earn toward debt or take a more measured approach, shame should never enter the conversation. Hell, if you need to *stop* paying on debts for a while, it's OK. As long as you're consciously deciding on a plan, rather than pretending your debt doesn't exist, you're good. Taking ownership of your financial stability means working with creditors, not ghosting them.

So, all that being said, let's discuss the alternative options.

The first is simple: *Talk to your creditors about options available to you.* This sounds so basic and silly to mention, but people are often so afraid to tell their creditors that they can't make their payments that they stop logging into their accounts, don't answer phone calls, or, much less, return any voicemails. The self-imposed shame over not being able to pay keeps people from finding solutions that could actually work for them.

But here's the thing about being so behind in your payments: you're actually the credit card company's *ideal* customer. Banks don't offer credit out of the goodness of their hearts. They offer credit as a form of *making money*. And they don't make money off of people who pay off their balance every month, never accruing any interest on their purchases.

Banks make money off of credit cards *specifically* through interest built up from not paying off the full balance *plus* late fees. If every credit card holder paid off their balance every month, what incentive would banks ever have for offering credit cards in the first place?

So, rather than hiding from your creditors, call them up like you're their *very best customer*. Your delinquency is what keeps their lights on and their salaries paid.

When you sack up and contact them, tell them the truth. Explain your circumstances and ask what options are available to you. Calling up my three credit card companies was how I learned that they all offered different COVID-19 relief plans. For six blissful months, I was able to pause *all* my credit card payments. That option alone allowed me to build up some stability in my money. By the time my payments resumed, I was in a much better place to start making those monthly payments.

Next is my favorite method for debt repayment, credit counseling.

Credit counseling is one of the best options you can pursue if your debt is so overwhelming that you don't seem to have any money left at the end of the month to pay your debt.

How it works is that you ask your credit card company for their preferred credit counseling organization and its contact info. Once you reach out, a financial counselor will ask you about all your monthly expenses and income, do some math, help you figure out which bills you can scale back, and then come up with a monthly payment you can afford.

From there, they call up your credit card company (or compan*ies*) and negotiate terms to get you that affordable monthly payment.

Now, this *will* require you to close your account with the credit card company, which will negatively impact your credit score for a bit. However, if you can't afford to make your monthly payments, your credit score is probably already shit anyway. Would you rather have a shitty credit score while you can barely breathe because of your crushing debt or have a temporarily shitt*ier* credit score that lets you make more progress toward paying off your debt?

Remember, motivation is everything in personal finance!

The best part about credit counseling is that they can roll several debt sources into one account. So, rather than paying minimum balances to multiple banks, you could make one blanket payment that the credit counselor divvies up to the banks. Your monthly payment will also include a fee for using the credit counseling service, but it's usually around $75 and factored into your monthly payment.

What's great about pursuing credit counseling is that you're essentially getting a free financial counselor out of the deal. You can call up your counselor anytime to help with budgeting or financial planning. Their entire job is to help get you fluid enough so that you can repay the bank(s) and *not* go back into debt.

I often don't like making specific referrals for products or services within personal finance because it's too easy for things to change in between writing and publishing, but this is my exception.

I highly, highly recommend GreenPath Financial Wellness. They're the de facto credit counselor for most of the big credit card companies specifically because they're so kind to their customers *and* they help those customers get out of debt for good.

Not all credit counselors are created equal, and many of them have plenty of complaints about harassing customers. If your bank prefers another credit counselor, just make sure you do your research on the company they recommend.

If you're more interested in a debt repayment option focused on expediency, you can hire a debt settlement attorney. These lawyers will call all your creditors and negotiate settlements on your behalf, arrange payments, and close the accounts. All you need to do is call them and sign on the dotted line.

The main benefit is that you'll usually pay 40 to 60 cents on the dollar to what you owe. But the main drawback is that you'll pay plenty more to the attorney than to a credit counselor. It won't be all up front. Many of these firms will offer an affordable payment plan that doesn't accrue interest for their services.

Basically, if you decide to hire an attorney to settle your debts, just do the math. Make sure that you'll be saving enough money to make this option more beneficial to you than the credit counseling route.

Finally, I want to *briefly* touch on bankruptcy. Now, I don't necessarily want anyone to declare bankruptcy, but I do think that not discussing it as an option just creates more unnecessary stigma around it. There's nothing shameful about any forms of relief as long as you know you've selected the right course of action for you.

Now, when I say brief, I mean *brief.* I can't possibly cover this all in a couple paragraphs, but I can give you enough info to help you determine if this is an option worth looking into for yourself.

Bankruptcy is the nuclear option when you have nothing else available to you. In other words, your payments exceed 50 percent of your take-home pay, you're getting sued by creditors, and/or you see *no way* to pay off your debt in five years.[1]

Two types of bankruptcy exist: Chapter 7 and Chapter 13. The main difference between the two is how they affect your debt and property. Chapter 7 will discharge all your debt, but you'll lose your assets in the settlement. Chapter 13 will reorganize your debt to make it more affordable and allow you to keep some assets like your home or car. Bankruptcies also stay on your credit for different amounts of time—ten years for Chapter 7 and seven years for Chapter 13.

Essentially how it works is that you hire an attorney to submit an application to a bankruptcy court on your behalf. The phone calls, lawsuits, and wage garnishments will all stop. Your credit score will immediately plummet, but the good news is that it should come back up within a year or two.[2]

However, the bankruptcy will impact your credit score for *years* and come up in background checks. It can affect your ability to rent, buy a home, get loans, or otherwise acquire credit.

Perhaps the biggest drawback, though, is that bankruptcy is *expensive*. You need to have the money to pay an attorney along with all the court fees. You can imagine that the costs would rack up pretty fast.

Figures that the main avenue for getting out of debt would cost money, right?

Bankruptcy might not be the best option for a lot of people, but at least it's there. If you think it could work for you, go ahead and reach out to your local or state bar association to find a bankruptcy attorney near you. Trust me when I say this is not a hobby you want to pick up in an attempt to save money.

Releasing Shame and Building Emotional Resilience

If you thought I was done with science in this book, well, *guess again*. I'm wrapping all this up with a mind-body solution that is scientifically proven to transmute shame into peace.

Sound too good to be true? I guess you'll need to try the emotional freedom technique and find out for yourself.

EFT is a type of therapy in which you reinforce positive beliefs while tapping a series of acupressure points on your hands, face, and torso.[3]

Although it's relatively new to mainstream psychology, more research is coming out regarding its effectiveness, especially for the treatment of anxiety, depression, PTSD, stress, chronic pain, and more. Studies have also found that it lowers heart rate, blood pressure, and cortisol—the

OG stress hormone. It's been consistently ranked by study participants as equally effective as talk therapy.

And, considering you can do it by yourself, it's a fantastic free resource!

Here's the most effective way to approach it.

When you're feeling anxiety, shame, or some other nasty emotion regarding money, boil it down to the belief or worry you want to work on. Rate the intensity from zero to ten with ten being the level right below a panic attack and zero being "I'm on a beach and just smoked a joint."

Then, start writing. Dump all your worries onto your paper along with every single thought that's upsetting you in regard to this money concern. Follow up by journaling on it in a broader sense. Does it remind you of any memories or people? Where did these anxieties and beliefs come from? You don't need to go *super* deep, just enough to provide some context to the anxiety you're experiencing.

Once you have that out of your system, write about all the ways you want to feel and the logic-based arguments and explanations that you *know* to be true, but don't *feel* very true right now.

When you're done, it's time to tap. I'll explain where and how to tap first before applying the statements you just listed.

These are the places where you'll tap:

- The side of your palm,
- The top of your head,
- The beginning of your eyebrows,
- The sides of your eyes,
- The cheekbones under your eye bags,
- The space between your lip and nose,
- The tip of your chin,
- The point where your collarbone meets your sternum and first rib, and
- Under your arm, on the side of your torso where a bra strap would lie.

When you tap the side of your palm, you'll do so by karate chopping it into your opposite hand. When you tap the top of your head, a flat palm or long fingers will do. For the rest of the points, you'll tap with the tips of two or more fingers. You'll want to make sure to tap each spot at least five times. For those that come in pairs—eyebrows, eyes, collarbone—you'll tap on both sides of your body. For the others, tapping with one hand is good enough.

Now you're ready to apply your written beliefs.

First, you'll begin your setup. This is where you go over all the anxieties and beliefs floating around in your head at this moment. You'll rephrase a lot of your worries to sound more accepting of the experience you're having.

For example, if you wrote, "I'm so afraid that I won't be able to make any money in my business. If I never make money, I'll never be able to leave this shitty job. I hate the fact that I need to spend eight hours a day working at something so unfulfilling," you'll rephrase it to sound like a series of statements around accepting these feelings.

- "Even if I never make any money in my business, I truly and deeply love and accept myself."
- "Even if I never leave this shitty job, I truly and deeply love and accept myself."
- "Even if I always spend eight hours a day working at something unfulfilling, I truly and deeply love and accept myself."

While you say these phrases aloud, you'll karate chop the side of your hand into the palm of your opposite hand. When you feel like you've covered all the current worries and thoughts, you can move on to tapping the remaining pressure points for the rest of the statements.

You won't rephrase these, however. You're going to engage in a type of one-on-one conversation where you speak each statement aloud while tapping. Speak one statement for each tapping point. Start with all the negative memories, beliefs, or people and eventually move your way through all the positive ones.

When you're done, pause for a moment and take a few deep breaths with your eyes closed. Then, rate your anxiety again on a scale from zero to ten. If it still feels heightened, restart your tapping process. Generally, though, this should be enough for you to feel relaxed and energized around taking new types of actions.

EFT is a great tool for any sort of anxiety or limiting beliefs, not just regarding money. Yes, it looks a little funky, but thankfully, you can do this in the privacy of your own home where you're less likely to get stares of concern. Although, I would consider giving anyone who lives with you a heads-up just in case they walk in on you and think you've finally snapped.

If you're not sure how to create your own effective narrative for EFT, you can use this one to reinforce a feeling of safety and stability.

Rate the level of your money anxiety from 0 to 10 and write your number down:

While karate chopping:

- Even though I'm afraid of spending all my money, I truly and deeply love and accept myself.
- Even though I'm afraid of losing all my money, I truly and deeply love and accept myself.
- Even though I'm not accustomed to financially thriving, I truly and deeply love and accept myself.
- Even though I'm irresponsible with my money, I truly and deeply love and accept myself.
- Even though I don't deserve money, I truly and deeply love and accept myself.

Tapping circuit, starting at the head and repeating the pattern:

- I'm so stressed out about money. (top of head)
- It feels like there's never enough to go around. (beginning of eyebrows)
- Everything I make is already spoken for. (sides of eyes)
- I suck at managing money. (cheekbones)
- I always have. (space between lip and nose)
- This feeling is exactly why I've never tried to manage my finances. (tip of chin)
- I hate always feeling so anxious about money. (where collarbone meets sternum)
- But I don't know how else to feel. (side of torso/bra strap area)
- I've always felt this way, even growing up. (Return to the top of head and repeat the sequence with the following statements.)
- I remember X.
- But then Y.
- It was like Z.
- And that's probably when I first realized that I couldn't have everything I wanted, but especially not money.
- I could have enough to cover my expenses.
- But being rich was never going to happen to me.
- Being rich is for other people.
- Rich people are bad.
- They're selfish and keep all the money to themselves.
- I don't want to be selfish, so I don't want to be rich.
- Then again, Dolly Parton is rich and she's a good person.
- She's taken care of so many people with her money.
- If I were rich, I would be like Dolly.
- I would give money away to people who need it.
- I would take care of the people I loved.
- I would follow my dreams.

- Maybe being a good person is why I deserve money.
- Because if I had money, I could change the world.
- And the world needs changing.
- Plenty of rich people started off broke.
- Some of them even went totally bankrupt.
- I've always bounced back from everything in my life.
- I'm still alive and standing tall.
- I'm resilient and strong.
- If I made it this far, I can live through anything life throws at me.
- Even if I spend or lose all my money.
- It won't be forever.
- I can always make it back.
- I can make back *even more* than before.
- I know I'm capable of doing it.
- I've taken a new approach to my money.
- I stopped being passive and started taking action.
- If I'm doing something different, it means I'll get different results.
- And if I don't, it just means I'm not an expert yet.
- But I will be!
- Everything I do, every lesson I learn, is making me better at managing money.
- That's why I'll be rich.
- This is just a moment in time.
- It won't define my lifetime's success.
- And it will make a great story on Oprah's podcast one day.

Now, close your eyes and take a couple deep breaths. When you're done, score your anxiety again from 0 to 10 and write it down. If it's a 5 or under, off you go. If it's still high, feel free to run through the prompts again or write your own!

Show Me the Money (Magic)

- **Age before beauty.** The older your money, the better. When you focus on giving every dollar a job and earmarking your dollars for future bills, you will slowly but surely build the cushion you need to start feeling safe.
- **Where to start.** If you're brand new to managing your money, you'll always want to start with an emergency fund of $1,000 to $1,500. From there, it's all up to you. If you would feel safer building up your savings to cover three or more months of expenses, that's fine. If you would rather throw everything at your debt, that's cool, too. If you want to save for a purchase that gives you something to look forward to and keeps you motivated, go for it. Follow your intuition.
- **Discharge your debt.** No matter how much debt you have, there's always a way out. Take charge of your debt instead of hiding from it. Make phone calls instead of letting your payments slide without warning. Don't be afraid to ask for help. More information will never hurt.
- **Tap it out.** The truth about living on the money manifestation wave is that it comes with a lot of emotional ups and downs. Emotional freedom technique (EFT) can help alleviate the stress and shame we carry around our finances. It involves tapping on acupressure points and speaking aloud our worries and then the beliefs we want to think instead.

ACTIVITIES

- Watch the basics videos from YNAB (You Need a Budget) on giving every dollar a job and aging your money. How can you incorporate the idea of aging your money so you can break the feeling of living hand to mouth?
- Look around your home right now and see what you can sell. Take a glance at some easy, local gig jobs. Set yourself the challenge of seeing how fast you can make $1,000 to $1,500 to put in your emergency fund. If you don't feel motivated, ask your friends to join you and turn it into a group challenge!
- If you're carrying debt, call your creditors to ask about what relief options they have available. Call a credit counselor and figure out what options might be available to you for repaying your debt.
- Try the EFT practice at the end of the chapter on your own or in the video I recorded, which you can find using the QR code at the bottom of this page. Then, practice writing your own EFT script. Use it every time you start feeling stressed about money.

Wrichcraft for Keeping Money

When it comes to magical approaches for keeping manifested money or consistently manifesting money, we're going to look toward anything that gives feelings of steadiness and/or openness.

Typically, the inconsistent nature of your manifestation comes from unstable feelings or habits. Grounding and cleansing are two of the most important activities you can do when you're in an inconsistent cycle.

That's why the deities, crystals, and rituals listed in this chapter will allow you to get in touch with that centered feeling to quiet your mind. When you're better able to get to that place, it will be easier for you to hear your intuition.

Rituals for Keeping Money

By now you know that the key to hanging on to manifested money is learning to build and maintain stability in your life. As such, the rituals that follow are all around crafting security, clearing stagnant energy, and removing obstacles.

Far more rituals than just these exist, so consider this a place to get your wheels turning. Feel free to seek out other resources or rituals that feel more aligned with what energy you're trying to build in your life.

Root Chakra Refresh

One of the best ways to build stability in your life is to give lots of love to your root chakra.

In an earlier chapter, I briefly explained where the chakras sit along your body, but what I didn't include is that they also correlate with the major nerve groupings that form the foundation of our nervous system.

The inferior hypogastric plexus is a bundle of nerves that exit the base of our spinal columns, wrap themselves around our reproductive organs, and travel down our legs. It corresponds to the root chakra, which is associated with our ability to feel safe and grounded.

This makes sense. If you didn't feel safe, the brain would send signals down these nerves to tell our legs to run. Our brains would prioritize protecting what evolution would consider our most important organs.

So, balancing this chakra is key to learning how to feel more stable internally, which, of course, will bring more stability *externally*.

Here are a few easy ways to open and balance your root chakra:

- Place your bare feet or sit directly on the earth.
- Eat root vegetables or meat.
- Lie on the ground with your legs propped against a wall or supported by a chair or other furniture.

- Meditate to consciously relax your body by tightening and releasing your muscles from the top of your head, all the way down to your feet.
- Stomp your feet or roll your feet out on a massage ball when you first wake up.
- Lie on your back and pull each knee to your chest one at a time.
- Jump, kick, jog, or do any exercise that uses strong legs.
- Incorporate yoga poses that open your hips, loosen up your back, or use your legs, such as forward fold, chair pose, yogi squat (a.k.a. garland pose), half locust or full locust pose, or bridge pose.

Focusing on creating a physical sensation of safety and stability can do wonders for promoting the internal, emotional experience of safety and stability.

Alchemize Your Bullshit Spell

This is a spell I wrote inspired by the energy of the full moon in Capricorn. This event combines the energies of Cancer and Capricorn, the mother and father of the zodiac, respectively. It's the moment when all the bullshit arising from Cancer season (or even as far back as the Scorpio full moon) starts to make sense. Finally, you see why you've been experiencing certain trials and how they will turn into lessons and blessings for the future.

This spell also draws on the narrative within the tarot's major arcana, the set of cards that don't fit into one of the four suits. As we cycle through the major arcana within our lives, we find inspiration in the succession of two cards: the Tower and the Star.

We come to learn that so-called "Tower moments"—the lowest points in our journeys—always lead to our Stars—the highest moments in our journey. The energy of this spell seeks to speed along the process that transmutes that energy.

TOOLS/SUPPLIES:

- Your altar (a table, desk, even a windowsill is fine)
- Paper (preferably origami paper, but you can also use loose-leaf paper cut into a square)
- A writing instrument

Directions

- Tidy your space for spell casting.
- Open your ceremony with a prayer of gratitude and protection to your higher power, the spirits of the four directions (north, south, east, and west), any deities you're working with, and the goddess Hecate (Heck-*uh*-tee), who oversees all witchcraft and spells.
- Swing your finger around yourself clockwise.
- Recall all the "negative" emotions you've been experiencing. Feel them until they're vivid in your heart and mind. Allow them to flow through you.
- Write down on your paper all of the shit you've been experiencing. Then, write about all the ways this shit is setting you up for your greatest future successes.
- Once you're done, fold your paper into an origami star (you can find the instructions at the link in the QR code at the end of this chapter).
- Now, while holding your star, think about all the blessings on their way and feel gratitude for the difficult moments you've had lately. Say the following refrain:

  Oh Mother, Father, hold me dear.
  Keep me safe from all my fear.
  Take my hand and lead the way.
  Give me strength on this day.

Take my tears, so wet and raw
And build a tower to inspire awe.
Give me hope to visualize.
I'll take my shit and alchemize!
From this day on
I see successes.
When things go wrong
I still feel blesséd.
I turn garbage to gold,
Just call me King Midas.
I'm bad and I'm bold
Thanks to this guidance.
As above, so below.

- Sit in gratitude for the blessings coming your way, if you feel so called.
- Close the circle with a prayer asking that your will be done with harm to none and finishing with the phrase "With this sound, my circle is down."
- Clap or otherwise make a noise to indicate that your protection circle is now closed.
- Swing your finger around yourself counterclockwise or just in the opposite direction than you did at the beginning.
- Go forth and celebrate! Your energy will continue flowing toward your blessings.

You can keep the star on your altar as a reminder that our tower moments always lead to our stars. However, if your star came out looking terrible and it's definitely *not* reminding you of beauty, you can discard it. Feel free to burn it in a fire-safe bowl and discard the ashes by burying them outside, releasing them into the wind, or flushing them down the toilet.

Getting to Know You(rself): Human Design

The newest astrology kid on the block is Human Design, a complex, self-knowledge practice that synthesizes a bunch of ancient systems into one. It includes astrology, the tree of life, the chakra system, the I Ching, and others.

To know exactly what your Human Design or "HD" details are, you need to know your *exact* birth time and place. Even a few minutes can affect your chart. If you have no way of figuring this out, you might need to hire a forensic astrologer (yes, that is a real thing) to help you reverse engineer the time based on your life so far.

While HD is known for its complexity, I'm only going to discuss the three most fundamental concepts. These will help you learn how to better interact with other people and make decisions in a way that will allow you to feel more secure and confident.

Those three aspects are your energy type, not-self theme, and your authority. These are especially helpful for manifesting money because they make it easier for us to (1) work better with our ideas and people around us, (2) identify when we're not on the right path, and (3) better listen to our intuition when we're making important decisions.

Now there are literally entire textbooks out there to teach HD, so consider these descriptions the most basic of introductions. I'm only going to focus on the most relevant points to help you live more easefully and decide more peacefully.

So, first up, let's discuss the five energy types. Your energy type explains the best way for you to function in the world—whether that's with other people, ideas, opportunities, and so on. It does so by defining your *strategy* for interacting. Let's get into the types:

- **Manifestor**—Your strategy is *to inform*. That means when you decide to take action on anything, even an idea, you need to tell people before you do it. Keeping plans to yourself oddly gets you into hot water. People seem to get offended that you didn't tell them sooner or get their opinion before you decide. This is because your energy is like a whip you can use to lasso the right people and repel the wrong ones. Walk around confident in the knowledge that you can literally speak your manifestations into existence—you just need to tell people your plans first.

- **Generator**—Your strategy is to *wait to respond*. That means you likely experience resistance to initiating or pursuing something that's not happening naturally. You like *something* to initiate, whether that's a person's request or a bolt of inspiration. And, thankfully, you're getting a constant onslaught of things to respond to from the universe all day. It's a bit like tennis practice where balls shoot out from a machine at different angles and you have to decide at which ones you want to swing. Whichever ones you pick will ultimately work out because when you're lit up by what you do, your energy feels like the sun's glow, warming everyone around you.
- **Manifesting Generator**—Your strategy is *also* to *wait to respond*. You have the option to inform others after that, but it's up to you whether you feel the pressure to speak up. If not, that's fine. One thing I'll tell you right now that will immediately make you feel better about incarnating in this world is that you are literally *designed* to be a multi-passionate person who gives up on hobbies and skills as soon as you're bored with them. That's because you only take what you need as you move through life. Your energy is like a shooting star, burning bright and speeding by people on your way to the next fun interest. Don't let anyone try to pin you to one thing, *ever*. You won't thrive in that monotony.
- **Projector**—*Our* strategy is to *wait for the invitation*. This is usually pretty annoying advice because we're the know-it-alls of HD. And

we really do know it all. The problem is that without an invitation, our advice can come off as offensive. That's because our energy is like a laser beam that connects straight with people's hearts. We can see into them, so if they haven't *asked* us for an opinion, we have a good chance of either hurting their feelings or pissing them off. The best thing you can do *instead* is share all your knowledge with anyone who *is* interested—even if that's just shouting it into the void of social media. When we show up as experts and share what we know, people are naturally attracted to our knowledge. And unlike Generators and MGs, we don't need to continually accept invitations. It's like a vampire getting invited into someone's home. Once you invite us in, we're here to stay, bitch.

- **Reflector**—Your strategy is to *wait an entire lunar cycle* before making any decisions. Yep. I know that's super inconvenient. But the unique issue for you is that it can be difficult to separate which preferences or emotions are yours versus which belong to others. Giving yourself the full lunar cycle puts you in the position to retreat and reflect in different environments and around different people. Your energy is like the moon. The moon doesn't create its own light; it reflects the light of the sun.

So, now that you know the best way for you to function in the world around you, how can you use HD to tell if you're living authentically? That is the not-self theme.

Your not-self theme is the specific emotion you experience when you do not feel like your authentic self. Get it? Hence, *not-self.*

Now, that doesn't mean you should never experience these emotions *at all*. It means that if you experience these emotions *more often than not*, you are likely living out of alignment or, in other words, "out of your design." Here are non-self themes for each energy type:

- Manifestors—Anger
- Generators and Manifesting Generators—Frustration
- Projectors—Bitterness
- Reflectors—Disappointment

The last piece of your HD puzzle for today is your authority. This is the way you are uniquely designed to make aligned decisions. Seven authorities exist, and they're designed to help you find clarity in making medium to monumental decisions.

For example, you would *definitely* use your authority to make decisions about your career, long-term commitments, or deciding where to live. You don't necessarily need to consult your authority for an invitation to brunch.

However, if you find that every time you go to brunch, you have a bad time, you can use your authority to help you determine why that is—whether it's the people, the places you're going, or other factors in your life.

Your guiding authority will be one of these:

- **Emotional**—Those of us who live with emotional authority naturally live on an emotional wavelength. That means we have natural highs and lows that cycle on multiple levels, such as over the course of a year, a month, a week, or a day. The key is that we're never supposed to make decisions in the moment. We need to wait until we cycle through all the emotions and arrive at a stable place before deciding. We are the people who always need to sleep on a decision because we automatically know in the morning. The easiest way to get people used to not getting an immediate response out of you is to answer with "maybe" instead of a straight yes or no in the moment. For example, "Maybe! That sounds super fun! Let me check my calendar and get back to you tomorrow."

- **Sacral**—Not all generators and MGs have sacral authority, but *only* generators and MGs can have sacral authority. It's most often described as an immediate gut feeling. This is almost the opposite of emotional because you *are* supposed to answer on the spot. And your choices are *only* "Fuck yes!" and "No." This should go without saying, but only say yes to things that feel like a "fuck yes." Anything that feels like a maybe is probably a no. If you struggle with making choices on the spot, that usually means the question wasn't phrased the right way.

  One way to help arrive at a decision is to ask yourself some tester questions you already know the answers to (for example, "Do I like coffee?" "Do I like white cheddar Cheetos?" "Am I 5'2"?) and only answer with guttural sounds. In English-speaking countries, that would sound like "Uh-huh" for "yes" and "Uh-uh" for "no." Sneak in the question you need to answer and you should know right away. Also, this authority can be used for decisions of all sizes. Generators and MGs who have emotional authority can default to their sacral authority for smaller, in-the-moment decisions like what they want to eat for dinner.
- **Splenic**—This is basically intuition based on fight or flight. Unfortunately, I can't really describe it deeper than that because it varies so much among people. All I can say is that when your intuition speaks on a big decision, it feels like you will die if you don't follow it. Your intuition makes everything high-stakes, and you probably can't explain it to anyone else without sounding a little nutty.
- **Ego**—This varies based on whether you're a manifestor or a projector. If you're a manifestor, this is called ego-manifested authority and it means you arrive at decisions based on talking it out. However, you're not talking it out so you can hear what others have to say. You're talking it out to hear *how you* speak about the issue at hand. So, you need to both talk aloud *and* listen to yourself speak.

- If you're a projector, it's called ego-projected authority. Basically, you can either get your dick up for something or you can't. There's no talking yourself into it. Projectors are tired folks. We're only meant to work like four hours a day. So, if the invitation doesn't get you revved up, then it's not worth getting out of bed for.
- **Self-Projected**—Similar to the ego-manifested authority, self-projected authorities need to talk things out. While an ego-manifestor could talk aloud to themselves, self-projected authorities need people to bounce ideas off. But, again, that's not to hear what the other person has to say, but to hear how *they themselves* are talking about the issue.
- **Mental/Environmental**—This is sometimes also called "No Authority." What this means is that your authority is external and based on your immediate environment. Your brain *really* wants to take over and overthink, but do not let it! Figure out first if the environment is right or wrong for making a choice—and that includes not just surroundings, but people as well. When you're in the right environment, you're safe to reflect and decide. Reflectors can use this authority for smaller decisions that can't wait a full lunar cycle.
- **Lunar**—This is the authority for reflectors, during which they wait a full lunar cycle before deciding. This gives them time to experience different situations, and that will bring up the six other authority types to help them arrive at a final choice.

Learning to live in this way can be tricky, but like most things in life, it's just a matter of practice. It usually takes about seven years for someone to get used to living in their design this way, so don't beat yourself up if it takes time. It's supposed to.

Deities for Keeping Money

As I stated at the start of this chapter, all these deities will help you to either find your center to stabilize your money magic wave or open you up to more opportunities, or perhaps do both.

These are deities who can walk the road with you and offer healing and support. Think of them as the type of friend you call after a breakup because they're equally good at listening, shit-talking, and making you laugh.

As previously discussed, plenty of deities exist outside of this list. If you feel called to another, that's totally fine. Make sure they're part of an open practice and choose the one whose energy you want to embody. You can start your work with them just by having a dedicated space to act as an altar.

Abundantia

- Roman goddess of abundance in all forms, finding inner peace around your finances, and typically shown with a cornucopia

  Colors: May vary culturally, but anything associated with money or abundance. Those are generally green, red, and gold.

  Symbols: Coins, cornucopias, milk, honey, fruit, flowers, food, grain, and wine

  Days: None that we know of, so go with any day prominently featuring money, like the deadline to file taxes or Chinese New Year if you celebrate it.

  OG myth: Hercules broke off the horn of the river god Achelous and gave it to the river nymphs. They decided to turn it into an abundance portal that constantly spewed coins and gifted it to Abundantia. No idea why, but what a nice gesture, nonetheless. She carries that cornucopia to any homes that invoke her help, and she's always happy to share her plenty. The best way for working with her is to ask her to help you be more like her—carefree and peaceful, secure in the trust that you can and *will* always make the money you desire.

Ganesh/Ganesha

- Known as "The Remover of Obstacles"; Hindu god of wisdom, success, good luck, the arts, sciences, intellect, writing, and communications; portrayed as a four-armed man with a fat belly and an elephant head with one broken tusk

  Color: red

  Symbols: Elephants, lotus flowers, and food, especially rice and sweets like modaka and laddus

  Days: A ten-day festival usually occurring around late August to early September. The first day is known as Ganesha Chaturthi. His birthday in late January to early February is a feast day as well.

  OG myth: Ganesh is known as the son of Shiva, the supreme being, and Parvati, his wife and feminine complement who split from Shiva when the earth formed. Parvati created Ganesh from her "body rubbings," so he could guard the door while she bathed. She forgot to send a telegram to Shiva about her impromptu birth, so when he got home and saw a stranger standing outside his house and barring him from entry, he did what any reasonable person would do and cut Ganesh's head off. Parvati got out of the tub only to realize her baby-man-son was murdered and she despaired. Shiva tried to undo the damage by grabbing the head of the first living being he encountered—an elephant—and popping it back onto Ganesh's body and bringing him back to life. If that's not the ultimate comeback, I'm not sure what is.

Aje Shaluga, a.k.a. Ajé, Aye, Ajé Shaluge

- Yoruban water deity of wealth, money, the economy, markets, abundance, trade, dyes, and pigments

  Colors: All of 'em

  Symbols: Tiger cowrie shells, white pigeons, fruit, water, golden treasure

  Days: Mondays and February 24

  OG myth: Aje is an androgynous deity who is worshipped as a god just as often as a goddess. Aje's most well-known myth is how they helped a woman who could not get pregnant after the fertility deities denied their assistance. Because Aje is an abundance deity, they were still capable of helping the woman become pregnant. A priest prayed and offered fruit to Aje, which successfully persuaded Aje to visit the woman and grant her request. The woman bore triplets she named Oja, Ona, and Ile. The next time Aje appeared to the woman, she gave great thanks to Aje and filled their arms with an abundance of fruit as a thank-you. Aje saw the woman and her family as deserving of more wealth, so they told the woman to poop in her fields once a month forever more. When she did, the family's crops became even more bountiful, giving them lifelong wealth and probably some sideways looks from their neighbors. Those who desire abundance but struggle with lack in *any* regard are told to pray and make fruit offerings to Aje Shaluga.

Working with these deities is no different than what I recommended in Chapter 9.

Create an altar space where you can leave offerings. If you use perishables like food in your offerings, give them back to nature when you feel like the energy has drained from them. That could be by the end of a meal or when they start to turn.

If your food-based offerings are pet safe, you can feed them to your animals or leave them out for your neighborhood wildlife. If not, you have my permission to chuck them in the trash when they start looking questionable. If you have access to composting, that would be even better.

You're also encouraged to learn as much as you can about your chosen deities so you can embody them on a more day-to-day basis. You could visit a body of water for Aje Shaluga, share sweets with Ganesh, or meditate before and after your budgeting with Abundantia. Whatever you feel called to do for your deity is usually the best way to bond with them.

Financial Stability Crystals

The last time I talked about crystals, I covered how to pick one and what you can do with it. All of that applies here. I would like to add that because many of these crystals provide a lot of stabilizing energy, they're perfect candidates for wearing or otherwise carrying around with you.

All of these crystals will promote financial stability. The best way to pick one is based on how you want to feel or in which way you could most use stability. Keep in mind that your general emotional climate is often how you attract money. When you think of it like that, it can make choosing a crystal easier.

- **Clear Quartz, a.k.a. "The Universal Crystal":** Energy enhancing, mental clarity, promotes balance and alignment, neutralizes negative energy
- **Tiger's Eye:** Energizing, luck, confidence, anxiety relief, protection, inspiration, mood stability, stress relief, willpower
- **Emerald and Ruby together:** Spiritual grounding and closeness, heart-opening, receiving, healing
- **Rose Quartz:** Self-love, attracts love, alleviates heartbreak and grief, builds trust, promotes forgiveness
- **Selenite:** Mental clarity, clear decisions, honesty, truth, clearing, protection, shielding, breaks negative patterns, calming
- **Obsidian:** Absorbs negative energy, strength, relaxation, restful sleep, balance, introspection, grounding
- **Amazonite:** Authenticity, self-discovery, harmony, truth speaking, compassion, mood and emotion stabilizer, compassion
- **Sodalite:** Energy enhancing, strength, intuition, confidence, courage, connection, perception, self-awareness
- **Garnet:** Energizing, memory enhancing, removing inhibition, love, lust, devotion, self-confidence, self-discovery, passion

I included one pairing here with emerald and ruby because they are often recommended together. Ruby amplifies the heart-opening effects of emerald, leaving you open to possibility and blessings. It's the perfect combination for anyone who struggles with receiving.

All of these crystals will help you attract money in their own way. Look at them as access points to the healings and lessons you need to stabilize your money magic wave. The goal is to find a new baseline that you can raise over time, rather than continuing with the radical high and low shifts you've been experiencing.

These stones are great for meditation, wearing as jewelry, keeping beneath a pillow, or keeping on or around you while you take actions related to money.

Magical Cleansing

Cleaning can be one of the best magical remedies you can employ. When people hear "magical cleansing," their minds often go straight to smudging. While smudging is a fantastic cleansing practice, it's often the last one you want to employ after some other magical cleaning techniques.

Generally, you can start with tidying your home, starting at the point farthest from the entrance and eventually working your way to the front. When you tidy with the intention to improve energy flow and create a more supportive environment, you turn a standard cleaning practice into a spell.

Another way to cleanse negative and stuck energy is to add some High John the Conqueror floor wash and bath to your counter spray and mopping solution. Also known as "High John the Conquistador," this root is a natural obstacle breaker that cleans out unsupportive energy. Although you can order the root, making a wash from it will likely be more expensive than just buying a premade wash from a practitioner online.

In the same way that you tidied, you want to cleanse your floors from the back of the house toward the front door. This ensures that all the negative and stagnant energy moves its way out of your home. As an optional task, you can combine some floor wash with warm water and use a clean rag or sponge to wash your front door.

Once your home feels like it's reached a baseline of cleanliness, that's the time for smudging.

Smudging is a Native American practice where you burn a bundle of dried herbs and allow the smoke to waft around your home to cleanse its energy. Anyone can do it—with some caveats.

First, there's a misbelief that smudging requires white desert sage. Not only is that untrue, but it is also a harmful misunderstanding that led to the overharvesting of white sage to the point that it became difficult for Native American communities to access it—and they're truly the *only* ones who need it for their practices. Using white sage when other herbs are readily available to you is a form of cultural appropriation, so just don't do it, mm'kay?

Instead, you can use base herbs like common garden sage, rosemary, or lavender to cleanse the energy within your home. You can buy a bundle online, use incense, or buy dry herbs straight from the produce section at the grocery store. Merely buy a bundle and hang them upside down until they become dry enough to burn.

When you're ready to smudge, open all the doors and windows you can to your home, set all your fans on a low setting, and drop the air conditioner setting a bit. You want to make sure the air is moving around so the smoke is able to get into all the spaces.

Light your bundle and stamp out the active flame so that you have a low smolder emitting curls of smoke. Don't forget to bring a dish to catch any falling ash!

Following the same path you did with your cleaning, go room by room and swirl the smoke around the room, making sure that it gets into all four corners of the ceiling. Every so often, repeat your intention. I usually say something like, "Please clear this space of negative energy, bad vibes, and anything that doesn't serve this home or the people living in it." Feel free to say whatever feels relevant and important to you.

When you're done with your home, make sure to cleanse items where you spend a lot of time and focus, such as your smartphone or computer, your pets (good luck with that), other people living in the home, and yourself.

Then you can close all the windows, return the AC to its typical setting, and shut the fans off.

If you want to create a simmer pot to fill your home with natural fragrance and the energy of specific herbs, this would be the perfect time.

A simmer pot is exactly what it sounds like. Think of it as a wet potpourri. You take a bunch of lovely smelling ingredients and let them simmer on the stove so your home smells lovely and everyone benefits from the aromatherapy that comes along with it.

If you've been waiting for an activity that will make you feel *super* witchy, this is the one.

Set the intention for your simmer pot, charge your ingredients as we discussed in Chapter 9, add them to a pot of water, bring everything to a boil, then reduce it to a simmer for it all to evaporate. Feel free to stir and restate your intention whenever you feel called.

You can use any of the herbs listed in Chapter 9 in addition to any seasonal scents or ingredients. Orange and lemon peels or slices are very popular year-round and their scents can be adjusted with additional spices.

Here are some fantastic herbs for promoting stability:

- Orange—peace, good luck, fortune, money, wealth
- Lemon—emotional healing
- Lavender—relaxation, love attraction, restful sleep
- Rose petals—relaxation, self-love, harmony
- Chamomile—healing, soothing, friendship, luck, money
- Peppermint—energizing, uplifting, physical healing
- Honeysuckle—willpower and inner strength

You can use any of the above in combination with the abundance herbs profiled in Chapter 9 to power your intention. Crystals are common ingredients for simmer pots as well—just don't forget to make sure your crystal of choice won't dissolve in hot water!

White Bath

Finally, if you feel like you've been carrying around some heaviness for a long time and it's too much to bear, you can take a white bath for purification.

This is especially helpful for empaths, who seem to carry the heaviness of everyone's emotions inside them.

A white bath contains the following ingredients:

- Cascarilla (powder made from finely ground eggshells)
- Pure cocoa butter
- Milk
- Dried flowers, usually white
- Florida water (This is an old-timey perfume, not swamp water.)
- Holy water
- White candle

You *could* make your own white bath mix. I won't tell you not to. But this is another one of those where it's often cheaper to purchase a premade mix or kit for yourself. Generally, you can buy a white bath mix, Florida water, and holy water in a kit from a practitioner online.

As per usual, you can use any kind of white candle, even a cheap tea light from the grocery store. All that matters is that it burns while you bathe.

Speaking of, a white bath is meant to be used for spiritual cleaning—not physical. That means you should shower before drawing your white bath.

Once you're clean, draw a warm bath, mix in your ingredients, and sit in the water for twenty minutes without allowing the water to touch your neck, head, or hair.

If you don't have access to a bathtub, you can still use a white bath for purification. Instead of drawing a bath, you'll fill a bucket with warm water, add your ingredients, get in the shower, and slowly pour the water all over your body, being careful not to let the water touch your neck, head, or hair. Some splashing on your neck is fine. You just don't want to douse your neck in it.

When you're done with your chosen method, sit on a towel and air-dry. Do not add any lotions, oils, or scents to your body after. Immediately go to sleep.

As a heads-up, this packs a punch and will leave you *exhausted*. The best time to do this is the first night of a weekend, not for any witchy reasons but because you will probably want to sleep way past eight hours after this.

Show Me the Money (Magic)

- **Let's get ready to (not) rumble.** When you're manifesting money in a wave, the best magical rituals to perform should focus on creating a sense of safety, groundedness, and stability. Working on your root chakra is easy to include in your daily routines. If you're carrying around some heaviness from your manifestation, use my Alchemize Your Bullshit spell.
- **To thy Human Design be true.** Everyone's Human Design type gives them advice on the most aligned way for them to make decisions, how it feels when they're not living in alignment, and how their intuition is most likely to present. Taking that advice can make surfing the money manifestation wave much easier by giving you clarity.
- **Stability sovereigns.** Certain money deities will be more helpful for you during the wave-based manifestation phase. Any deity who can help you find grounding and inner peace will be more helpful than those purely dedicated to making money. That's because you need the *feeling* of stability first so you can manifest money to *contribute* to that feeling.
- **Stability stones.** Think about the specific energies you want to experience in your day-to-day life. Find a crystal that promotes the most prominent quality you want to absorb. Carry it around in a left pocket or left bra cup, or wear it as jewelry on your left side. Think of it as a reminder to take a few deep breaths whenever you feel overwhelmed or worried about money.
- **Cleaning as magic.** One of the best ways to swipe your energetic slate clean is to literally clean your space. Turn your chores into magical rituals with intentions and herbs. It's a perfect seasonal change activity. Some witches even set their cleaning schedule to the moon phases.

ACTIVITIES

- How can you add root chakra work into your daily schedule? Focusing on creating a ritual around finding your center can make it easier for you to not only feel stable, but also hold yourself accountable on your goals.
- If you know your birth time, find your Human Design chart from Jovian Archive or Human Design expert Jenna Zoe. Familiarize yourself with your strategy, not-self theme, and authority. When have you naturally used them in the past and found success? When have you strayed from them and hit a wall?
- Find a deity around stability who works for you. Research them and learn as much as you can. Whenever you engage in rituals or behaviors focused on finding your center, imagine them sitting right there with you, helping you access peace.
- How can you work magical cleaning into your existing cleaning schedule? If you don't have one, how can you infuse your existing mundane cleaning with intention?

PART 4

How to Manifest Even More Money

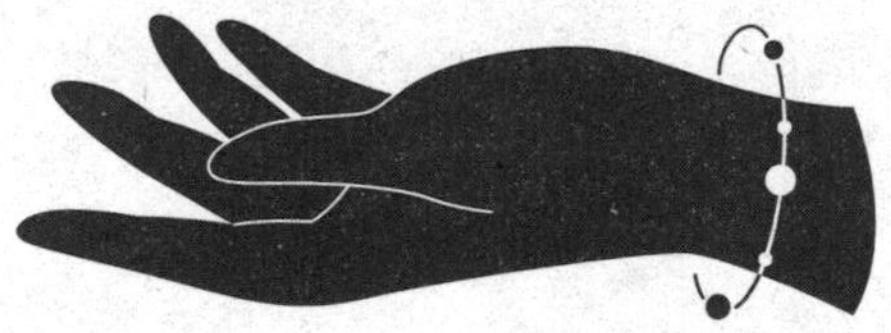

Deepen Your Authenticity

The final aspect of manifesting money is for those lucky bastards who called money in, found consistency, and now they've plateaued.

"Lucky?" I can hear them exclaiming from here.

But they are. A plateau is a juicy place to be! No matter at what point your momentum has petered out, jump-starting your money magic and manifestation from this place is fun! It's all about shaking up your routine, reevaluating what your version of wealth looks like, and being bold enough to become a radically authentic version of yourself.

These are my favorite clients. They come to me so frustrated and even angry because they've tried every solution they can and nothing seems to work. It feels like they're bumping their heads against a bulletproof glass ceiling.

The solution is almost always the same: have some fucking fun!

Using Joy to Level Up Your Financial Life

When people get to the point where they're consistent, financially sound, and thriving in their career or business, it's because they've been in workhorse mode. For so long, they've lived as a dedicated visionary, crafting a legacy or empire they can be proud of. So, when they start setting their sights on *more* and their tried-and-true methods don't yield results, they double down into that energy.

They turn into detectives, trying to learn whatever they can to fix the bug in the code of their success. They become so analytical that it's like they're the forgotten half of the Headless Horseman—just a head floating around wondering how their body managed to find a horse to run off with.

But people are like electronics—sometimes the best way to fix their issues is to unplug 'em and plug 'em back in again.

I went through a similar dynamic right before I pivoted in my business. You've heard the story of how I launched a program that fell right on its face. Well, what I attempted to do in the months that followed was to take the original plan for a six-month program and chop it into three two-month programs designed to lead from one into the other.

I gave people the option to enroll for all three or just one for different price points. After all, I had done so much work on preparing for this endeavor that I didn't want to give everything up now.

In theory, it was a smart idea and solid business advice. No need to throw the baby out with the bathwater, as they say.

The execution, on the other hand, felt like *such a slog*. I was essentially promoting a program for four straight months, which *wasn't* fun. I was so busy trying to recruit for each of these small programs that I hardly got a breather. By the time those six months were nearly over, I was sick of them. I made money from the programs, but only enough to cover my expenses, and I was wiped out.

Despite barely having money outside of my bills and right before a big cross-country move, I invested in a more straightforward business coach who could tell me what I had done wrong. Instead, he didn't see anything *bad* with what I had done and recommended I try launching a shorter but similar version of the program one more time.

Well, that flopped, too. I didn't get a single bite, despite so many people showing interest during the three days of free training I ran as a way to promote it.

My coach was surprised and had me sit down with the branding expert on his staff to review the launch and all my materials with me.

She had me close my eyes and asked a series of questions about how I wanted my potential clients to feel in my programs, what I did best, my favorite problems to solve, my favorite colors, my favorite outfits, and more. Some of it seemed relevant, but most of it seemed odd.

Once she finished her questions, she read back to me how I described my business, myself, the results I get for people, and how my clients feel about my programs. Everything I had said was related to magic, manifestation, glitter, fun, celebration, community, and more.

Then she read back some of my content and had me look at my website. All my written copy was *so* serious. It focused on hard business strategy and making it understandable. Although my website was *beautiful*, the photos of me weren't fun, inspiring, or lighthearted. Some of them definitely gave off bad-bitch vibes, and nothing about the content seemed to convey anything about magic at all.

I realized that I had been trying *so hard* to not come off like just another **manifestation** coach on the internet that I became just another **business** coach on the internet.

I'd effectively erased all of my eccentric personality and the fun parts of what I taught my clients inside my programs. I knew I needed to make a change.

So, I rebranded. I got new photos, rewrote the copy on my website, and started talking openly about money magic and manifestation for entrepreneurs.

And unlike what I had been doing in my business for *months*, I was having a ton of fun! I wore sequined jumpsuits and a gold dress in my photo shoot, and it left me looking like a fairy godmother in the best way possible.

Then I launched a three-month program called "Practical Magic."

I no longer hid behind the reputability of straight business strategy. I still talked about it, but I openly talked about magic spells, manifestation, astrology, and all the other parts of my business that I loved sharing alongside financial planning, sales strategy, and marketing.

Rather than putting my life on hold to launch from home, I decided to crash a trip with my sister and our best friend. They had come down to visit me for my birthday, and I spontaneously chose to tag along. Launch be damned! I needed to let my hair down.

Manifestations began pouring in from the beginning.

We wound up with a free upgrade to a presidential suite in a luxury Orlando resort with an indoor Jacuzzi tub that could have fit three people. The suite had a huge balcony overlooking the city from which we could see surrounding lakes and watch fireworks from the theme parks at night. It also had three bedrooms and a fully functional kitchen. All the furniture and decor seemed to have come straight from Tommy Bahama. I had never been in such a fancy hotel room.

It was *perfect* for a working vacation.

So, after dropping the gals off at Disney, I worked from the penthouse balcony or the pool until it was time to pick them up. I had more fun just living in this little bubble of luxury while I ran my launch. When we drove down for the second half of the trip, I worked from the beach.

I felt so relaxed, happy, and inspired the entire time. Was it any wonder I could teach and sell with ease? Definitely not.

I signed one pay-in-full client during the ten days of vacation, and in the week that followed, six others signed up. I made $26,000 in sales and $14,000 in cash.

The reason those other programs failed and this one didn't wasn't just because of a rebrand. It was because I deepened into my authenticity. Up until then, I was able to achieve a certain degree of success from my knowledge alone.

Once the strategy and knowledge wasn't getting results, it became necessary for me to look at how my brand and offers aligned with who I was and what I enjoyed teaching. I had unintentionally followed the mantra "Sell them what they want, give them what they need" by not publicly discussing the influences of magic and manifestation I taught alongside my business consulting advice.

Had those programs succeeded, and I was forced to teach that much business strategy to more than the handful of clients I had, I would have been bored. The programs didn't sell because on some level *I didn't want them to*. I needed to be brave enough to let people think I was nuts talking about magic alongside strategy. I needed to publicly show up as the complete version of myself—the strategist *and* the witch—to find the clients I dreamed of coaching.

It was the same as I navigated my career change before business as well. For almost a decade I believed that if I could get a criminal-law reporting job, I could happily work in that capacity for the next thirty years. I got sick of it after three because it wasn't authentically me.

As much as I love to write, I'm someone who lives for problem-solving. I often joke that most of my hobbies are just various forms of thinking—crosswords, sudoku, puzzles, logic games, and so on. Once my job became routine, I couldn't muster up any passion for it anymore. That was why I needed a business in the first place: so I could finally ensure variety in my career.

So, if you feel like you've hit a cap on your income, investigate *how* you're making money. Does it still authentically align with who you are? Are you covering up tattoos you love at a job you've grown to hate? Do your coworkers, customers, or audience appreciate and respond to your personality, or are you hiding parts of yourself? I promise that whatever accommodations you're making, you'll have an easier time with finances when you can be your whole self in your career.

At the same time, I couldn't have arrived at the level of success I achieved through strategy alone. I needed the chance to unplug, have fun, and *be* that fun, inspired, sparkly coach I knew I was. It took a photo shoot and an impromptu vacation to get back in touch with that version of myself. Had I remained chained to my desk, I wouldn't have been able to let loose, rejuvenate, and feel inspired again.

It's time to start asking yourself questions like "When was the last time I had a vacation?" "When was the last time I had a deep belly laugh?" "When was the last time I practiced one of my hobbies?"

Trust me when I say that the best thing you can do for your money manifestation journey is to switch from actively trying to make money to learning how to give yourself joy and quality rest.

When your money stagnates after you've been able to achieve some consistent money, that means it's time to reevaluate and refresh. That means *not* focusing as hard on increasing your income. Inspiration comes much easier when we're not trying to force it.

Too often we decide to take some time off and then spend that downtime trying to rest productively. We'll read personal development books instead of fiction. We'll try to combine a work conference and a vacation. We meet up with friends to cowork instead of connect.

What if you just allowed yourself to rest without imposing society's love of productivity and business on it? Imagine how it might feel to rest without wondering about how you could become a better worker, parent, friend, or person.

And if you've been reading this on a vacation, I'm sorry, but I need to ask you to put the book down and step away. I know I'm a hilarious genius who's blowing your mind every other page, but I'll also be here when you get back. Take a break, friend.

Your Dream Life (Or So You Think)

Since you're already reevaluating your life, we might as well take the chance to look at our hopes and dreams while we're at it.

When you start a money magic and manifestation journey, you often go in with a laundry list of money and *stuff* you believe will make you truly happy. Sometimes we achieve it only to realize that it's not actually what we want anymore.

Sometimes you wind up on a money manifestation plateau because you haven't realized that you don't actually want your dream life anymore. And sometimes it happens when it feels like we're *so* close to achieving it.

No one gets this one better than I do. I spent the vast majority of my twenties desperately wanting to leave Florida. It felt like a crime that I would be forced to live out my hottest years in small towns rather than feeling as if I were starring in my own NYC-based HBO series.

Moving to Washington, DC, was a big deal for me. I had put so much time, money, effort, and worry into moving to a city I adored. For the longest time, I pictured myself there forever, eventually moving to a Virginia or Maryland suburb to raise kids and commute into the city.

But that had always been when I imagined a career in political journalism or the law. When I decided to leave that career behind and start my own business, I didn't exactly *need* to live in a city, even though I wanted to. Then my fiancé got accepted to a PhD program at The Florida State University in Tallahassee, where I had sworn I would never return.

At first, I insisted on staying in DC. Even though we were engaged, I insisted that we could do long distance again. My fiancé, God bless him, said he would never ask me to move somewhere I hated because he didn't want me to resent him.

But, *man*, was I bummed at the idea of us being separated for up to four years! And if we were planning to get married, living apart would suck even more. Still, I couldn't bring myself to say I wanted to move—at least not at first.

Around this time, we were rewatching the entire series of *Parks and Recreation*. It's one of my favorite ensemble comedies, about the employees working for a parks and recreation department in a fictional small Indiana town called Pawnee. I watched the show when it aired and had rewatched it at least once before. During this rewatch, I found myself thinking something I never had before.

Pawnee isn't that bad. I think I would enjoy living there.

Now, if you only knew how much trash I talked about small towns my entire life up until this point, you would be shocked. It shocked *me*.

What I appreciated this time around was how much community existed in Pawnee. The town had annual festivals and events, it had a lot of outdoor spaces, it wasn't terribly far from a city, and it felt cozy.

It wasn't just Pawnee. All of the shows I watched on my own took place in small towns—*Virgin River*, *Sweet Magnolias*, *Sabrina*, *Gilmore Girls*, *Riverdale*, and more. I found myself wishing I could step into those towns with their familiar haunts and faces. I was just a number in a city, and I hadn't even seen most of the neighbors I had in my building.

I also started noticing my own habits. Even with hundreds of restaurants at my disposal, I preferred my go-to spots that I frequented. The same went for theater. I had a couple favorites, and even then I didn't see every show. What was I really, really getting out of living in DC now that I didn't have a legal journalism career?

The pandemic only made it worse. The places where I did experience a small sense of community—like my rock-climbing gym—were closed. Whenever we went into quarantine, we had no access to outdoor spaces, not even a balcony. I occasionally snuck out to do yoga in the grass or sit under a tree and journal, but I was still keenly aware that I was in a city. I couldn't escape sirens, car horns, construction, and everything else that came with living in DC.

I craved easier access to the outdoors that could feel like an escape. I wanted a quiet neighborhood, friendly neighbors, and dark nights where I could see the stars—even if only a little.

When I revisited the list detailing the dream life I was manifesting, so much of it didn't seem to appeal to me anymore. I didn't want to live in a modern, renovated apartment near a park and restaurants. It's not like I could enjoy the perks of getting there during happy hour anyway. They all featured $10 appetizers, $12 cocktails, and $5 Coors Lite—*very* cheap for DC. "That's *not* a happy hour," I would grumble to myself every time I started a tab.

If this is how I felt, why was I still living here? It clearly wasn't the museums, restaurants, and theater anymore. So, I sat in meditation and asked myself what was the benefit of living in DC over Tallahassee. To my surprise, I heard the voice of my teenage self.

"Because only losers live in small Florida towns," she spat at me. "*Successful* people live in cities, obviously."

When I opened my eyes, I realized that my ego was clinging to what it believed was *the only* indicator of success. Living in a city, even if I was struggling, meant that I had made something of myself. It made me better than the bullies from middle school and high school—many of whom moved back to my hometown or to equally small southern towns.

I was so committed to not being like them that I had completely ignored my own needs.

As a fairly logical adult, I realized I could put that aside. Not *all* successful people live in cities, obviously. That was a mile marker of success I came up with as a teenager that had nothing to do with what *actual* success looked like. Not even all celebrities live in LA, New York, or London. John Travolta lives on a ranch in *Ocala*, Florida, which I can assure you has much less going for it than Tallahassee. Unless you're really into horses, in which case it has *everything* going for it.

It was time for me to admit that I had come to crave the small-town experience I spent more than a decade judging. I couldn't lie to myself anymore—not when I had a Netflix category called "Small-Town Charm" calling me out.

I realized how much Pawnee reminded me of Tallahassee in the way that it was kind of a dump, but a dump with heart. Tallahassee had around four annual food festivals and a county fair, more than a few good restaurants, and a solid arts and theater scene, thanks to the college's fine arts program. The only thing it was missing was four seasons. But, hey, it wouldn't be forever.

I sat with my realization for a few days, asking myself what I would need to feel happy and supported there. I wanted a two-bedroom apartment nowhere near college students in a quiet, tree-filled part of town so I could have a home office. I wanted to have enough funds to enjoy what entertainment was available in town. That was all I needed.

When I told my fiancé that I wanted to move with him at the end of the year, his eyes nearly fell out of his head.

I explained my reasoning and short list of necessities to him, and he was on board but wary. He didn't want me to feel forced or make a decision just to make him happy. But I stuck to it. Part of me worried that I was making a mistake, but I kept telling myself I could always move back.

Once I made the decision, everything fell into place. We found an apartment that was literally double the square footage of our place in DC at almost *half* the price. It backs up to trees that flower in the spring and summer, and the only thing we can hear at night is a chorus of frogs. It was so dark our first night there that we had to play Marco Polo so I could find the air mattress after turning out the light.

And I got my personal office to fit an L-shaped desk, lots of natural light, *my own bathroom* with a garden tub, and a door that closed. I would never need to work from a wall desk in the bedroom while my fiancé texted me to say I was being too loud over Zoom ever again.

I felt so much clearer-minded in this space, and with living expenses so much lower, it became much easier for me to pursue my money goals. I *felt* more like the business owner I wanted to be, so of course I was able to show up in that way.

To my surprise, I fell in love with the place I loathed. I found the best coffee I've ever had (and I've had so much over the years, my blood type is basically dark roast). I found go-to restaurants for all the cuisines I loved in DC. My only gripe other than the suffocating summers is that UberEats takes forever to get to us. So, I would say I'm faring pretty well.

Since moving here, not only did I rebrand my signature programs to be based around magic, but I got incredibly stable with my finances, started paying off my debt, went viral on TikTok, got featured in BuzzFeed and Yahoo!, became a contributing writer for *HR Exchange Network*, landed an agent and a book deal, and started getting paid for public speaking.

The only reason any of that happened was because I revisited my goals to see if they still authentically aligned. I needed to be brave enough to let go of what my ego was clinging to so fiercely as the only proof of success.

Whether you're on a juicy plateau or in a slump, it requires the same level of reevaluation. Look at the type of life you're manifesting and ask yourself if you still want it. Look at your sources of inspiration to see if they reflect what you say you want. Sometimes we achieve the entire list to realize it only brought us bragging rights instead of deep satisfaction. Checking on your list to ruthlessly eliminate anything that doesn't align is the best way to avoid that kind of outcome.

So, take a look at what you asked for at the beginning of this book. Now that you've learned as much as you have about yourself, does it still feel important? Do you still want it? There's no shame in deciding that something you thought was the be-all and end-all of life goals isn't actually something you want for your life.

Chances are, you've already been through some version of that so far. If I knew at fifteen what I knew now at thirty-five, my life would have turned out so differently. I probably would have gone to art school in LA to study theater and cracked my heart wide open experiencing the roller coaster that comes with pursuing a big, fantastical dream. Instead, I played it safe like so many of us do by going to a nearby college, studying a practical major, going to law school, and getting a respectable law job.

The important point is that eventually I chose to step off the treadmill of tradition and ask myself if I was happy—and I *kept asking*. Challenging your own thoughts and goals is one of the best ways to reawaken your magnetism because it requires you to either recommit to what you said you want *or* forge a new path based in passion.

Connecting the Dots

Whether you've now rewritten your money manifestation list or recommitted to the vision you've always had, the next best way to jump-start your way out of a plateau is to use a simple question.

Why don't I have my dream life yet?

I'm not talking about asking it in that whiny way when you've had a day of paying your bills and you ask, "Why couldn't I have been born to rich parents?" I mean asking it with 100 percent sincerity and actually answering it.

Like I said before, when we've been working on getting to a place of comfortable success, it's often after we've been keeping our head down and consistently working toward our goals. That doesn't always mean you've lacked passion or have been working mindlessly.

You can be working in absolute, total joy at your job or business to the point that you kind of forget to check in with your progress. Asking yourself, "Why don't I have this yet?" forces you to pause and look at the distance between where you are and where you want to be.

I realize this sounds silly at first.

"If I knew why I didn't have it, I would obviously fix it."

But would you? That's the point of asking this question. When you've been working consistently and getting consistent money results, but you can't seem to *increase* the money results you've been getting, it's usually because you haven't stopped to reevaluate.

That doesn't necessarily mean you need to discard everything you've done. It often means you just need to tweak it. When you're in a juicy rut, you have to accept that what got you to this level of success is *not* what will get you to the full realization of your money goals or dream life.

For example, let's say you have no problem attracting clients in a business and making money. If you ask yourself, "Why don't I have my dream life?" and the answer is "Because I don't have time to take on new clients to make more money," that's going to require you to look at how you're spending your time to start closing that gap.

You'll need to take inventory of how you spend both your work and free time to see where that extra time could come from. That's naturally going to lead to a few solutions:

- Take away free time to work more, which would probably make you feel like you're moving in the opposite direction from your dream life.
- Outsource some of your work to an employee or independent contractor, which might free you up to take on more clients, but won't help if you're already feeling spread thin.
- Raise your prices so you can take on fewer clients, or keep taking on the same number and increase the money coming your way.

I asked myself this question once my business felt stable enough for me to think about writing a book: "Why don't I have a book deal yet?"

I wrote out my list of reasons:

1. I haven't actually written anything.
2. I don't have an agent.
3. I don't have enough of a social media following.
4. I don't know how to write an agent query or book proposal.

Once I had that list, I began checking off the items as if this were a to-do list. I started with one hour of writing every day. I began with an outline and eventually fleshed that out into chapters. I did this about five days a week for three months and wound up with four chapters.

At the same time, I was teaching one of my signature programs, Embodied Uplevel, for business owners looking to become thought leaders. I brought in speakers with different areas of expertise to cover topics like paid public speaking, starting and monetizing podcasts, and writing books.

I desperately wanted a guest in the publishing industry, so I asked my virtual assistant to send some outreach emails from me to any agency she thought would align with my brand. One responded and when I saw who it was, I squealed.

It was the head of my favorite agency, whose website had been solidly sitting in my bookmarks bar for over a year.

Now, she *did* ask if this was a paid speaking engagement, and I knew I likely couldn't meet her rate. So, I asked my VA to schedule a Zoom call so I could discuss the opportunity with her.

And once I got on that call, I had a PowerPoint ready to go. I pitched her on me, my program clients, all of our manuscripts, and offered a package of services for her and her staff that I thought might come close to what she normally charged to speak. She was kind and receptive and told me to keep in touch, but she ultimately said no to speaking.

I didn't even care. I was flying high on the presentation. The fact that I got face time with my dream agent and *she asked me to stay in touch* was enough of a milestone for me to celebrate.

So, I marked my calendar for her next workshop on how to write an agent query letter a month later. My goal was to attend that, then write a query I could send by the end of the year. That would easily check off that last list item, which would cinch almost the rest of the gap between where I was and where I wanted to be.

A book deal felt closer than it ever had in my life. I just needed to play my cards right.

I felt so electric after that call that I kept working long after I normally shut my laptop. I checked the daily newsletter of reporters looking for experts to comment on their stories. I saw a request that I knew I could speak on, but knew that my opinion would *never* make the cut purely based on how the request was phrased.

It asked for sources who could talk about "what perks companies could offer that would keep millennials in the workplace." Being a millennial myself, I knew the *only* legitimate answers to this question were money and benefits.

Since I was already fired up, I typed back a long response explaining that millennials don't give a shit about perks and just want jobs with good pay and benefits. I ranted and raved about how managers assume all millennials are twenty-two when the vast majority are in their thirties with kids, about how we're still financially impaired from the 2008 recession, and why upper management can't seem to wrap their heads around the fact that company loyalty is a two-way street.

Yet hitting Send didn't release enough of the energy I had from the presentation and that rant. People needed to hear this. So, on a whim, I decided to upload a video of myself reading it to TikTok.

I didn't have a ton of followers, but I didn't care. I figured at least my friends would cheer me on and feel vindicated that I stood up for them.

I felt better and finally went to bed. When I woke up, my phone had hundreds of notifications. My TikTok went viral and it wasn't stopping!

Later that day, an editor reached out to ask if she could post my written response as an essay on her publication's website.

By the end of the week, a reporter from BuzzFeed asked if she could write about the video and send me more questions to pick my brain. Thanks to the publicity, I wound up with more than 70,000 followers on TikTok, checking off that third list item.

At the end of the month, I had a message on LinkedIn from an editor at a publisher saying she loved my TikTok and the rest of my content then asked me if I had ever considered writing a book. I was gagged. Could it finally be happening?

I used the opportunity to reach back out to the agent and ask if she had any advice. She told me to take the call, don't sign anything, and let her know how it went.

That's exactly what I did. I pitched my four book ideas to my editor, who zeroed in on the one she wanted. I told the agent, and the agent asked if I wanted to be her client. I signed, she helped me craft my proposal, and off it went. My book got picked up about a month later.

Now, this is obviously not how people generally wind up getting book deals. I know this. But the truth is that success in *any* endeavor can never be replicated exactly the same way.

Everyone has their own story of actions that led them to success. I mean, *Fifty Shades of Grey* started out as a *Twilight* fanfic with 56,000 reviews, was then self-published, and eventually picked up by Penguin's imprint Vintage. No two people can take the same actions and get identical results.

That is why asking the question "Why don't I have it yet?" is so important.

When you zero in on exactly *why* you don't have the money or life of your dreams, you will essentially come up with a to-do list that only you can complete to attain your goals.

A quote often attributed to Roman philosopher Seneca states that "Luck is when preparation meets opportunity." When you create your own to-do list and focus on checking those points off, you're laying the groundwork to make sure that you won't miss your opportunity once it presents itself.

Had I never stopped working on my business to ask myself why I didn't have a book deal, I might have let my busy schedule keep me from writing, reaching out, and speaking my truth on social media. The answer to that question couldn't be found in how I was running my business or making sales.

Just like the answer to why you don't have what you want isn't in what you've been doing this entire time.

Villains Can Be Role Models, Too

There's a surprising demographic of people who make the perfect role models for those whose money magic and manifestation is in need of resuscitation.

Villains.

And I mean *all* villains—fictional and real ones. The thing about villains that makes them the perfect source of inspiration for anyone in a manifestation plateau is that they truly and completely do not give a flying fuck about the opinions of others.

Think about it: If they're hell-bent on taking over the world, making a coat out of puppies, or seeking revenge, caring about what other people think of them is directly at odds with that goal.

And while I know you can't have gotten to this point without stripping back your ego and showing up authentically, I guarantee you have more layers to peel back.

When we plateau in our manifestation journey, it's often because we're keeping ourselves small in some way. Even though we're definitely more authentic and much braver than we've been in the past, there's always room to go deeper.

Remember, worrying about what other people think is a valid evolutionary survival tactic left over from our days of living in tribes. It's deeply ingrained in our psyche. So, even when we start showing our authenticity, it's still naturally going to come out as a watered-down version of who we truly are capable of being.

I've always internally struggled over my desire to be famous. I felt like I was born knowing I was destined for stages and greatness. When you're a kid talking about those things, adults find it cute and indulge you. Past a certain age, everyone starts to worry about whether you're losing touch with reality.

As a child, I was convinced I would be a famous actress, but the moment I hit high school, my parents began pressuring me to pursue a *real* career. Of course, I know they were looking out for me and trying to encourage me to prioritize financial security over artistic expression. I get it and I don't hold any of that against them.

The issue is that kids, even teenagers, don't really understand nuance.

So, when they experience these misguided, loving attempts at protection, they don't see them as parental concern. They see them as rejection. Encouragement to find a safer, more palatable career gets rooted in the psyche as an extreme judgment like "Who I am is not acceptable, so I must hide my true self so my caretakers will continue to love me."

I was no exception to that.

So, even though I had arrived in my career as a coach with media appearances and a book deal, I didn't feel deserving of it. I didn't feel capable. I had talked such a big game about aiming for a bestseller and I felt like I would inevitably wind up a giant disappointment. Even though *everyone* around me felt completely certain about my success and how good my book would be, it was like I suddenly lost faith in myself.

My hero and inspiration came from a controversial, modern villain whom everybody loves to hate: Ye, or, the artist formerly known as Kanye West.

In the midst of writing this book, *Jeen-yuhs*, the three-part documentary about Kanye's rise to fame and fall(s) from grace, was released on Netflix. I had been a Kanye fan for a long time before I took a break after all his nonsense with Donald Trump. But knowing that *Jeen-yuhs* begins the story years before the release of *The College Dropout*, Kanye's 2004 debut album, I was always going to watch.

And, holy shit, did it change me.

Watching Kanye at nineteen, popping out his retainer to play his demo and rap for office workers and DJs while they ignored him and took phone calls broke my heart. And seeing him not let that faze him while he continued to write, record, and mix glued it back together again.

No matter what he experienced, he refused to let it deter him from thinking he was meant for fame and greatness. Seeing him write and rap through an almost sealed jaw after a car accident that nearly killed him put so much of his behavior in perspective.

Of course he didn't give a shit what anyone said about him in the media. He had to spend *years* as the only person other than his mother who deeply believed in his grand vision. When one of his friends called Jay-Z a genius and said Kanye couldn't call himself a genius yet, he immediately shot back that he was and he didn't need someone else to give him that title.

Why couldn't I have that level of assurance in myself? After all, I had actually made it to a major life goal. Now wasn't the time to question myself. Whenever my doubt creeped in, I would think, "WWKS: What would Kanye say?" And the answer was never meek, humble, or steeped in self-doubt.

I shared my thoughts with my fiancé, who took the opportunity to say he noticed I seemed fixated on arguing with people everywhere. He said I cared way too much.

"Stop casting your pearls before swine like Jesus or whoever it was in the Bible said," he told me.

I had never heard that verse despite thirteen years of Catholic school, so having my atheist-turned-Buddhist partner quote it compelled me to look it up for confirmation.

"Do not give what is holy to the dogs; nor cast your pearls before swine, lest they trample them under their feet, and turn and tear you in pieces." Matthew 7:6

Damn! I couldn't believe my partner, who had only studied the Bible as a literary manuscript for his PhD, had dropped a verse on me that was straight fire. It was a before-and-after moment where I couldn't unsee all the ways I gave so much value to people who didn't appreciate it.

It's exactly how Kanye wound up getting his first album picked up. When Roc-A-Fella Records dragged its feet on giving him a deal even though he was actively producing for them, he continued shopping it around to other labels until they decided they didn't want to lose him to a competitor.

Executives would later say they didn't know how to sell a rapper who didn't write about drug dealing, grew up in the suburbs, and wore pink polos and Gucci loafers. They claimed there wasn't a market for rap like Kanye wrote.

The dismissals only fueled his fire even more.

Yes, it's safe to say that fire has burned him many times over. Kanye West is definitely an asshole about 90 percent of the time. But that willingness to not give a shit what anyone says to or about him is what made him famous.

For someone who spent so long trying to make sure she didn't offend anyone, that spoke to me.

The truth is that even though I was living a more authentic version of my life, I still showed up too small and too nice.

I realized I needed to learn how to be an asshole.

If I could be willing to let people think I was rude or delusional, then I was probably doing a better job of honoring my needs and boundaries instead of twisting myself into shapes to fit their convenience.

I became far more direct in my communication. When people felt unsure about hiring me, I told them it likely wasn't a match. I stopped following up with potential clients who *said* they wanted to work with me, but could never seem to find the time or money. When people ghosted on a free call with me and asked to reschedule, I told them no. I unfriended all the coaches and entrepreneurs who only sent me friend requests because they saw me as a potential client instead of a collaborator, an equal, and a thought leader.

Unsurprisingly, no one seemed to care about any of it.

What I realized in the end was that in trying to be an asshole, I just became more selective and self-assured. I wasn't an asshole at all. I had just spent so long on the people-pleasing side of the pendulum that I had to aim for the total opposite side just so I could land somewhere in the middle.

I promise that as authentic as you are at this moment, some important part of you is still showing up too small.

If you're unsure of how to escape the smallness, look to the villains you judge the most. The more you hate someone, the more likely it is that they're showing you some qualities you need to embrace.

I hated that Kanye, whose music I loved, couldn't seem to ever communicate his thoughts well enough for people to understand what he was getting at, and in doing so, he undermined any and all good that he did.

But the reason I hated that was because I needed to care less about how people received my words.

Imagine how much more powerful you could become if, instead of dismissing your villains for being villains, you began asking them what they're trying to teach you.

Show Me the Money (Magic)

- **Are you having fun yet?** When we're making decent enough money, it becomes all too easy for us to focus on how to catapult ourselves into the next income bracket. Instead, we need to check back in with ourselves to make sure that our methods for bringing in cash flow are still fun. If they're not, you might be subconsciously pushing away success because on some level, you know that means more dullness and sacrifice.
- **Touch (base with) yourself.** As we evolve and become more authentic in how we live, our goals often change. What we wanted at the beginning of our money manifestation journey is no longer what we consider our dream life. Sometimes our income plateaus because the life we've been manifesting money for isn't in alignment with the person we've become.
- **Ask the obvious question.** We're all a lot smarter than we give ourselves credit for. It might sound ridiculous to ask yourself, "Why don't I have this yet?" but if you treat the question seriously and answer it, you'll be surprised at how easily you identify the solution to breaking out of your plateau.
- **Be bad. Be very bad.** People who piss us off or whom we judge as villains are usually highlighting qualities we need to integrate. You wouldn't feel so activated if some part of you didn't crave the freedom that came with a total disregard for societal norms, morality, or what's considered polite behavior.

ACTIVITIES

- Are you manifesting money when you really need joy? What can you do this week that would bring some fun into your life?
- Revisit your manifestation list. Does it still align with what you authentically want? If not, what does?
- Why don't you have what you want yet? How can your answers serve as a to-do list for getting closer to it?
- Who is someone you can't stand—real or fictional? Why do you hate them? How could their main qualities indicate traits you need to embrace within yourself?

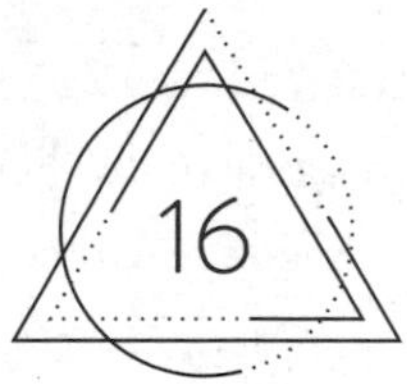

Living in the Zone

Once you've been able to consistently make the money you need to survive, thrive, and leave that old life behind, that feeling doesn't change overnight. You will naturally look to money as the solution to any issues that continue to come up. And that's because up until now, making more money *was* the solution that fixed your problems.

It's easy to understand *in concept* that money can't buy happiness. But anyone who's lived through financial scarcity or instability—even more so through financial trauma—can tell you that about 90 percent of their problems could be easily resolved by more money.

Yet hanging onto the idea that money will solve everything for you is often why your money magic will begin to stagnate.

When you've gotten to a place of stable abundance and you're focusing on building wealth, you can't look at money as the source of all your solutions anymore. That implies that if you don't receive money, you will lose your stability. It's another form of scarcity mindset.

Instead, you need to focus on money as the natural by-product of a life lived in joy. In other words, you're shifting your focus from the result (money) to the process (living).

The Power of Joy

In his books *The Big Leap* and *The Genius Zone*, Gay Hendricks distinguishes between living in your zone of excellence and zone of genius.[1]

The zone of excellence is where you're excelling at something in which you are skilled. You're experiencing success, but not necessarily fulfillment and joy.

The zone of genius, however, is the place where you are doing work that comes from your innate talent, seems to cause unending inspiration, and produces work that is not only uniquely *you*, but far exceeds what anyone else is producing.

It's the difference between when I was a practicing attorney and journalist versus a coach, speaker, and now author.

I was *damn good* at appeals, thanks to my innate talent for writing and public speaking. I carried a caseload of 200 appeals and once delivered three oral arguments in a month. On average, most people argued about four to five *a year*.

I won all of them.

I was also a *damn good* journalist. I wrote fascinating deep-dive series, published quality coverage from important criminal cases on Twitter, and gave a number of effective radio interviews.

I covered the confirmation hearing of Jeff Sessions when I had strep throat like I was Michael Jordan playing with the flu in the 1997 NBA finals.

I was performing so well that the vice president of the news division sent me to the 2016 Congressional Correspondents Dinner and tapped me for TV interview training. I was on *fire*.

These were my zones of excellence. I was producing quality work and getting impressive results. In both places I was one of the shining jewels of the organization. And in both places, I lost my passion after a while.

My innate genius is and always has been in giving intuition-based advice, explaining esoteric concepts, helping others reach their goals, and testing shit out on myself like a manifestation lab rat.

I was writing and speaking in both roles where I lived in my zone of excellence, but because both jobs excluded my innate abilities, it wasn't enough for me to really thrive.

More money might have incentivized me to stay, but it wouldn't have been enough for me to feel fulfilled. In fact, I felt happier and more fulfilled in the first year of my business, which made half of the money of my legal career, than I ever experienced in *any* job.

This is why, before I ever read any of Gay Hendricks's work, I always referred to this space as the "zone of joy and genius" to my plateauing clients. The more time you spend doing work that brings you joy *and* you are naturally good at doing, the easier it is to attract money.

That's because joy and fun are natural forms of surrender.

I've touched on surrender earlier in this book, explaining how people in manifestation spaces often refer to "letting go of the results" when you're actively manifesting them.

Plateaus require you to double down into that space of release. When you find work that meets the dual needs of passion and talent, you naturally stop worrying about money. Instead, you're doing the kind of work that absorbs your entire focus and inspiration. You know the type. It's the work you do for hours on end only to come up at 2:00 p.m. and realize you're starving because you haven't eaten.

When that becomes the bulk of how you spend your time, money is no longer the main focus of your work. You've come to understand that the entire point of living an authentic life is to find fulfillment. *That* is what money can't buy.

That means your new mantra in this phase of money manifestation needs to be, "Just because I'm good at this doesn't mean I need to keep doing it in this way—or at all."

Get in the Zone

Now that you see why it's crucial to live in the sweet spot that encompasses both passion and talent, it's time to filter your life through this perspective.

Take a moment to draw a Venn diagram like this:

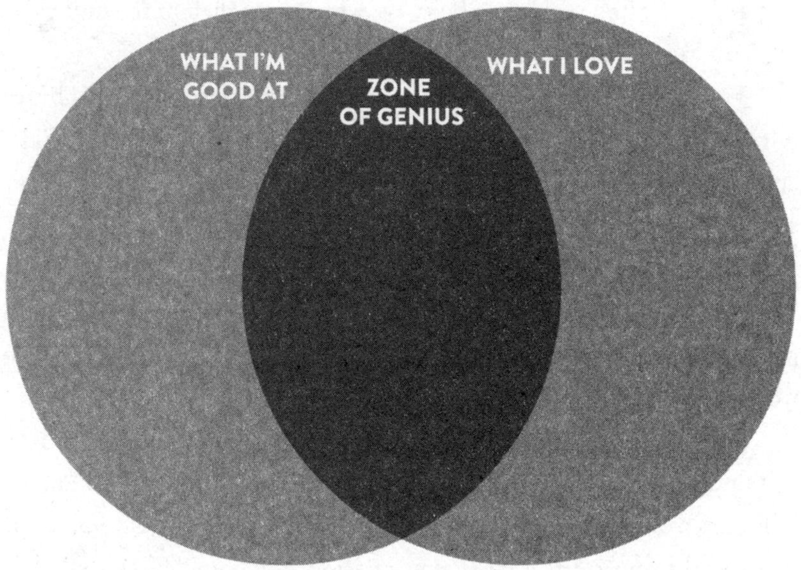

Now, brain dump. List anything that comes to mind in all three categories, but really prioritize your job or career because that's how you receive the money you're making.

Sometimes this process is what makes people realize they're in the completely wrong career. Sometimes this actually reassures people that they're doing all the right things, but with the wrong focus.

Even when the answers aren't incredibly obvious, they can still inform how you can spend more time in your zone of joy and genius.

For example, this is how my diagram looked when I began turning my attention toward finding a book deal and becoming more vocal about empowering workers to find better-paying jobs at more supportive companies:

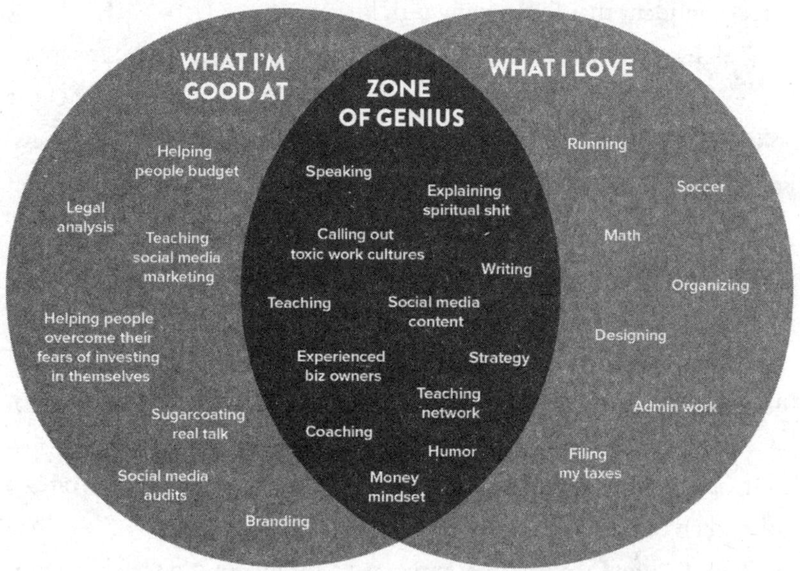

Some of these might sound silly or irrelevant, especially the category of things I love but am not good at. I admit I'm full of myself, so I tend to think I'm good at a lot of things, but I still forced myself to list activities there. Starting with irrelevant topics I *knew* I loved but could easily admit I was *not* innately good at helped me come up with more topics within my career and business.

Those topics I didn't love and I wasn't good at were the first things I got off my plate. I came up with a system for onboarding clients with prewritten contract templates, welcome emails, payment forms, call links, and more. That way when I onboarded a client, all I needed to do was copy and paste their information to send it out. As I worked through my process, I filmed a video for future employees who could take over those duties.

With designing and taxes, I bit the bullet and hired someone to do them for me. As much as I've always loved doing my own taxes (yes, seriously), it was time for me to admit that it had gotten too complex for me to feel confident that I was doing it right.

Taking those off my plate already opened up so much time for me!

When I turned my attention to the rest of the list and looked at it holistically, I saw how I needed to refocus my time and efforts in business. I advertised a lot of that left category as services I could do for potential clients, but I didn't really *enjoy* doing them. Some of it I couldn't completely dismiss, so instead, I looked at how I could provide those activities in ways that limited the time I spent doing them.

For example, I took my best practices for social media marketing and turned them all into videos I could upload in an online course. That way, my clients could watch the videos and learn how I used social media. That opened up our sessions to solely focus on their unique strategy, rather than covering the basics.

It's also how I realized that it was time for me to bring back my job-hunt coaching offers. I had an entire course that I'd recorded and hadn't promoted or sold in two years, so I updated everything to account for post-pandemic job hunting and added in more resources on leveraging social media in a job hunt. I started offering those coaching sessions again, and in no time, I signed two of my favorite clients to date.

And since they could learn the basics from the course, we spent all our time together addressing issues at their miserable jobs to make them more tolerable, zeroing in on what their dream jobs and companies were, and making quality contacts that actually led them to great opportunities. One of those clients learned to set boundaries in her job and, as a direct result, got a promotion with a $20,000 raise within three weeks of working with me!

I also started talking about all my favorite topics on social media, and this time, I wasn't sugarcoating any of it. I spoke my mind about work culture, job hunting, toxic business practices, ethical business strategy, calling out manipulative sales tactics, and more.

It was exactly what I needed to supercharge the stalling money in my business and reignite the passion in my life. It happened because I was able to shift so much off my plate that I was spending the majority of my time in that zone of joy and genius.

Making that shift is the entire reason I was able to start showing up for my next level and seeing the results. I'm essentially living my dream life.

I might not have the lake house, designer wardrobe, or the gay, drag-queen son of my dreams, but I only have active calls two days a week, I spend one writing and creating content, and I always have three-day weekends.

I might not be totally out of debt yet, but I make good enough money and I can see the light at the end of the tunnel, which is way more than I could say about myself three years ago.

I don't feel the pressure for the *stuff* in my dream life because I'm living a version of it now, and the feelings matter way more than the rest.

Isn't that why you're manifesting more money anyway? The goal is to enjoy your life. What's to stop you from enjoying it right now?

That is the power of spending all your time in the zone.

Habit Inventory

Just as we can keep our head down and work without taking a moment to reevaluate our plans to see if we need a new approach, we also need to take a step back and look at our habits.

This isn't necessarily about how we spend our time, though. It's more about the mindless actions we take in the name of saving money that, once we take a step back, don't always make sense or leave us with a low-key feeling of brokeness.

My mom is the *queen* of these. Some of her greatest hits are:

- Hanging up a square of paper towel to dry because she only used it to dry water off hands.
- Collecting hotel samples and hoarding them for years to display in a guest bathroom, even though nobody uses them.
- Getting a free refill of popcorn at the movie theater to bring home to pack up in the pantry as a snack.
- Collecting plastic cups at stadiums after sporting events to wash and use at home.

I realize this list sounds like a list of sustainability hacks, and if my mom were doing them to lower her carbon footprint, I probably wouldn't see them as cringeworthy. However, she's doing this not because she *can't afford* extra paper towels, guest samples, popcorn, or cups. She's doing it because she always has.

These are completely mindless habits. She's probably never stopped to ask herself if she needs more plastic cups or even wants that movie popcorn tomorrow.

And the truth is, we *all* have a list of habits like this. I asked my siblings to share their examples because we love calling each other out every time we do something like our mom does. Here were some of their gems:

- Rewearing clothes because they're not *that* smelly,
- Sneaking food into movies or events,
- Stocking up on free food from work or school whether you like it or not,

- Sourcing your furniture from people's trash piles at the curb or your apartment building's trash room,
- Watching bootleg movies,
- Using a student ID when you graduated *years* ago,
- Sneaking a flask into bars or stadiums,
- Bringing bags or Tupperware containers to a buffet or bottomless food event, and
- Taking free T-shirts from events that you don't actually want to wear.

They gave me plenty of other options, but I had to stop there or I would need to write a whole other book.

I know plenty of people probably want to jump down my throat right now to tell me that a lot of people *need* to do these things because they truly can't afford not to. Rest assured that I agree with you. I'm not talking about those people. I did plenty of these for *years*, especially when I was in college and just starting out in my career.

I'm talking about the people who make solid money and can afford to toss a paper towel after drying their hands.

If you're wondering why your money manifestation has plateaued or stalled, it's often because you're still living like you're broke by mindlessly engaging in behaviors like this.

For example, the only cereal I really like in this world is the OG Special K from Kellogg's with freeze-dried strawberries in it. At first, Kellogg's was the only one who made it, so I always bought a box when I went food shopping.

Yet when stores started releasing their generic brand version of it, I started buying it without a second thought—even though I didn't like it *nearly* as much as I liked Special K. I never questioned my own logic. Isn't that what financially responsible people *do*, buy the cheaper generic whenever they can?

Well, sometimes the generics just don't stack up to the name brand. And the generic cereal I bought from Safeway was one of those things for me.

It wasn't until I had been really craving some Special K that I found myself sighing in the grocery store, legit sad that I had to buy "Red Berries Cereal" instead of Special K.

Suddenly, it dawned on me. I don't *need* to buy the generic brand just because it's cheaper. I could afford an extra $1.30 for Special K. That wouldn't break my budget in the least.

Once I saw that, I started looking around at these other habits that left me sighing because it felt like I had to do them.

And even though it made me cringe at first to do things like let the waiter take away a small amount of leftovers I knew I wouldn't want to eat the next day, I began to feel less financial pressure.

It's odd that spending more money helped me feel financially free, but it's only because all these actions were money-saving habits that just made me feel broke rather than feeling pride from saving money.

And to be clear, Mama loves a deal. I love thrift shopping and I almost never pay full price for clothes. But that's because I feel really good about saving clothes from winding up in a landfill and getting clothes closer to their cost of production instead of the super markup stores place on them. If I'm going to drop some serious cash on clothes, I would rather buy a quality item from a small designer where my money makes a real difference.

But Special K tastes better to me than Great Value's "Strawberry Awake." It's not worth saving less than $2 to compromise on a flavor craving.

It's a lot like that old adage, "Don't spend a dollar to save a dime."

Just as Marie Kondo encourages you to think about all your unused clutter costing you money in terms of rent, storage space, and stress, I want you to think about your money habits in this way, too.

That doesn't mean you need to get rid of them all at once. I happily buy store-brand candles, even though I would prefer to get some fancier ones. They're just not at the top of my list of priorities as far as what I want to spend my money on.

When I'm rich and famous, though, I won't think twice about spending $50 on a three-wick, soy-blend candle.

Part of living your dream life is giving up the small shit that makes you feel broke. Perpetual disappointment costs way more than the dollar you're saving because it continues to place distance between you and your dream life.

Role Model Refresh

Of course I couldn't let you go without talking about finding role models for the new level you're achieving in your finances and life.

Initially, I talked about how important it was to collect a variety of role models who showed you what you were capable of having. Not just the rich and famous ones, but those who were only a few steps ahead of you as well.

This is your chance to look around and see if you like the people around you.

I'm not necessarily talking about friends, though they could be included here. Rather, I'm talking about the people you know who have reached the type of success you want.

Now that you have a better understanding of how to live in your zone of joy and genius and the individual to-do list that will help you connect with the authentic dream life you're manifesting, it's time to reevaluate those role models.

That doesn't mean you need to strike people off your list. It's more about looking at them collectively to see if they're still a match for you.

For example, when I decided it was time for me to focus on writing this book and public speaking, I started looking at who was around me in all facets of my business.

I loved all my clients, but had noticed more than a few had gotten into a habit of not actually watching the videos to teach them how to run successful businesses or apply any of the advice I had given them.

Having been a coach for three years, I obviously knew at this point that clients like that happen. They'll pay for containers, not take any real action, and wind up with shitty results. That's out of my control. I can't *blame* myself that they didn't get what they wanted out of it.

What I *could* control, though, was how I screened potential clients and who I chose to take on as a client. The biggest part of that was learning not to chase people down about working with me.

I've always said that fortune is in the follow-up. Most people genuinely don't mean to ghost you or forget to pay you, and they'll be grateful for the reminder. However, that's not what I was doing.

I would pitch people on working with me because I liked them or their business, even if I felt like they weren't sold on me. It was as if I became solely focused on proving myself to people who didn't show enough interest in working together.

So, I started letting people go, choosing instead to look for the people who would see me as a *fuck yes*. If I was on a call and I didn't feel like they were just as excited about me as I was about them, *I* chose not to pursue a sales call.

The other part of this is looking at your industry peers.

It took me unplugging from promoting my business and signing clients while I wrote my book to realize that (1) I hated Facebook as a platform, (2) I hated writing long-ass captions for social media that no one seemed to read, and (3) I lived in a bubble of coaches and entrepreneurs who all seemed to sell the same shit in the same way to the same people.

I was so sick of what my client acquisition efforts had become, but because I kept my nose to the grindstone and kept working, I hadn't had the time or space to realize that the people around me weren't aligned with what I wanted. I hated that all the coaches I knew seemed to advertise their services with the same kinds of copy. And I hated that everyone seemed like they were fighting each other for the same clients.

Too often had I asked the question, "Are you considering any other coaches or programs?" and heard a potential client mention someone who was nowhere near as talented as I was. Yet because those coaches felt comfortable making promises on results and posting pictures of expensive luxury goods, I felt disadvantaged somehow.

It wasn't that these people ran their businesses in a bad way. It just wasn't *my* way. And the fact that I was attracting the same potential clients as them left me feeling some kinda way—and it wasn't good.

So, I began ruthlessly clearing out the people I followed in all my news feeds. If I didn't find someone funny or interesting and they weren't already a personal friend, then away they went.

After I decluttered my contacts, something beautiful happened.

I enjoyed my social media feeds again.

I loved the posts I saw and the people who shared them. I wasn't feeling less-than anymore. I began sharing more personal posts, memes, and information I cared about. And I didn't see everyone who commented as a list of potential clients anymore.

Instead, I was having fun and being a *real* person. When I sat and thought about it, it made sense. I had essentially violated the rule of one of my favorite quotes: "If you're the smartest person in the room, you're in the wrong room."

Rather than engage in bitterness over the fact that people couldn't see how much better of a coach I was than them, I instead chose to leave the room I was in for a new one. The result was that I felt less pressure about my business than I had ever before, which did wonders for my confidence and creativity.

I'm not saying you need to unfriend everyone on social media and ditch your childhood friends. Instead, look at who your peers are and whether you feel like they're an accurate reflection of the more authentic person you've become.

Sometimes we outgrow our role models and that's OK. I don't have the same role models I did when I thought I was going to be an actress, a journalist, or a lawyer because I no longer want to be any of those things.

Running through your role models to see if they are truly living the life you want and showing up the way you want is a necessary step in learning how to bust through the glass ceiling. If you can't see everything that's up there, you need someone to give you a preview.

Show Me the Money (Magic)

- **Excellence versus genius.** Just because you're good at something and you make money from it doesn't mean that you need to continue pursuing it. If you prioritize joy over performance, you'll inevitably find more success because you'll enjoy the ways you make money.
- **Creatures of habit.** In the same vein as plodding along without examining whether we still enjoy how we make money, it's easy for us to overlook habits we don't need anymore. When you engage in behaviors from a place of scarcity—even though you no longer need them—it will subconsciously feel like you're still broke.
- **Take a look around.** Often, when we plateau in our money manifestations, it's because we've outgrown our spaces. If you can step back and look at the people you've been following, the places you're hanging out, and more, chances are you'll see that you're ready for fresh faces, spaces, and inspiration.

ACTIVITIES

- Are you functioning in your zone of excellence or zone of genius? What are you doing just because you can and not because you *want* to?
- What realizations did you have when you made your Venn diagram to discover your zone of genius? How can you spend more time in that middle space?

- What ridiculous habits are you still engaging in that make you feel broke instead of abundant? What's your version of Special K?
- Do your role models still align with the life you want? What gaps do you need to fill in to believe you can have everything you want?

Practical Magic for Increasing Your Money

If you've made it this far, congratulations. I'm so proud of you for sticking with me this whole time. It's not easy to stick with a book that tries really hard to poke at your wounds until you decide to clean them out and stitch them up.

At this point, all that's left for me to discuss is how to bring newness and calculated risk-taking into your life to speed out of the money-manifestation cruise control you're in.

It probably won't surprise you that the first piece of advice I have for you is to do more (a) shit that scares you and (b) shit you think you don't like.

By now, I'm sure Point A makes sense. Whenever we face our fears, we get a nice confidence boost when we realize that actions or activities we've feared are nowhere near as intimidating as we initially believed.

I'm not just talking about things that scare us in money or career either. I'm talking about literal activities that you find scary, like skydiving or telling your crush you like them.

When you make it a habit to confront fears anytime you feel like you're plateauing, you'll easily bounce out of that place once you've experienced something you would have never considered doing before.

This is actually how I started rock climbing! I wanted to confront my fear of heights and wound up loving it so much that I joined a gym, bought all the necessary gear, and started going three times a week.

The logic extends to doing things you don't like or, rather, things you don't *think* you like.

Getting over Yourself

In previous chapters, I talked about how attaining a certain degree of success is often accompanied by a mindless degree of hard work. Well, the same goes for everything we say we like.

It's almost like our brains go into lockdown to maintain the status quo by neutralizing any stimuli that could cause even minimal disruption of our workflow. It might make logical sense, but that lockdown of likes is actually what kills the inspiration we need to step outside of where we are and find the way to our zone of joy and genius.

Think of it like a relationship. In the beginning, everything is new and exciting. You've got the giggles and the butterflies and everything feels fun. Because of that, you're more willing to try activities or interests you wouldn't choose to engage in yourself or even see movies that normally wouldn't appeal to you.

Fast-forward two years later and it takes two hours just to pick a movie on Netflix because neither of you wants to compromise on what to watch. You're locked back down in your likes, and because you trust that your partner loves you, you don't feel like you need to win them over by giving their movie genres a try.

I know better five-and-a-half years later than to ask my fiancé to watch any British romantic period drama. It's not happening. And I don't care because I'm done watching any documentaries about Japan or movies where various British men go on road trips. Netflix made separate profiles *for a reason*, OK?

However, if you *never* decide to try anything new with your partner, you would both get bored, start living parallel lives, and feel disconnected.

It's the same thing with manifesting money.

That's not to say you need to buy things you don't like or compromise on your goals. Rather, I want you to start thinking about everything you've always said you don't like or would never do and be bold enough to try something different.

This could start off as small as brushing your teeth starting on the opposite corner of your mouth. It's about creating a habit of questioning yourself so you can learn more about who you're becoming as you reach your dream life.

The easiest way to do this is anytime you feel tempted to say—even internally—"No, I don't like that," instead say, "I don't know if I don't like that." It automatically puts you in the mindset to try something before ruling it out forever.

It makes sense. For example, our palates change about every seven years. It's why you can hate onions as a kid and think they're too spicy, only for you to sauté them in everything as an adult.

Similarly, our interests can change every few years. I'm pretty sure the vast majority of kids hate getting clothes at Christmas until they hit high school and clothes become *everything*.

Assume that you're still growing and give yourself a chance to get to know yourself again.

One of the best ways to do that? Assume you're wrong more often.

When Keeping It Real Goes Wrong

I've already told you how fiercely I love being right, so rest assured this comes from personal experience.

The more certain we feel about our rightness, the more important it is for us to assume we might actually be totally off base.

Being right was a huge issue in my relationship for a while. I never listened to anything my fiancé said, even if I asked for his opinion. The result was not just a good amount of arguing, but lots of "I told you so." And if being right is orgasmic, then hearing "I told you so" is probably the equivalent of being kicked in the cooter.

The worst bout of this was when I started my business. My fiancé did not approve of me jumping into a business without a job to keep me financially secure, but I did it anyway. And I said one of the most hurtful phrases I've ever uttered in our relationship.

"I love you, but, frankly, I don't care about what you think. My business needs to come before your needs right now because I don't know how else to do this with a job."

Oof. Had I been on the receiving end of that, I'm not so sure I would have stayed with me.

Was it any wonder that my new career caused so much friction for us?

A couple years later, my friend Michelle Keinan, a relationship coach who calls herself "The Satisfied Wife," told me one of the secrets to her happy marriage was "I would rather be in love than be right."

Not only that, but Michelle's story focuses on how she gave her husband complete control over her business. If he ever thinks her business is *harming* her, their relationship, or their family, he can tell her to pull the plug and she'll listen.

The first time I heard that, I judged her so hard. Like, why not give up your right to vote and stop wearing pants while you're at it?

When I put aside my initial shock, I realized what she was getting at was trusting the people *you already consider safe* to have your best interests at heart.

So, I stopped fighting. I started assuming he was right all the time. One of the biggest shifts I made was learning how to stop getting defensive when he gave me criticism.

Instead, I began saying, "Thank you for helping me get better at X."

And when my business looked like it was hitting a low point and he asked me to get a job, I started job hunting. I chose to see all of his feedback as coming from a place of love and wanting the best for me. I knew he would never cross my boundaries or ask me to do anything that would harm me or our relationship—just as I would never ask those things of him.

Not only did our relationship improve, but I began making *more* money. Job hunting myself helped me rediscover my passion for job-hunt *coaching*, and I started offering it as a service again.

Three weeks into that job hunt was when everything turned around. I went viral on TikTok, landed my agent and book deal, and began making the most consistent money I ever had in business. I no longer needed the job, but I made some great contacts and landed a few clients in the process.

If you are so focused on always being right, you'll miss so many opportunities where you can improve—not just as a person but in the ways you make money.

The practice of assuming you're wrong is good to use in most situations, even with shitty people who might not have your best interests in mind.

By listening to those people, you'll be able to see what kind of feedback makes you feel defensive. Those are the places where you need more healing and confidence. After all, we never get defensive over qualities or motives we know without a doubt we don't have.

Saying "Yes" Again

Generally speaking, one of the biggest lessons people learn before reaching success is how to say no. We've discussed this before in terms of setting boundaries with other people *and* with yourself.

By this point, you become a master of boundaries—someone who knows just how precious their energy is and how important it is to protect it.

Well, now that you're *so* good at saying no, it's time to start saying "yes" again.

When you've spent so long in a place of protection and focus, it's easy for your default setting to adjust to declining invitations or sitting on ideas. And that's a good thing! *No* is one of the more difficult words to say when we've been so thoroughly programmed around wanting others to like us.

The only problem is that it falls into the mindless-hustle category along with so many other behaviors we develop on the way to predictable success.

Of course, this doesn't mean you need to violate your boundaries around working. You don't need to take on clients you're not excited about or start automatically saying yes to anything your boss throws at you. Rather, reserve yes for the times when the options presented to you *could* be fun, but your knee-jerk reaction is to say no because you're tired or uncertain.

It's easy for "no" to become a defense mechanism to protect ourselves from saying a more difficult "no" later.

For example, it's much easier to say no to a date altogether than it is to say no once you're twenty minutes into a date.

That exact scenario happened to me during one of my "Say yes" phases. After about six months of refusing dates, I had recently decided that I was open to invitations again as long as they were from people in person. I didn't want to linger on the apps anymore because they felt like too much work. Well, not long after I set the intention, an invitation arrived.

It was a hot, sticky summer evening in DC, and I was heading home late from work after running an errand. I was wearing my favorite white sundress when a handsome stranger jogged across the street toward me. He stopped and said, "Miss, I'm sorry to bother you, but you are absolutely stunning in that dress and I just had to come tell you. Wherever you're going, can I walk you there?"

He seemed fine, so I said OK and started chatting. He was British and visiting DC on his way to another city for some kind of work. I found him interesting and was enjoying the conversation, so when he asked if I wanted to grab a drink before hitting the Metro, I agreed.

We popped into the nearest bar, which was in a basement, during what appeared to be karaoke night. We each ordered a beer and sat at a table to keep talking. That's when the energy shifted.

He started bragging about his work and how much money he made. He kept invading my personal space to whisper instead of talking loud enough for me to hear him. I also didn't like how touchy-feely he was getting, even though none of it was exactly *pervy*.

At the same time, I had been on dozens of dates just like that one and would generally smile and nod my way through until it felt like I had given someone enough of a chance that I could leave without them feeling bad. But the thought of doing that made me cringe.

I got up to use the bathroom and looked at my phone. We had only been there *fifteen minutes*. I realized I would rather be at home with my cat than sit here for another minute.

I went back out, sat down, and said, "I'm leaving."

He looked shocked. "Is everything OK?"

"Yes," I said. "I'm just not enjoying myself and I want to go home."

I left my nearly full beer on the table and walked out. Once I was outside, I felt *empowered*. I didn't lie about why I was leaving. I told some guy straight to his face that I was straight-up not having a good time and went home. It made saying yes in the first place worth it to me because I gave myself the confirmation I needed that I had truly broken the pattern around seeking validation in men.

Six months later, when I decided that January 2017 would be a month of yes to kick off the New Year, I let a friend give my phone number to my now fiancé.

She had asked me twice before, but I declined out of habit. What good was it to meet anyone who wasn't local?

Had I not decided on a month of yes, that third invitation might have been the last and I would never have met the love of my life.

So, give it a shot. For the next twenty-four hours, switch your default setting to yes and see what magic might happen when you're up for anything.

Leveling Up Your Financials

All of the advice to this point is well and good, but how can you start managing your finances like a boss once you're at this point? Obviously chaos energy and changing things up isn't as helpful when it comes to money management. After all, you spent all that time getting used to stability. You don't want to jeopardize that, right?

Well, the best advice I have for you is to decide that you want to learn about personal finance and take an interest in your financial future.

Looking for resources to attain the next level in your finances depends on the goals you have in mind.

If you have your emergency fund, a Fuck-You Fund, and you've paid off your debt, it's probably time to either start reading some personal finance books or talk to a financial advisor.

Now, plenty of gurus will tell you that financial advisors are full of shit, that they can't predict the market any better than you, and they'll charge you out the ass for the most minimal investment management. I'm not disagreeing with them. It's kind of like how people think lawyers are shady. A good number of my old classmates alone confirmed that for me.

Rather, you want to make sure you're looking for a financial advisor who fits your needs. Some financial advisors work off commission when you purchase life insurance or mutual funds from them, rather than charging astronomical fees for managing your account. Sometimes banks and credit unions provide free financial advisors.

Like most things, you'll be best served by shopping around for someone who fits your needs, your budget, and your vibe. Your intuition will never steer you wrong.

Yet even if you decide to hire someone, knowing some basics of personal finance will help you feel more empowered in those conversations and help you screen people even better. Reading books like *I Will Teach You to Be Rich* by Ramit Sethi or listening to podcasts like *So Money with Farnoosh Torabi* will help you develop an understanding on what financial goals you want to pursue.

The same goes for accountants. Honestly, if you're paying the high-end service from TurboTax, which comes with all the assistance and guarantees, you're going to wind up shelling out like $300 anyway. You can probably find a small accounting firm that charges the same price and will do everything for you. Some CPAs even offer sliding-scale options or a take on a certain number of pro bono clients every year. Getting financial help is not as out of reach as you think.

And for those of you in business, just know that the first person you should hire is a coach and the second is a virtual assistant. Why not the other way around? Because the coach will help you see the ways you can increase your business income and what you can offload to that virtual assistant when the time comes to hire them.

After that, it's all about unloading the tasks that you don't enjoy or the places where you need support. Just make sure that when you're hiring people, you're paying a livable wage. Plenty of virtual assistant firms from abroad, such as in India or the Philippines, seem to offer tempting rates, but their employees are earning far less than what they need to live—and what the legal minimum wages are in those countries.

That's a perfect segue into the last method for jump-starting your money manifestation: Fulfilling others' manifestations.

Be the Person You Needed

When you finally attain a level of consistent income that you're looking to increase, one of the best practical actions you can take is to pay it forward.

That's not meant as a platitude either. This is literally a method for more deeply understanding and tapping back into the concept of money as energy.

When you know there's more than enough to go around for everyone, it becomes much easier for you to see others' success as a foretelling of your own. If you're able to assist in that process, it's like getting a peek behind the curtain of the universe. You start to realize all the ways that other people's successes and destinies are intertwined with your own.

This is also the perfect time to see how you can start changing the world around you for the better. Back in the beginning of this book, I talked about how so many of the people I meet want to be rich so they can make a real impact in their communities.

Chances are, that resonated with you.

You probably started this journey imagining the ability to pay off the school lunch debt in your town or tipping a waitress $1,000 at Christmas.

My sister is truly the best example of this. She spent nearly a decade never making more than $40,000 a year. When she finally landed her dream job with a six-figure salary, she immediately looked for ways to pay it forward.

Sometimes it's small things like treating one of her pro bono clients to her first-ever Starbucks latte or giving 50 percent tips to her servers. Sometimes it's big, rich-bitch moves like secretly paying the bill on my parents' anniversary dinner for the family or spotting her friend the $500 it cost to attend BravoCon and letting her repay it over time.

No matter what it is she does, she tells me the same thing.

"It's what I needed when I was in their position."

She never forgets her experiences as the server, barista, intern, broke friend, broke daughter, broke sister, and because of that, she makes it a point to give as much as she can, whenever she can.

What's so wild to me is that the well never seems to run dry. Yes, she makes a good living, but she also lives in a big city with a massive cost of living. It would be all too easy for that to create tightness in her income. Yet she's somehow always winding up with money heading her way from surprise refunds or other random sources.

I truly think it all comes from her giving nature. She knows that whatever she pays out, she'll receive even more. And even if she didn't, the joy she gets from being a kind stranger makes it all worth it to her.

The truth is that we're all equally capable of answering the prayers from others manifesting money. Achieving this level is when you realize that the universe isn't some cosmic being creating miracles from mist.

The universe is all of us. It's the magic that happens when we create lives of joy with the intent of spreading it to others.

So, if you want to manifest, fulfill the manifestations of others.

Show Me the Money (Magic)

- **You don't know best.** The easiest way to break out of a plateau is to assume everything you thought was a *truth* about yourself and how you make money might not be. When we reach a certain degree of financial success, it's easy for us to dig our heels in over strategies or habits that got us to this point. But what got you to this goal is not what will get you to your next one. Be open to the idea that you might not know yourself or your income as well as you think.
- **Please say yes.** Finding success often comes with laser focus that makes us pros at saying no to protect our time, money, and energy. That means if you're at a plateau, it's time to swing in the other direction so you can find new inspiration and shake up the energy you've been in.
- **Get rich.** Now that you have money, it might be time for you to look into the ways you can make money work for you. There are countless strategies for learning to invest and create passive income for yourself. It's up to you to become fluent in the language of personal finance and, if you so choose, find a trusted advisor.
- **Give back to move forward.** Make sure that you share the wealth after you've attained a new level of success. When you use money to benefit others, it always comes back to you—often with interest.

ACTIVITIES

- What do you *think* you dislike that might be more of a habit than a preference? How does it change your perception of yourself to say, "I don't know if I don't like that"?
- Is wanting to always be right getting in the way of your abundance? Who makes you feel the most defensive and how could they be right about you?
- What financial professionals or resources do you feel like you need to uplevel your money?
- How can you be the person you needed when you were broke? Do you know anyone who could use a leg up that you could offer?

Wrichcraft Practices for Increasing Money

Magic around increasing money after you've stagnated means you need to focus on newness and shaking things up. Most of the information in this chapter will cover the ways you can magically reignite your spark.

The most important part of this, of course, is learning to remain open to *anything* coming your way. If you're willing to face whatever the universe wants to throw at you, even challenging experiences, you run a better chance of actually blasting through that glass ceiling above your head.

Make a Magical U-Turn

By now you know that everything around the plateau is all about change and newness. We want to release what isn't serving us and remain open for what will. That's why I like to use a change-of-course spell for those in plateaus.

You can do a change-of-course spell anytime, according to the moon phases and astrology outlined in Chapter 2. However, my favorite time to cast a change-of-course spell is on a lunar eclipse.

Some witches don't believe in doing magic on eclipses because the energy is so erratic, but I find that fully leaning into the chaos supercharges the effects by causing an about-face that will get you on the right path much faster.

The same thing goes for making moonwater, which many witches make by leaving a glass of water out under the moon. Many won't make eclipse water because of the scattered energy, but you *can* if you want. Just keep in mind that this is the type of water you need to label, date, and keep in the back of the fridge to save for when you need a bit of chaos magic in your life.

I would still recommend starting with this change-of-course spell to test out the energy and see if you can handle it first.

This ritual is ideal for an eclipse during a new moon. New moons are generally times of manifestation, but eclipses are times for change. Put these two together and you've got the energy for turning your luck around!

Change-of-Course Spell

We are working with the goddess Hecate because of her nature regarding duality.

"Hecate is a goddess of Greek mythology who was capable of both good and evil. She was especially associated with witchcraft, magic, the Moon, doorways, and creatures of the night such as hellhounds and ghosts. She is often depicted carrying a torch to remind of her connection with the night and in sculpture with three faces, representing her role as the guardian of crossroads."[1]

She embodies exactly what we're trying to do—move from darkness to light and draw up a crossroads for ourselves to move in a new direction.

She's often represented by dogs (the ancient Greeks sacrificed dogs and puppies to her) and keys.

As such, you'll want to have something to represent her. You could use a picture of a dog or merely a key.

TOOLS/SUPPLIES

- Your altar (a table, desk, even a windowsill is fine)
- A key or picture of a dog/puppy for Hecate
- A white or black candle (You can even use one based on what you're trying to change, such as red/pink for love life, green for money, etc.)
- A red ribbon (If focusing on love, you can include a black ribbon with it. If money, you can include black and blue ribbons.)
- A bowl
- 1 tablespoon of salt
- 1 tablespoon of water
- Paper (preferably green, but it doesn't matter that much)
- Writing instrument
- Optional lavender and/or bergamot oil (Lavender/bergamot spray or scent of any kind is fine, as is another essential oil for a specific purpose related to your spell.)

Directions

- Tidy your space for spell casting.
- Open your ceremony with a prayer of gratitude and protection to

your higher power, the spirits of the four directions (north, south, east, and west), any deities you're working with, and the goddess Hecate (Heck-*uh*-tee), who oversees all witchcraft and spells.

- Swing your finger around yourself clockwise.
- Place your key or doggo on your altar for Hecate.
- Use your hands, voice, body, etc., to drum up energy—sing, dance, chant, scream, beatbox, whatever you want.
- This is the part where you need to focus on your intent for the spell. Think about what you're calling in or releasing. Is it for your greatest good? You need strong desire and passion for what you're calling in.
- Write a list of three new things you want to bring into your life during this moon cycle (the next four weeks). These could include a new job, a relationship, an apartment, or whatever else.
- Anoint the paper with your oil and fold it seven times toward you.
- Tie your ribbons around the candle as best you can.
- Take your candle and place it in a bowl. Place the tablespoon of salt around the candle. Add the tablespoon of water around it as well.
- Light the candle and say the following words:

On this Lunar Eclipse, I stand before thee,
To ask for your guidance, oh, Goddess Hecate.
The darkness of the Moon and light of the Sun,
Compel me to move, walk, or run.
I, (say your full name), stand tall in this place
A product of Goddess and God's divine holy grace.
I am my ancestors' wildest dream.
I'm healing their trauma, I will wipe this slate clean.

From my habits I am free. (Think about the habits you want to let go of.)
From my addictions I am free. (Think about the addictions you want to let go of.)
From my problems I am free. (Think about the problems you want to let go of.)
From this moment on, I'm starting anew
As blessings and actions come into view.
Let the Sun guide me each step of this path.
Let the Moon guard me, 'til my dreams come to pass.
I thank thee!
I thank thee!
I thank thee!

- Think of affirmations that go with what you're calling in. ("It is safe for me to make X amount of money" or "It is easy and effortless for me to find a date" or "I am easy to love." Say whatever feels right.)
- Burn your paper in the candle flame. Say your affirmations three times while it burns.
- If it's still burning when you're done repeating your affirmations, just imagine what it will be like to receive your manifestations/be on your new course of life.
- Close the circle with a prayer asking that your will be done with harm to none and finishing with the phrase "With this sound, my circle is down."
- Clap or otherwise make a noise to indicate that your protection circle is now closed.
- Swing your finger around yourself counterclockwise or just in the opposite direction than you did at the beginning.

- Go forth and celebrate! Your energy will continue flowing toward your blessings.

Getting to Know You(rself)

To reignite your money manifestation magic, we're going to revisit astrology for some inspiration. Two aspects present the perfect jumping-off points for self-exploration: the nodes and Lilith.

The nodes are two placements in your birth chart called the North Node and South Node. The North Node covers the way you are most likely to find self-fulfillment in life. It's the theme around what qualities you need to embrace and grow into to evolve as a person. With that, it also describes the type of lessons you'll face in life to help you stretch past your comfort zone and grow.

The South Node denotes the past—typically your early life and the qualities you've needed to heal and those you can take with you as you begin to embody your North Node. It's both the version of you that you're leaving behind and the wisdom you learned as that person. Some even say it indicates who you were in your most recent past life.

The nodes are always polarities, meaning the signs directly across from each other on the zodiac wheel. This is why you'll typically only see the North Node on your chart. It's assumed the South Node is its exact opposite.

Here, we're focusing on the North Node. Remember, whenever we want to fully understand a placement, we need to look at both the sign and the house it's in. This is because the signs describe the personality traits and the houses explain in what area of life they show up.

Let's take mine for example. I have my North Node in Aries, which makes my South Node its opposite—Libra.

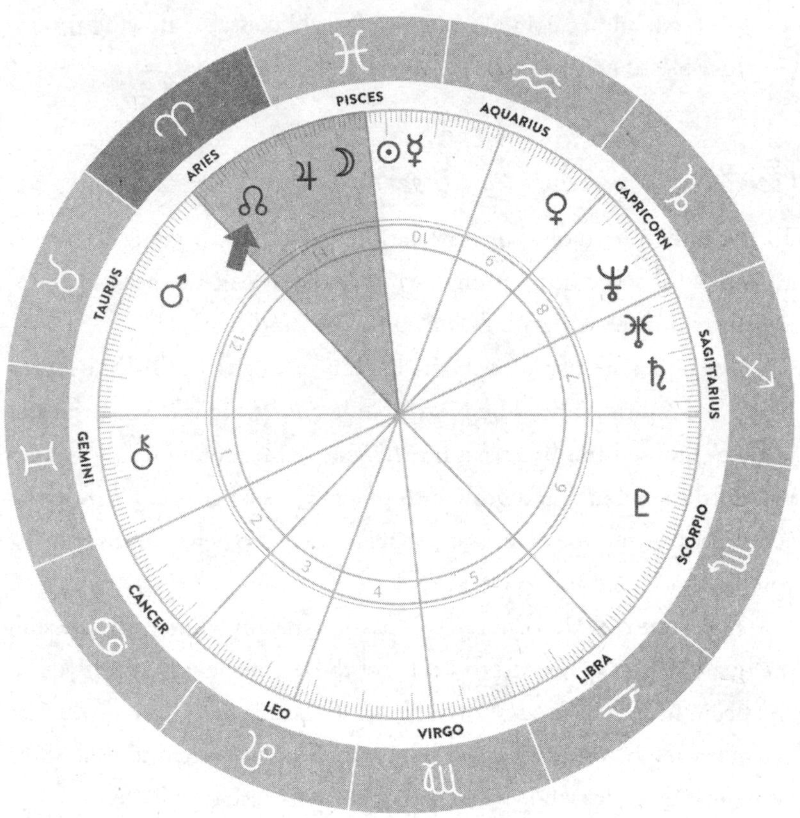

If we look at the signs and their qualities alone, it's easy to gather that in my early life, I struggled with people-pleasing, codependency, making decisions, and being argumentative. Even though that's a surface-level description of Libra's qualities, it's all true. However, my south node in Libra also gave me some natural gifts like charm, beauty (*flips hair*), keen artistic sense, and a knack for mediating.

Meanwhile, my North Node in Aries pushes me way outside my comfort zone. I'm challenged to be a leader, solely focus on myself and my goals, and to act swiftly and decisively. I'm being called to stand up for myself and to build independence. Can you see how that would naturally be scary for someone whose comfort zone is solidly in the opposite type of dynamic?

The houses are just as important here, too. Having my North Node in the Eleventh House means that my destiny is wrapped up in my community—both my friends and mankind as a whole. My purpose is to advocate for a group, find belonging in a group, and move all of us toward a more compassionate, humane future.

Even though these descriptions barely skim the surface of what the nodes truly mean, I can see how that's played out for me so far. I've definitely made that journey in my life from someone who deeply cared about the opinions of others into creating a highly self-reliant career focused on changing the world through community.

Looking at the nodes' signs and houses can often provide you with insight on what direction you're being called in and the best way to show up for it. When you're in a manifestation plateau, the North Node serves as a reminder of what qualities you can lean into to better connect with your destiny.

When it comes to money in particular, Lilith is one of my favorite positions to explore. "Black Moon Lilith," as it's also known, is a mathematical point in your birth chart. It's named after the fabled first wife of Adam in the Bible. Lilith refused to lie beneath him during sex because she was not below him—which is funny only because anyone who's been in a committed relationship long enough knows that being on the bottom is prime real estate because it means less work.

Anyway, she rebelled, left Eden, and not even the angels could persuade her to return. She became a demon who apparently stole men's "life force" in the middle of the night so she could reproduce more demons. In my opinion, it sounds like she had it better than Eve.

Lilith in the birth chart carries a similar theme to her namesake. She's full of duality—rebellion and obedience, sexual freedom and repression, trauma and healing. There's a reason astrology enthusiasts so often refer to her as your "inner bad bitch."

Looking at the sign and the house will indicate both the trauma you need to heal and the power you carry in this life.

For me, that's Cancer and the Second House. With Cancer, it conveys difficulty in a childhood where I felt neglected or unseen. Not getting that nurturing I craved means that now I am the Mama Bear of my chosen family and friend group. The Second House being about money tells me that my power comes from living through financial lessons that force me to learn how to let go of the scarcity mindset and allow myself to live in luxury.

When I'm in a plateau, I know I can look at these placements and see what kind of healing I need to focus on to feel more confident. Lilith helps me love the negative qualities associated with those placements.

Generally speaking, that means confronting all those feelings from childhood around being told I was too sensitive that made me retreat into myself and how that affected my financial life. It also means anytime I experience some sort of financial chaos, it's my job to find the lesson in it that I can teach others so we can all learn to live the good life.

Alexa, play Ariana Grande's "7 Rings."

Deities for Increasing Money

The deities included here are all about getting in touch with your power. Yes, they're associated with wealth and fortune, but more importantly, they're associated with being a fucking badass.

These are the gods and goddesses who don't play. They will happily work with you, but you also better be ready to get called off the bench and put into the game.

You know how "nothing works unless you do"? The same goes for these three. If you want big results, they'll expect a big commitment.

Hathor

- Egyptian fertility goddess of love, the sky, joy, the sun, birth, alcohol, and the harvest; often depicted in a headdress of cow's horns with the sunset between them

  Color: Red

  Symbols: Cattle, gazelles, mirrors, cats, drums, beer, wine

  Days: Her birthday on September 17, the Egyptian new year on August 7, and a festival for harvesting papyrus on November 2

  OG myth: Honestly, so many great myths about Hathor exist to show what a party girl she is. In her early days, she caught a taste for murder after slaughtering hundreds of humans for insulting her father, Ra. He tried to call her off, but she found the rampage too fun and wouldn't stop. So, he offered her a bunch of beer dyed red with mandrake and told her it was blood. She drank it, *loved it*, fell asleep, and woke up cured of her thirst for bloodshed. One of her favorite offerings is booze. In another myth involving a trial, Ra stormed out of the courtroom after an insult, leaving everyone without a judge. Hathor followed him and started doing a funny dance in which she kept flashing her coochie, which made Ra laugh enough to get over the offense and return to court. I have a feeling we would see even more lawyers if this were still a common practice.

Jupiter (Jove)

- Roman king of the gods who oversaw the sky, thunder, lightning, wisdom, wealth, and abundance

  Color: Blue

  Symbols: Eagles, lightning bolts, walnuts, or anything you would associate with a rich, good-natured grandfather or sugar daddy

Days: Thursdays, the Ides of each month, and a bunch of other festival days he shared with other Roman deities throughout the year

OG myth: Romans weren't big on storytelling with their deities, but they do believe that Jupiter was integral to the foundation of Rome. As they explained it, Rome was struggling under its second king, Numa. So, Numa persuaded two lesser deities to summon Jupiter. Numa pleaded with Jupiter for his protection, so Jupiter outlined his demands around worship and sacrifices. In exchange, he taught Numa how to avoid lightning bolts. This acted as a metaphor as most of Rome believed the success of its empire was because of their worship of Jupiter. I wonder who they credit for its fall.

Freyr

◢ Norse god of peace, prosperity, pleasure, good luck, the harvest, rain, and the sun; king of the elves

Colors: Brown, gold, and green

Symbols: Boars, ships, the ocean, water, beer/wine/ale/mead, erections (seriously)

Days: February 2, August 1, and the twelve days of Yule (the original Norse-Germanic holiday that inspired Christmas)

OG myth: Freyr sat on Odin's throne, which gave him a view of the whole world. He saw a giantess named Gerdr, whom he thought was so beautiful that he immediately lapsed into a deep depression over the idea that he could not have her. Freyr's father, Njord, sent a servant to help his son, who asked the servant to woo Gerdr on Freyr's behalf. As payment, the servant asked for Freyr's sword that fought on its own. Freyr turned it over, and Gerdr agreed to his proposal. It turned out to be quite the sacrifice as without his sword, Freyr died in the battle of Ragnarok. It just goes to show that thinking with one's dick has a long, rich history.

Crystals for Shaking It Up

While all the crystals I'm discussing in this section are capable of manifesting money, I'm going to take a moment to dive in on one in particular because it's uniquely suited for those of you in plateaus.

Yes, I'm talking about none other than the tektite known as moldavite.

Moldavite came to fame on TikTok as a powerful manifestation crystal, which left everyone scrambling to get some, despite its high price tag.

Even though moldavite is technically a good crystal for manifesting, it's meant for people who have already done a lot of healing work. That's because they're usually more willing to embrace difficult lessons and stay grounded through the process.

Because what moldavite does is strip you of *anything* in your life that's standing in the way of you and your alignment.

Without some healing or attempts to get your life into alignment before buying moldavite, you should prepare yourself for some earth-shattering changes in your life. I'm talking breakups with people you thought you would marry, getting fired from your job without a backup plan, deep betrayals revealing a friend's true colors, and so on. It's the kind of shit that will leave you scream-singing to Natalie Imbruglia's "Torn" on repeat.

Of course, all of it will inevitably lead to the type of life you've been craving, but it's going to come after a lot of pain.

All of that being said, if you've been working on your shit and are stuck in a juicy plateau, *this* is the crystal you want. It will shake things up in the best way, and the more open you are to whatever it brings, the better your experience.

Also, keep in mind that moldavite is a limited-quantity tektite because it *all* comes from the same crater in the Czech Republic. Naturally, that means there's a lot of green glass sold as moldavite on the market. Make sure you buy from a reputable seller who can certify its authenticity.

Now that that's out of the way, let's jump into the rest of the stones for ceiling shattering.

- **Malachite, a.k.a. the less intense version of moldavite:** Transformation, trauma healing, pattern breaking, empowerment, protection
- **Black Obsidian:** Introspection, strengthening, mirroring inner self, relaxing the mind, protection, absorbs negativity
- **Amethyst:** Inspiration, cleansing, invigorating, enhancing responsibility, clearing aura
- **Yellow Sapphire:** Gratitude, appreciation, positivity, bliss, physical power, wisdom, wit, optimism, enthusiasm
- **Black Agate:** Connects you with your spiritual purpose, good fortune, mental clarity, laughter, emotional balance
- **Bloodstone:** Heightens intuition, increases creativity, reduces grief, absorbs pain from challenging situations, protection
- **Goldstone:** Ambition, confidence, endurance, mental clarity, abundance

These will all work when it comes to getting clear on the ways you can peel back any layers blocking your authenticity and live in the zone of joy and genius. You'll find yourself inspired in new ways and thinking creatively about your life and the ways you bring money into it.

Flower Power

Just as with crystals, I like to use rituals and resources that will shake up the energy I've been in so I can start attracting newness into my life.

One resource I haven't covered yet is flower remedies.

These are tinctures that specialized practitioners make from plants that promote certain emotions. By consuming them, you improve your overall emotional state and rebalance those that feel like they're holding you back from reaching your full potential.

You drip about four drops under your tongue about every four hours, every day for at least one month. Generally, a full course can span up to three months, but you can basically stop when you start forgetting to take them. It's your body's signal that they're no longer needed.

Now, it's important to clarify that flower remedies are intended as a supplemental treatment for balancing emotions and unblocking those that seem to get in the way of taking action.

The effects are really subtle with flower remedies, but they build over time.

For example, the first flower remedy I ever tried was mimulus for support in facing my fears. It was about a year into my entrepreneurial journey and right after that program that bombed. It felt like I was afraid to move in any direction because I was so unsure of myself.

I had bought two flower remedies months before and forgotten about them. So, in the midst of my fear paralysis, I decided to give the mimulus a shot.

I began taking it religiously, and about three weeks later, I found myself craving something I never had before—scary movies and TV shows.

Now, it *was* October, but just to make it clear, I've never enjoyed the fear part of Halloween. When I was a kid, my mom had to hide the life-sized, glow-in-the-dark skeleton at night because I would get too afraid to use the bathroom or get a glass of water. My parents forbade me from watching *The Nightmare Before Christmas* until I was in middle school because I scared so easily.

It didn't change as an adult either. Most of my Halloween decorations are different variations of teddy bears dressed in classic costumes like ghosts and witches. I only let myself watch *Supernatural* and the Netflix reboot of *Sabrina* during the day because I would get too shook up at night.

So, it was *bizarre* that after thirty-three years of living as a scaredy cat I would suddenly want to start watching horror. It started with Mike Flanagan's *The Haunting of Blair Manor*, which my fiancé and I binged (at night!) in about three days. We immediately moved on to *The Haunting of Hill House*.

It didn't stop there either. My fiancé, a horror nut, capitalized on this newfound interest and kept picking movies he thought I would like. I couldn't get enough of them!

The stark change led me to read as much as I could about fear. I found it fascinating that I could have such an immediate change of heart that found me appreciating all the physical and emotional sensations that fear caused inside me.

Inevitably, I began craving the same kind of rush in my business. I knew I had been hiding—behind a copywriter, behind guest speakers. I realized that even though what I wanted more than anything was to be seen, I was *terrified* of what that really meant. Anytime I took a big step forward in my business, I seemed to pull myself back.

I knew I needed to share these thoughts with the world and began sharing my revelations on social media. I talked about fear and how important an emotion it was when it came to making money. If you weren't afraid, I said, then you weren't pushing yourself enough outside the comfort zone to truly succeed.

All that talk about fear, Halloween, and manifestation caught the eye of a former client who had paid to take the original version of my job-hunt course about a year earlier. She had been playing with the idea of starting a boutique public relations firm and asked if she could use me to test whether she could pull it off. I liked her and didn't have anything to lose, so I said yes.

Three weeks later, I was featured in *Forbes*.

That's how flower remedies support your emotional well-being. They don't repress the emotions you're struggling with. Rather, they amplify the feelings that can help you move through those blocks to help you reach your full potential.

You can find a whole smorgasbord of options from the original producers at Bach Flower Remedies or find a practitioner who can create a custom blend for you. One I love in particular is Alexis Smart, who features custom blends on her website to help with common issues.

Show Me the Money (Magic)

- **Change lanes.** Sometimes it's not just about taking different actions, but also intentionally changing your energy's directions. Whenever you're in a plateau and nothing you do is yielding results, a change-of-course spell will always switch things up. As long as you're willing to lean into a bit of chaos, you might just enjoy the new path that follows!
- **Destiny's child.** If you're in a financial rut, it's a great opportunity to examine your North and South Nodes and Lilith. Find the sign and house for your North Node to get an idea of whether your goals are aligned with your destiny and to identify qualities you need to lead with to get there. Then, use Black Moon Lilith to guide your healing and embrace your shadow self.
- **Energy investors.** Deities for breaking out of a plateau should help you tap into new inspiration and leadership qualities. This is the time to break out the big guns. Go for powerful figures who can show you how to crack out of your shell.
- **Don't make moldavite your first crystal.** Technically a tektite, moldavite is not a stone to mess around with if you're a beginner. That being said, if you're completely willing to break down and lose it all to align with your fate, it might just be the right option for you. If you're scared, start off with malachite or opt for a stone focused more on empowerment than extremities.
- **Flowers for the win.** Flower remedies create small yet powerful shifts inside you over several weeks. If there's a quality you've struggled to

access, a flower remedy can help you get there. Rather than picking one willy-nilly, asking a practitioner or expert for recommendations will probably be more fruitful (pun intended).

ACTIVITIES

- If it feels like you've been stalled out in your energy for a while, try your hand at the change-of-course spell. Make sure to document when you cast it and any developments along the way.
- Check out your birth chart again and make notes about the signs and houses for your North and South Nodes and Lilith. Journal on the qualities of these signs and houses, how they've been playing out in your life thus far, and how you can better utilize them moving forward. Do some research to see what else you can learn about yourself.
- Find a deity who feels as powerful as you want to feel in your finances. Create a space on your altar for them and ask for them to lend you strength whenever you engage with your career or money.
- If you feel ready for moldavite, make sure to research reputable vendors who can offer certificates of authenticity. Otherwise, journal about what kind of power you would like to channel right now. Find the crystal that would match that flavor of empowerment.
- What's been the hardest emotional shift for you to make lately? Research some flower remedies and see

what options might help you tap into that quality. If in doubt, reach out to a practitioner for advice.

Conclusion

When we met way back in the beginning of this book, I explained that a general tenet of witchcraft is that *magic is science, and science is magic*.

That formed the basis of my goal when I began learning what I could about manifesting money and money magic, leading me to adopt my own mantra: *Money magic is finance, and finance is money magic*.

Eighteen chapters later, I hope you see that, too.

I'm sure my wordy ass has you overwhelmed with information—excited, but a little unsure of what to do next. My advice? If you've never tried your hand at money manifestation or money magic, go back to Part 2 and start implementing the advice that feels easiest. If you've *been* manifesting money, go back to the section you resonated with the most and do the same thing.

Just make sure that you take a balanced approach to your manifestation strategy. If you *only* use the magic methods without the personal finance, you probably won't get the results you wanted out of this book. Similarly, if you seek to *only* solve your problems with straightforward financial solutions, your mindset (and the universe) will probably ruin the fun like my college neighbors who always called the cops on my parties an hour in.

Yet no matter where you start, it's crucial to make the mental shift around how you think about money. You need to give up the view that money is scarce and finite, instead adopting the viewpoint that it *flows* (remember that *current* and *currency* share the same Latin root) and it's in the air around us all the time. Part of that is also giving up the idea that money is good or bad. It's how we use it that matters.

Then there are the basics of magic. Understanding the moon phases, the zodiac signs, and the importance of intention and visualization make all the difference when we're investigating magical solutions to money.

Of course, science is a huge part of this as well. Learning exactly how our brains work in the grand scheme of the world and existence itself makes it more believable that you contain enough power to shape your destiny.

Once you have that foundation under your belt, you can start manifesting money.

For those beginners, keep in mind that a massive aspect of manifesting money is understanding neuroscience and psychology. Our brains are wired to protect us from a range of traumas they experienced when we were growing up, and our psyches love to play along by hiding the beliefs that are holding us back in our subconscious.

Thankfully, now you know that once you access those subconscious beliefs, you can also change them. It's all about seeing to believe, listening to your body when you need to rest, prioritizing fun, and following your intuition to the results that only you can achieve in your own unique way.

That's when it's time for some strategy. Manifesting money starts with some practical strategies to increase your income or save more of it. That can look like finding a new job, asking for a salary adjustment, starting a business or side hustle, creating a strategic spending plan, or, most likely, a combination of several of those options.

Approaching the practical first will only give your spells more juice. After all, those are the types of actions you would take if your rituals were successful.

And speaking of rituals, don't be afraid to give them a try! Keep them simple to start and never forget that intention is *always* more important than the words or actions. Between astrology, deities, crystals, and herbs, you have so many magical tools at your disposal—and a lot of them are probably already in your house.

Now, if your manifestation journey is focused on *keeping* the money you manifest, that will require some tweaking. You first need to focus on finding stability in your finances. I like to say that stability is the stepping-stone to wealth. You can't manifest abundance without first manifesting stability.

So, take an honest look at your dramatic ass to see if money has become a tool for you to wreak havoc on yourself because drama feels more predictable and secure than security. Once you see it, accept it. It's OK that you've used spending money as a trauma response. Forgive yourself and release the shame. Otherwise, it will be difficult to find a real solution.

The truth is that sometimes we manufacture bullshit in our lives because we get some sick satisfaction from it. That's OK, too. I'm not here to kink shame your brand of existential masochism.

Instead, accept all of this when it comes to your finances. Start assuming that you will fall short of big goals and dare to aim lower. Budget for the worst-case scenarios. And instead of running from your debt, take initiative and reach out to your creditors and/or a credit counselor. When you choose not to shame yourself, it becomes easier to take action.

As far as your magical approach, focus your rituals and energies around staying centered and removing anything that's zapping your energy. No matter how big or small that may be, you'll feel *much* better when it's all out of your life.

Finally, when it feels like you've been in a juicy financial place for a while, but can't seem to scale the money coming to you, it's time to shake things up. Revisit all your goals, role models, and information sources to ensure they're still in alignment with what you want. Chances are, you've outgrown one or more of them. Just as we donate outdated clothing, it's probably time for you to do some inspiration shopping. You're not the person you were when you started this journey, so what got you here *won't* be what gets you to the next level. You might even need to overcompensate by playing the villain a little bit, but I promise you'll never be as bad as you think you are.

Once you've cleared out all those old strategies, influences, and habits, you can start spending the rest of your time and energy in your zone of joy and genius—all the stuff you're *both* good at *and* love doing. That's the key to your next level.

Switching up your energy will also require you to take new approaches. You'll probably need to consider hiring help, whether that's a financial advisor, coach, or virtual assistant. At the very least, you'll need to question what you think you know and remain open to the feedback from people who value you. The truth is you *don't* know it all.

Rituals, spells, and tools at this point should focus on changing the energy or direction of the path you're on. That could be as extreme as buying a piece of moldavite—the tektite known for its vicious stripping back of anything keeping you off your authentic path—or as gentle as a flower remedy to help you access a particular feeling of power you've been craving.

No matter what phase you're in or what path you take, what's clear is that you can create your own formula for manifesting money. Despite what personal finance gurus want you to believe, there's no one-size-fits-all strategy for creating financial abundance.

If you take nothing else away from this book, I hope you know that no matter what financial circumstances you're in right now, you *can* change them. And you can change them *your* way.

After all, that's exactly how I learned to crawl out of all the embarrassing or hopeless situations I've been in over the years. I had to learn how to embrace the chaos, shame, success, and pitfalls to get where I am today.

And if the only reason for all of it was so you could feel fully seen and empowered enough to find your own financial strategy that leads you to pay it forward *even more*, then I would happily fall on my face all over again.

So, don't let me down. Go out there and manifest some money. **The world needs you to be rich.**

Notes

Chapter 1

1 Heather Long, "Amazon's $15 Minimum Wage Doesn't End Debate over Whether It's Creating Good Jobs," *Washington Post*, October 5, 2018, https://www.washingtonpost.com/business/economy/amazons-15-minimum-wage-doesnt-end-debate-over-whether-its-creating-good-jobs/2018/10/05/b1da23a0-c802-11e8-9b1c-a90f1daae309_story.html.

2 Nicole Spector, "Global Catastrophes Jeff Bezos Could Fix and Still Be the Richest Man in the World," *Yahoo*, October 13, 2020, https://www.yahoo.com/video/global-catastrophes-jeff-bezos-could-120012088.html.

3 Madeline Berg, "Dolly Parton's Net Worth Revealed: The Staggering Success of America's Country Music Queen," *Forbes*, August 5, 2021, https://www.forbes.com/sites/maddieberg/2021/08/05/dolly-partons-net-worth-revealed-the-staggering-success-of-americas-country-music-queen/?sh=344bc9676a28.

4 Rania Aniftos, "A Timeline of Dolly Parton's Good Deeds," *Billboard*, August 3, 2022, https://www.billboard.com/music/music-news/dolly-parton-good-deeds-timeline-9487782/.

5 Gabrielle Sanchez, "10 Times Dolly Parton Was a Literal Angel," *Vulture*, November 19, 2020, https://www.vulture.com/2020/11/dolly-parton-vaccine-donation-history.html.

6 Sudiksha Kochi, "Dolly Parton Gives Royalties from Whitney Houston's 'I Will Always Love You' to Black Community," *USA Today*, August 2, 2021, https://www.usatoday.com/story/entertainment/celebrities/2021/08/02/dolly-parton-gives-black-nashville-property-whitney-houston-song-money/5452329001/.

Chapter 2

1 Iain Duguid, "The Real Prayer of Jabez," Westminster Theological Seminary, January 8, 2018, https://faculty.wts.edu/posts/real-prayer-jabez/.

Chapter 3

1 The Editors of the Encyclopedia Britannica, "Matter," *Encyclopedia Britannica*, https://www.britannica.com/science/matter.

2 Mauro Manassi and David Whitney, "Illusions of Visual Stability through Active Perceptual Serial Dependence," *Science Advances*, January 12, 2022, https://www.science.org/doi/10.1126/sciadv.abk2480.

3 Lisa Feldman-Barrett, "The Mind-Blowing Science Behind How Our Brains Shape Reality," *Science Focus*, May 17, 2021, https://www.sciencefocus.com/the-human-body/the-mind-blowing-science-behind-how-our-brains-shape-reality/.

4 Anil Ananthaswamy and Kate Douglas, "Can a Robot Ever Be Conscious and How Would We Know If It Were?" *NewScientist*, July 7, 2021, https://www.newscientist.com/article/mg25033420–600-can-physics-explain-consciousness-and-does-it-create-reality/.

5 Tam Hunt, "The Hippies Were Right: It's All about Vibrations, Man!" *Scientific American*, December 5, 2018, https://blogs.scientificamerican.com/observations/the-hippies-were-right-its-all-about-vibrations-man/.

6 Cell Press, "People Synchronize Heart Rates While Listening Attentively to Stories," *Science Daily,* September 14, 2021, https://www.sciencedaily.com/releases/2021/09/210914111238.htm.

7 Inga Timofejeva1, Rollin McCraty, Mike Atkinson, et. al., "Global Study of Human Heart Rhythm Synchronization with the Earth's Time Varying Magnetic Field," *Journal of Applied Sciences*, November 2021, https://doi.org/10.3390/app11072935.

8 Cymaman, "Water Out of Chaos: Cymatics Reveals the Hidden Geometry of Water," YouTube Video, 4:15, January 15, 2015, https://www.youtube.com/watch?v=fTI4ZmiuOrs.

9 Rongxiang Tang, Karl Friston, and Yi-Yuan Tang, "Brief Mindfulness Meditation Induces Gray Matter Changes in a Brain Hub," *Neural Plasticity* (November 2020), doi:10.1155/2020/8830005.

10 Brynne DiMenichi et al., "Effects of Expressive Writing on Neural Processing during Learning," *Frontiers in Human Neuroscience*, no. 6 (November 2019), https://doi.org/10.3389/fnhum.2019.00389.

11 Bruce Ecker, "Creating Juxtaposition Experiences to Relieve Trauma Symptoms," *Psychotherapy Networker*, https://www.psychotherapynetworker.org/blog/details/676/a-brain-science-strategy-for-overwriting-traumatic.

12 Lexi Krock, "Fertility throughout Life," *NOVA Online*, October 2001, https://www.pbs.org/wgbh/nova/baby/fert_text.html.

13 Lauren Wilson, "Mothers, Beware: Your Lifestyle Choices Will Even Affect Your Grandkids," *News.Com.Au*, May 23, 2015. https://www.news.com.au/lifestyle/parenting/kids/mothers-beware-your-lifestyle-choices-will-even-affect-your-grandkids/news-story/3f326f457546cfb32af5c409f335fb56.

14 Olga Khazan, "Inherited Trauma Shapes Your Health," *The Atlantic*, October 16, 2018, https://www.theatlantic.com/health/archive/2018/10/trauma-inherited-generations/573055/.

15 Jocelyn Kaiser, "Mom's Environment during Pregnancy Can Affect Her Grandchildren," *Science*, July 10, 2014, https://www.science.org/content/article/moms-environment-during-pregnancy-can-affect-her-grandchildren.

16 Jill M. Goldstein, et al., "Impact of Prenatal Maternal Cytokine Exposure on Sex Differences in Brain Circuitry Regulating Stress in Offspring 45 Years Later," *PNAS* 118, no. 15 (February 1, 2021), https://doi.org/10.1073/pnas.2014464118.

17 "Witch-hunts in Early Modern Europe (circa 1450–1750)," *Gendercide.Org*, https://www.gendercide.org/case_witchhunts.html.

18 "Vietnam War U.S. Military Fatal Casualty Statistics," *NationalArchives.Gov*, https://www.archives.gov/research/military/vietnam-war/casualty-statistics.

19 Tim Newman, "5 Bizarre Medical Techniques from History," *MedicalNewsToday*, October 3, 2018, https://www.medicalnewstoday.com/articles/323221#1.-The-tobacco-smoke-enema.

Chapter 5

1 Mariam Arain et al., "Maturation of the Adolescent Brain," *Neuropsychiatric Disease and Treatment* 9 (April 2013): 449–61, https://doi.org/10.2147/NDT.S39776.

2 Elyssa Barbash, "Different Types of Trauma: Small 't' versus Large 'T'," *Psychology Today*, March 13, 2017, https://www.psychologytoday.com/us/blog/trauma-and-hope/201703/different-types-trauma-small-t-versus-large-t.

Chapter 6

1 Katie Nodjimbadem, "The Racial Segregation of American Cities Was Anything But Accidental," *Smithsonian Magazine*, May 30, 2017, https://www.smithsonianmag.com/history/how-federal-government-intentionally-racially-segregated-american-cities-180963494/.

2 Debra Kamin, "Black Homeowners Face Discrimination in Appraisals," *New York Times*, August 25, 2020, https://www.nytimes.com/2020/08/25/realestate/blacks-minorities-appraisals-discrimination.html.

Chapter 8

1 James Wellemeyer, "This 29-Year-Old Just Boosted Her Salary by $22,000—Here's

How She Did It," *MarketWatch*, August 24, 2019, https://www.marketwatch.com/story/more-people-are-job-hopping-tempted-by-better-salaries-and-the-highest-number-of-openings-since-2000-2019-08-08.

2 Sarah Brady, "49% of American's Who Switched Jobs Received a Pay Increase," *ValuePenguin,* March 3, 2022, https://www.valuepenguin.com/news/switch-jobs-income-increase.

3 Kevin Gray, "Problem-solving Skills Top Attributes Employers Seek on Resumes," National Association of Colleges and Employers, November 12, 2021, https://www.naceweb.org/talent-acquisition/candidate-selection/problem-solving-skills-top-attributes-employers-seeking-on-resumes/.

4 Kaleigh Moore, "Study: 73% of Employers Want Candidates with This Skill," *Inc.*, April 7, 2016, https://www.inc.com/kaleigh-moore/study-73-of-employers-want-candidates-with-this-skill.html.

5 Sebastian Rupley, "Meet the Buyer of the Broken Laser Pointer," *Ebay Inc*, September 11, 2015, https://www.ebayinc.com/stories/news/meet-the-buyer-of-the-broken-laser-pointer/.

6 Tiffany & Co., https://www.tiffany.com/accessories/decor/everyday-objects-sterling-silver-tin-can-60559139/.

Chapter 9

1 Mike Greenberg, "Caishen: The Chinese God of Wealth," *Mythology Source*, January 4, 2021, https://mythologysource.com/caishen-chinese-god/.

Chapter 10

1 William M. Francavilla, "Of Course You Are Way Too 'Smart' to Be Scammed. Think Again," *CNBC*, April 30, 2018, https://www.cnbc.com/2018/04/30/of-course-you-are-way-too-smart-to-be-scammed-think-again.html.

2 Tom Ajamie and Bruce Kelly, "Why Smart People Fall for Investment Scams," *Forbes*, October 20, 2014, https://www.forbes.com/sites/nextavenue/2014/10/20/why-smart-people-fall-for-investment-scams/?sh=7126a9727f48.

3 Neil Bhutta et al., "Changes in U.S. Family Finances from 2016 to 2019: Evidence from the Survey of Consumer Finances," *Federal Reserve Bulletin* 106, no. 5 (2020): https://www.federalreserve.gov/publications/files/scf20.pdf.

4 Noah N. Levey, "100M People in America Are Saddled with Health Care Debt," *Pennsylvania Capital-Star*, June 23, 2022, https://www.penncapital-star.com/health-care/100m-people-in-america-are-saddled-with-health-care-debt-analysis/.

5 Kimberly Zapata, "Financial Stress Is a Leading Catalyst for Suicide—How to Help Save Lives," *Health*, August 25, 2021, https://www.health.com/money/financial-stress-suicide-risk.

Chapter 12

1 Carolyn Elliott, *Existential Kink: Unmask Your Shadow and Embrace Your Power* (Newbury Port, MA: Weiser Books, 2020).

Chapter 13

1 Sean Pyles, "Chapter 7 vs. Chapter 13: Which Bankruptcy Option Is Best for You?" *nerdwallet,* December 14, 2021, https://www.nerdwallet.com/article/finance/chapter-7-vs-chapter-13.

2 Liz Weston, "When Bankruptcy Is the Best Option," *nerdwallet*, August 6, 2021, https://www.nerdwallet.com/article/finance/bankruptcy-best-option.

3 Jayne Leonard, "A Guide to EFT Tapping," *MedicalNewsToday*, September 26, 2019, https://www.medicalnewstoday.com/articles/326434.

Chapter 16

1 Brianna Wiest, "How to Get into the 'Zone of Genius' and Unlock Your Highest Potential," *Forbes*, September 26, 2018, https://www.forbes.com/sites/briannawiest/2018/09/26/how-to-get-into-the-zone-of-genius-and-unlock-your-highest-potential/?sh=21bed0de5672.

Chapter 18

1 Mark Cartwright, "Hecate," *World History Encyclopedia*, June 22, 2017, https://www.worldhistory.org/Hecate/.

Acknowledgments

No one tells you that writing a book is like giving birth from your mind, heart, and soul. My vagina might be intact, but trust that all three of those parts of me are scarred and strong from this process. And just as every mother needs a whole community of support in the birth of a child, I needed one for bringing this book into the world.

Thank you to my editor, Meg Gibbons, and agent, Jessica Faust, who saw my potential, my magic, and my hunger, and took a chance on a new author with an affinity for F-bombs.

Thank you to my vision-holders and best friends for hyping me up along the way. You know who you are. Thank you to Lacy Phillips and To Be Magnetic for introducing me to a topic that I would expand to become my life's work.

I obviously need to thank my parents for fucking me up just enough to be funny. Thank you, especially, to my dad, who has always been the ultimate hype man when it comes to dreaming big. Whether it was because you were on board with my goals or trying to reign me in so I wouldn't get crushed by risk, I wouldn't be the delusional, stubborn dreamer I am today without you.

Also? I'm going to thank myself. After all, I lived through all the bullshit and had the bravery to put it on paper. So, thank you, Past Me, for taking risks, making mistakes, and abandoning any sense of embarrassment a long time ago. We did it, hot stuff. You're an author now.

Finally, the deepest thanks goes to the love of my life and favorite writer, Iain Grinbergs. I could not have done this without your constant reassurance, genuine laughter at the passages I read aloud, and tolerance of my slovenly ways. I might have written a book first, but I know you're next.

About the Author

Photo © HeatherDrymon

Jessie DaSilva, dubbed "The Millennial Money Witch" by *Forbes*, is a thought-leader, speaker, business consultant, and money mindset coach. She helps businesses increase profits by attracting and retaining top talent, small business owners balloon profits without burnout, and job hunters find dream jobs at dream companies for dream pay.

Jessie is known for her millennial worker rants on TikTok and unique brand of coaching that combines realistic, actionable strategy and magical mindset adjustments.

When she's not changing the world, you can find her jogging a trail in Tallahassee, hyper-focusing on a kitting project, or binge-watching *Shark Tank* with her fiancé and cat.

Connect with me!

Tag me in a post of you reading *The Witch's Way to Wealth* for a chance to be featured on my social media!

Plus, enjoy readings, funny videos, learn about my events, special offers for followers, and more!

- TikTok: @millennialmoneywitch
- Instagram: @j_dasilva
- Twitter: @jdasilva
- YouTube: youtube.com/@millennialmoneywitch
- LinkedIn: linkedin.com/in/jessicadasilva/
- Pinterest: pinterest.com/jessie_dasilva/
- Facebook: facebook.com/CoachJessieDaSilva

Special Offer for Readers!

Get your first month to the online membership version of *The Witch's Way to Wealth*, my money magic school, completely free!

Learn more about the manifestation processes described in the books, along with monthly workshops about money, career, business, and more.

Network with other witches manifesting their way to wealth!

Get it all here with the code WW2W:

Hire Jessie to Speak at Your Next Event

Looking for a dynamic, funny speaker for your next conference, meeting, or event?

Jessie is available to speak on talks about the magic of money mindset, how to turn your dreams into reality, networking your way to a job, and what Millennials and Gen Z want in the workplace.

Check out her speaker demo here:

Proof & Praise for Jessie DaSilva Coaching

"Before I started working with Jessie, I worked with coaches who were helping me understand the manifestation and deep healing process. Yet I didn't understand the pragmatic steps I needed to take. I needed someone to look at my business as a consultant that the spiritual work alone could not help me enough. Since working with Jessie, not only have I gotten clear guidance on exactly what I needed to do, it's allowed me to think about my business in a more linear fashion. My biggest win was seeing myself as an elite coach. That mindset shift made me feel powerful and magical, which totally changed how I showed up online. Beyond that, I cracked the $20k-month mark after three months of working with her and consistently made more than that every month since, including $50k in January 2021. Jessie gave me full permission to be human and spiritual. There's a perception that for coaches like me, we need to be 100% spiritual all the time. Jessie has a similar flavor of reality that allowed me to feel good about my own brand of coaching. When I get off Zoom, I feel reassured that I'm on the right path, I feel like I have course correction on what I need to course correct, and I just feel like a baller overall. And that is a profound gift."

—Dr. Liz DuBois, Dr. Liz DuBois Coaching

"Before working with Jessie, I knew what I did from a professional side, but manifestation was at an ethereal level. Jessie brought that understanding to me. So much of getting to the next level was about having faith and going past the unknown. You need intuition in your business, and part of intuition is connecting with your inner witch. I needed permission to do that, which Jessie gave me. I also just would not put myself out there because I was striving for perfection. Jessie said to strive for excellence instead. So, I started to put what I create out there unapologetically. That led to being showcased in Today.com in January for my programming with a video I made as part of the write-up! I also had a whole page in Plate magazine devoted to me and my work around diversity, which I'm really proud of. And that's a national magazine! I was invited to write for Yankee Magazine a second time, and all my local programs were covered by all three New Haven newspapers. I was also awarded so many fellowships and grants for my work. I was awarded $5,000 from the Center for Arts & Activism. I was the creative-in-residence for the New Haven Public Library. My biggest win was getting selected as one of about 40 chefs for James Beard's Chefs' Boot Camp for Policy & Change from 800 applicants. I would not have applied had I not been in Practical Magic, creating alchemy and manifestation on my own terms. I also had my first in-person show in a New York City gallery. Accepting myself and my quirkiness, along with Jessie's suggestions, resources, and guest speakers have made me feel great about manifestation and what I have to offer. It just shows that with intentional thought and action, you can manifest your dreams."

—Nadine Nelson, Global Local Gourmet

"Before I started working with Jessie, I went through a breakup with my fiance—then COVID hit and shut down the yoga studios where I worked. It became a stark reality that all I'd known was now non-existent. No fiance, and now no job (way to treat a girl, universe)! I had ideas of what I wanted to do but it was mixed up in a nightmare of having to generate immediate income and not having a real structure for this new way of working.

"Our world collided when I read one of Jessie's posts. I messaged her to congratulate her on her transformation – I was really inspired by it and thought this was the girl who would catapult me. To be fair I've been approached by a lot of coaches but I was drawn to the no nonsense, no bullshit, get-shit-done attitude. She seemed fearless and in that moment I intuitively knew she was my girl. I didn't know how I was going to pay her, mind you, and wasn't really in the market for a coach. But with no man and no job I thought f*** it, it can't get any worse!

"After working with Jessie, I created three one-on-one programs. I went from teaching 12 classes a week to teaching three and making more money. I created a new modality, Yoga by Design, that offers yoga and movement practices that correspond to your Human Design and astrological placements. I fired a private client for not being committed enough when I would have acted out of scarcity before.

"I've been able to become really self-employed and independent from the studios in a way I didn't think was possible. I love what I am creating. I cannot wait to wake up in the morning and be me—it's totally awesome! Work life balance is on fire—I have more time to myself than I ever thought was possible!"

—Mary Smiley, Yoga by Design

"When Jessie and I started working together, I was making around $700-$800 a month from my business and working 20-25 hours a week on DoorDash to make up the difference. I was struggling to make ends meet, which was financially challenging because I was the only person in my home who was able to work. Since working with Jessie, I've more than tripled my income and my business has grown to 18 times its original size. I'm completely comfortable paying my bills, having things that I want, and celebrating the fact that I'm living the life I dreamed of. I always had a positive outlook on life, even from the beginning. I've also always been a really dedicated person. But my time working with Jessie definitely helped me step into my power, keep the faith, and have patience for the things I wanted. She reminded me that sometimes we need to take big leaps of faith so we can get what we want out of life—that gentle push made all the difference."

—Claira Reign Kruse, Holistic Contentment

"Gift after gift, call after call, she poured value and kindness and empathy and incredible manifesting goodness into my life. I had to wait until I was more solid before I could join her program, but as soon as I did, I signed a client that was *more* than her pay in full price. After participating in one of her free three-day workshops, I feel more grounded, more centered, and more excited to welcome in what I'm manifesting. The tests seem less significant, the silence less deafening and I am *prepared* to meet the call of what I want. She is more than just a coach. She is someone who believes in you, shows you your true levels that you can achieve, and helps you until you get there—*even* before you pay for her services."

—Jenny Ambrose, Purée Fantastico